Aliens and Sojourners

Divinations: Rereading Late Ancient Religion

Series Editors: Daniel Boyarin, Virginia Burrus, Derek Krueger

A complete list of books in the series is available from the publisher.

Aliens and Sojourners

Self as Other in Early Christianity

BENJAMIN H. DUNNING

PENN

University of Pennsylvania Press

Philadelphia

For Bob

Copyright © 2009 University of Pennsylvania Press

All rights reserved. Except for brief quotations used for purposes of review or scholarly citation, none of this book may be reproduced in any form by any means without written permission from the publisher.

Published by
University of Pennsylvania Press
Philadelphia, Pennsylvania 19104-4112

Printed in the United States of America on acid-free paper
10 9 8 7 6 5 4 3 2 1

Library of Congress Cataloging-in-Publication Data

Dunning, Benjamin H.
  Aliens and sojourners : self as other in early Christianity / Benjamin H. Dunning.
    p.   cm. — (Divinations: rereading ancient religion)
  ISBN: 978-0-8122-4156-3 (alk. paper)
  Includes bibliographical references and index.
  1. Self—Religious aspects—Christianity—History of doctrines—Early church, ca. 30–600. 2. Theological anthropology—Christianity—History of doctrines—Early church, ca. 30–600. 3. Strangers—Religious aspects—Christianity—History of doctrines—Early church, ca. 30–600. 4. Alienation (Theology). 5. Identification (Religion). 6. Other (Philosophy).   I. Title
BT713.D86   2009
270.1—dc22   2008035362

Contents

Introduction: Aliens, Christians, and the Rhetoric of Identity

All Christians placed their citizenship in heaven. On earth they were but pilgrims and strangers.

—*Roland Bainton*

At the close of the first century C.E., the early Christian text *1 Clement* (c.93–97) opens with a greeting from one group of Christian aliens to another: "The church of God residing as aliens (*paroikousa*) in Rome to the church of God residing as aliens (*paroikousē*) in Corinth."[1] This was not the first text to characterize Christians in terms of their status as aliens or sojourners. But as the first century came to a close and the second century progressed, the trope proved to be an increasingly useful one. Other Christian writers made use of it in epistolary prescripts and elsewhere. Polycarp addresses his *Letter to the Philippians* (c.117–120) to the resident alien church at Philippi, while the *Martyrdom of Polycarp* (c.155–160 or 170–180) figures not only its specific audience as aliens but in fact the entire "holy and catholic church" as a body that sojourns.[2] Similarly *2 Clement* (mid-second century) seeks to reassure its audience and strengthen their resolve by reminding them that their sojourn in this world is of short duration.[3]

In all these ancient texts, we see instances of what I will call "the resident alien topos"—the designation (one that quickly became traditional) of the Christian self as a stranger, sojourner, foreigner, and/or resident alien in order to communicate varying forms of Christian alterity. In view are Greek terms such as *paroikos*, "resident alien," *xenos*, "stranger-foreigner," *parepidēmos*, "sojourner" and *politeia*, "citizenship" that together form a linguistic complex repeatedly used by early Christians to speak about who they were and what it meant for them to be Christian.[4] In light of the evidence for the widespread use of this topos in the first and second centuries C.E., numerous historians of Christianity have drawn conclusions along the lines of the epigraph from Roland Bainton cited above: the claim to outsider status on earth must have served as a universal identity marker in the early Christian movement. According to this argument, the first Christians followed the Apostle Paul in looking to their heavenly citizenship (Phil 3.20) and thereby became a kind of spiritual "resident aliens." As the Epistle to the Hebrews puts it eloquently, "they confessed that they were strangers and sojourners on the earth" (Heb 11.13). By drawing on a particular language of stranger and alien status, these Christians articulated their difference, their marginality—in a word, their "otherness"—from the world around them.

Nor was the vibrancy or usefulness of the topos limited to the context of the first and second centuries. Indeed it proved to have staying power not only through the systematic persecutions of Christianity in the third century, but also through the transition to imperial religion in the fourth century and beyond. Perhaps most famous is the theologically laden contrast that Augustine draws between saintly strangers (represented by Abel) and citizens of this world (represented by Cain) in *The City of God*: "When these two cities began to run their course by a series of deaths and births, the citizen of this world [Cain] was the first-born, and after him the stranger in this world [Abel], the citizen of the city of God, predestined by grace, elected by grace, by grace a stranger below, and by grace a citizen above. . . . Accordingly, it is recorded of Cain that he built a city, but Abel, being a sojourner, built none. For the city of the saints is above, although here below it begets citizens, in whom it sojourns till the time of its reign arrives, when it shall gather together all in the day of the resurrection."[5]

Even in contemporary theological reflection, the image of the Christian as a stranger, alien, and sojourner continues to enjoy a broad purchase. For example, in *Resident Aliens: Life in the Christian Colony*, Stanley Hauerwas and William Willimon issue a provocative manifesto regarding their vision of present-day American Christian identity:

A colony is a beachhead, an outpost, an island of one culture in the middle of another, a place where the values of home are reiterated and passed on to the young, a place where the distinctive language and life-style of the resident aliens are lovingly nurtured and reinforced. We believe that the designations of the church as a colony and Christians as resident aliens are not too strong for the modern American church—indeed, we believe it is the nature of the church, at any time and in any situation to be a colony . . . an island of one culture in the middle of another. In baptism our citizenship is transferred from one dominion to another, and we become, in whatever culture we find ourselves, resident aliens.[6]

This vision of what normative American Christianity ought to be is one that is both enthusiastically embraced by some and vigorously contested by others. What cannot be contested, however, is that Hauerwas and Willimon place themselves here within a rich and extensive interpretive tradition, one that hearkens back to a very ancient rhetorical move: figuring the Christian self in terms of its resident alien status. Theologian Miroslav Volf in fact locates Hauerwas explicitly within this stream: "By the second century, being 'alien' had become central to the self-understanding of Christians. Later it was essential to monastic and Anabaptist movements alike, to Augustine and Zinzendorf, and, in our own time, to Dietrich Bonhoeffer (*The Cost of Discipleship*), no less than to Jim Wallis (*Sojourners*) or Stanley Hauerwas (*Resident Aliens*)."[7]

This orientation toward Christian identity is not the only one in the history of the tradition. But as the above examples show, it is one that is so prominent that it can easily appear to be natural, given, and self-evident. Yet when we look back at the roots of this motif in the earliest texts of Christianity, a clear question emerges: *why* did the first Christians speak about themselves this way and *to what ends*? To be sure, speaking one's alien status was a means of claiming a space of difference—though this by no means entirely settles the question. For one thing, "difference" is itself a fluid and flexible category, one that can be deployed to define the world (and one's identity within it) in variable and historically rooted ways. So what kinds of difference did early Christians enact in claiming the resident-alien as a ground for identity? And why resort to this particularistic language of alterity to do so—especially insofar as it stands in a certain tension with the universalistic imperative to proclaim the Christian witness to the ends of the earth? (Matt 28.18–20, Acts 1.8)

One issue historians can clearly agree upon is that the early Christian use of the resident alien topos is in some sense dependent on traditions drawn from the Hebrew Bible. The paradigmatic figure of Abraham is repeatedly characterized as an alien and stranger (see in particular Gen 23.4), and the motif appears multiple times throughout both the Hebrew Bible and its later Greek translation. (This appropriation of cultural material from the Jewish scriptures will be explored at length in later chapters.) However, simply noting this textual dependence tells us little about the meaning or use of the alien topos in the earliest extant Christian texts. Was it in fact a central and indispensable trope of formative Christian identity, as both Bainton and Volf seem to imply? Perhaps more importantly, did the topos always work to the same end, interpellating Christian subjects as "aliens and strangers" in a singular, stable, and uniform way?[8] Or (pace Bainton's bland ascription of a universal function to the topos), were there multiple uses to which it could be put in the first centuries of the new movement?

Insiders, Outsiders, and Identity

The alien is that which stems from elsewhere and does not belong here . . . it suffers the lot of the stranger who is lonely, unprotected, uncomprehended, and uncomprehending in a situation full of danger. Anguish and homesickness are a part of the stranger's lot. . . . All this belongs to the "suffering" side of alienness. Yet with relation to its origin it is at the same time a mark of excellence, a source of power and of a secret life unknown to the environment and in the last resort impregnable to it. (Hans Jonas)[9]

What makes an "alien" or an "outsider" worthy of the name? In his innovative study, *Religious Outsiders and the Making of Americans*, R. Laurence Moore examines the motif of outsiderhood as a self-designation for religious groups in nineteenth- and twentieth-century America. Of particular interest is his chapter on the early days of the Church of Jesus Christ of Latter-Day Saints and the hostile polemic surrounding the group. Here Moore poses a simple but critical question: why did "most everyone who wrote about Joseph Smith's church, and above all this included the Mormons themselves, [assert] that Mormons were not like other Americans"?[10] What exactly was so different about this group? Even more to the point, what made Mormon difference so significant in nineteenth-century America?

Potential "objective" answers to this question may seem straightforward: polygamy, perceived sectarian behavior, and/or theological innovations. Yet when we take into account the movement's birth in "an era fecund in religious inventiveness," the issue becomes decidedly more complex.[11] As Moore perceptively points out, "a generation that read almost daily about the claims of various men and women to new religious revelation might have been expected to greet Joseph Smith's Book of Mormon more calmly than one vociferous part of it did."[12] The question this raises for the study of the Latter-Day Saints is this: how one can account for the historical and cultural *significance* of perceived Mormon difference?

In light of this dilemma, Moore concludes that any attempt to mount an "objective" case for Mormon difference proves unhelpful and is best abandoned. Instead he contends: "Mormons were different because they *said* they were different and because their claims . . . prompted others to agree and to treat them as such. The notion of Mormon difference, that is, was a deliberate invention elaborated over time. . . . [By declaring their outsider status,] they built a usable social identity for themselves."[13] Here Moore highlights the role that the figure of the Mormon self as outsider played in forming communal religious identity against the backdrop of a disorienting array of religious options in nineteenth-century America. In his view, the early Mormon community put the idea of their own marginalized difference to work in order to construct and maintain their distinctive religious identity in a confusingly pluralistic universe. The issue at stake then is not primarily about difference in any absolute sense, but rather about proximity: how the members of a group mark out their own sense of self over and against cultural others who are in many ways too much like them. By inventing themselves as outsiders with respect to American culture, the early Mormons were in fact able to create a powerful notion of *insiderness*—one that defined group boundaries and also reinforced communal solidarity against the threat of the overly proximate within a complex and diverse cultural environment.

What then are the implications of Moore's analysis for understanding the uses of the resident alien topos in early Christian texts? The dangers of overly facile comparison never lurk far from the surface in the study of religion—and early Christians are not Mormons or vice versa. In view are two very different sociohistorical and political milieus (not to mention distinct theological and hermeneutical frameworks), making any straightforward comparison a risky and problematic project. But nonetheless, Moore's thesis concerning the construction of difference by a new religious movement in nineteenth-century American may still function as an illuminating analogical tool for thinking about the figure of the alien in early Christianity. At the very least, his work pushes us to consider the crucial strategic functions that a rhetoric of alienation can have in the project of articulating communal religious identity. In other words, just as the Latter-Day Saints made use of a discourse of outsiderhood to invent and maintain "a usable social identity," so we need to consider whether early Christians were also able to use the language of alien status to achieve similar ends in a vastly different cultural context.

Could this mean that early Christians were not in fact "really" all that different from their environment and the people around them? To constitute the question this way, I would argue, is already to assume too much about the stability of "difference" as a category. On the one hand, I do not wish to deny a historical referent (or referents) to the early Christian difference that was articulated through textual appeals to the resident alien topos. But on the other hand, the modes and degrees of that difference (in varying times and places) need to be interrogated. Thus it is important to acknowledge that the problem of *what sort of otherness* the alien topos encodes is a profoundly rhetorical one, intimately connected to language and politics. As Jonathan Z. Smith has argued, "perhaps the most basic sense of the 'other' is generated by the opposition IN/OUT. That is to say, a preoccupation with boundary, with limit (in the primary sense of threshold) seems fundamental to our construction of ourselves and our relations to others."[14] From this perspective, alterity emerges as a question—a shifting and variable proposition—enmeshed in this preoccupation with boundary and its resultant implications for the formation of identity.

Again, this is not to imply that substantive difference did not exist on either side of the boundaries separating early Christians from everybody else. Yet as Smith elaborates elsewhere, "difference" is itself not a fixed or static entity (as the phrase "substantive difference" might seem to imply), but rather "a mode of both culturally encoding and decoding, of maintaining and relativizing internal as well as external distinctions."[15] What this more flexible definition highlights is that the way an individual or group chooses to demarcate what counts as difference (and then talk about it) is a social process, always rooted in a context and network of relationships. As Smith astutely points out, " 'Otherness' is a matter of relative rather than absolute difference. . . . This is the case because [it] is a relativistic category, inasmuch as it is, necessarily, a term of *interaction*."[16] In other words, the designation of the other always exists, according to Smith, in relation to the construction of the self: "the real urgency of a 'theory of the other' . . . is called forth not by the requirement to place the 'other,' but rather to situate ourselves."[17] To formulate the other as "other" is to engage in a project of self-definition with powerful political and cultural implications.

Historians of antiquity have extensively studied this cultural dynamic as it plays out in the rhetoric of Greco-Roman literature.[18] But, of course, when it comes to uses of the alien topos, the primary project is not actually to articulate the self by formulating the other as "other." Rather, the center of gravity lies elsewhere: the topos lays claim to a rhetoric of marginality in order to formulate *the self as other*. This does not negate the relevance of Smith's insight about the relational dimension of self/other identity politics overall: constructing the self in terms of its alterity (what I am calling "the self as other") inevitably situates the actual other (i.e., the non-self) in some sort of relation to that self. But the rhetorical emphasis is different. More specifically, mobilizing the image of the alien as a designation for the self—rather than the other—serves (at least in most cases) to *valorize* that alien status.

In this way, the alien—a figure of reproach and ambivalence throughout so much of antiquity—could be revalued toward new and constructive ends. Aliens and foreigners had long occupied a conflicted space of both repulsion and desire in Greek and Roman thinking. And in this discursive tension there were further possibilities: the position of the alien could be exploited and appropriated—that is, turned into a usable and even desirable resource for formulating the self. In this appropriation, alien status becomes itself a site of a compelling doubleness: it retains its negative connotations of social estrangement and marginality, while also, and at the same time, being refigured (as Jonas notes above) as "a mark of excellence, a source of power"—and thus a doubly useful resource around which to figure the complexities of identity.

The Diverse Landscape of Early Christianity

Early Christians were not the first to figure out the usefulness of the topos. (The valorization of the alien/sojourner figure in Hellenistic philosophy and early Judaism will be examined in Chapter 2.) But they did capitalize on the space for rhetorical maneuvering afforded by its doubleness in ways that were particular to them, seizing on the elasticity of the topos to pursue a range of different identity projects. This diversity problematizes any simple or monolithic characterization of early Christian "difference" in relation to the topos. What emerges instead, I will argue, is a whole spectrum of uses whereby the alien topos functioned as a peculiarly malleable discursive resource—one that could be strategically drawn upon and variously put to use in order to negotiate identity and demarcate difference in a variety of ways.

At one end of this spectrum, as we will see, some Christians used the figure of the alien to construct a "usable social identity" (à la Moore's analysis of nineteenth-century Mormons) among the vast range of cultic identities and practices that proliferated in the ancient Mediterranean. This use of the topos could represent Christian identity on a rhetorical level as socially marginalized, while all the while seeking to position it as a force to be reckoned with very much *within* the Roman world, and in a nonresistant—or even assimilationist—stance toward many basic Roman cultural values (a dynamic often overlooked or downplayed by historical scholarship on this period). Or the topos could be used to argue for certain kinds of (selective) resistance to the dominant Roman social order, strategically calling Christians to differentiate themselves in particular practical ways rather than others. But on the other end of the spectrum, the topos could be flipped on its head; that is, it could be used to argue that the self-as-other approach to identity not only is fundamentally illegitimate but entails within it a wrongheaded understanding of what Christian life and salvation are all about.

Exploring this rich, pervasive, yet variegated discourse of early Christian identity is the project of this book. To this end, I will examine the uses of the resident alien topos in five early Christian texts from the first and second centuries C.E.: 1 Peter, Hebrews, the *Epistle to Diognetus*, the *Shepherd of Hermas, Similitudes,* and the *Apocryphon of James*. Though these are by no means the only Christian texts of this period that invoke the figure of the alien, stranger, or sojourner in their projects of identity construction,[19] they are the five texts that engage most substantially with both the concept and the rhetoric of the Christian as a foreigner or resident alien.[20] As such, these texts remain the most promising sites for an investigation into the distinctive flexibility of the topos and its generative possibilities for inflecting identity in different ways in the first two centuries of Christianity.

Though 1 Peter, Hebrews, *Diognetus*, and *Hermas* have been treated together on this issue (usually in the interests of drawing a conclusion about the significance of the topos in 1 Peter), the introduction of the *Apocryphon of James* into the conversation is (to my knowledge) a new step. *Ap. Jas.* is a text of the Nag Hammadi corpus that makes use of the alien topos and falls within the chronological scope of my inquiry.[21] But it has not played a role in previous scholarly discussion of the early Christian alien topos—probably in part due to a larger trend within early Christian studies to separate off Nag Hammadi literature somewhat artificially, confining it to discussions of "Gnosticism."[22] By giving *Ap. Jas.* a central place in this project, I am aligning myself with current scholarship that is working to integrate Nag Hammadi material into broader scholarly reconstructions of Christian origins.[23] This orientation also follows the growing scholarly tend to reject the Eusebian model of Christian history as the linear and triumphant progression of orthodoxy, in favor of one that recognizes the rich fluidity and diversity of Christianities in the early centuries of the Common Era.[24] As Denise Buell puts it, this approach "views Christianity not as an essence but as a contested site—one defined and claimed by competing groups and individuals—and Christian history not as an evolving totality but rather as a series of ongoing struggles, negotiations, alliances, and challenges."[25]

Within this contested site, the claim to be an alien or an outsider was not straightforwardly transparent. Rather it *did* something—or more precisely, it could do (and still can do) numerous things. As Vincent Wimbush argues, "Early Christiani*ties* . . . were discursive and rhetorical formations ever productive of new social formations—formations that represent not the inexorable *verweltlichung* or development toward world-church, but the constant cycle of problematization, protest, reform. Its social power lies in what it provides in imagination and discursive formation."[26] The resident alien topos as deployed by early Christians can thus be considered a particularly potent cultural resource—at the level of both imagination and discursive formation. Due to this potency, I maintain, it is that much more important that the topos and its spectrum of possible uses be investigated—rather than assumed to convey something singular and self-evident about Christian identity, either historically or in contemporary theological reflection today.

"I exhort you as resident aliens and sojourners": Alterity in 1 Peter

As noted above, I am not the first to question the role and function of the resident alien topos in Christian literature of this time period. In fact much scholarly ink has been spilt on the issue—though largely confined to a specific corner of New Testament studies: the exegesis and sociohistorical analysis of 1 Peter.[27] This is for a variety of reasons wrapped up in the specific intellectual politics and circumstances of biblical studies in the last thirty years. These include larger structural issues in the field such as: (1) a long-standing (and perduring) tendency among many scholars of early Christianity to give pride of place to texts in the New Testament canon; and (2) a general turn among biblical scholars in the 1970s and 1980s to methods of social scientific analysis. Here 1 Peter and its use of the resident alien topos was deemed especially amenable to such analysis, in contrast to the other principal (canonical) contender, Hebrews, whose use of the topos was generally considered too "Platonizing" to yield much in the way of useful social data. Also important, however, is the work of individual scholars that has functioned to define the conversation in specific and important ways (most notably John Elliott—see discussion below).

Yet when it comes to the figure of the alien, the biblical text in question actually presents its interpreters with a relatively modest quantity of relevant material. 1 Peter opens with an address to its audience as "elect sojourners of the diaspora" (*eklektois parepidēmois diasporas*, 1.1). Several lines later, the letter refers to the addressees' time of alien residence (*ton tēs paroikias hymōn chronon*, 1.17). Last, in chapter 2, we find a direct exhortation to these Christians as "resident aliens and sojourners" (*parakalō hōs paroikous kai parepidēmous*, 2.11). Granted, all these references to Christians' alien identity are tantalizing textual clues. But they in fact offer interpreters relatively little to work with. The evidence boils down to three elliptical phrases centered around two Greek terms, *paroikos* and *parepidēmos*. Given the sparseness of these data, scholars have tended to focus on a single question: what does this appeal to Christians as resident aliens and sojourners tell us about the identity and sociohistorical location of 1 Peter's original recipients?[28]

On one side of the debate is (most prominently) the early work of John Elliott. In his monograph, *A Home for the Homeless: A Sociological Exegesis of 1 Peter, Its Situation and Strategy*, Elliott laments the fact that "exegetical decisions concerning [the terms *paroikos* and *parepidēmos*] in 1 Peter in particular frequently ignore, or at least fail to mention, their political, legal and social import."[29] Instead he argues (on linguistic and sociological grounds) that 1 Peter's use of these terms reflects the legal status of

communities of Christians in Asia Minor at the end of the first century
C.E.[30] According to this view, "the actual political and social condition of
the addressees as *paroikoi* is used as an occasion to encourage their religious peculiarity and strangeness as well."[31] Elliott thus contends that the
use of the alien topos in 1 Peter represents a concrete and identifiable
social reality: 1 Peter is addressed to predominantly rural communities
of resident-aliens in Asia Minor, a social status based on a lack of citizenship, irrespective of religious considerations.[32]

Drawing on an impressive array of sources (Hellenistic, Hebrew
Bible / LXX, New Testament) to make his case for political-legal usage
of the terms, Elliott seeks to elucidate what he sees as the lynchpin of 1
Peter's theology: the correlation between legal resident-alien/*paroikos* status and the new collective home to which these aliens have come to belong
by becoming Christians—the household/*oikos* of God. This link between
paroikos and *oikos* (*tou theou*) is, in Elliott's view, "neither accidental nor incidental, but rather a basic component of the Petrine strategy . . . throughout the letter"[33]—urging a group of *legally* displaced outsiders to seek an
actual place of belonging in the *oikos* of the Christian community.[34]

Other scholars have offered a counterpoint to this position, maintaining that the alien language of 1 Peter is best understood "metaphorically."[35] One particularly prominent example is found in Reinhard
Feldmeier's *Habilitationsschrift, Die Christen als Fremde: Die Metapher der
Fremde in der antiken Welt, im Urchristentum und im 1. Petrusbrief.* Here Feldmeier argues that early Christians speak about themselves as strangers
and aliens in response to the reduced social status (or outright social
rejection) that has been thrust upon them at conversion and baptism.
He supports this position by reading the Petrine alien topos primarily
in terms of the use of the "stranger" as a metaphor for human existence
in Hellenistic philosophy, as well as the use of *paroikos* and *parepidēmos* as
theological metaphors in the tradition of the Hebrew Bible/LXX. Feldmeier thereby maintains that the author of 1 Peter "in an audacious turn
to a relatively narrow biblical and Jewish tradition, interprets the negative experience of non-identity as a specifically Christian identity."[36] In
other words, 1 Peter uses the topos as a metaphor drawn from the biblical tradition (contra Elliott's emphasis on Greco-Roman legal usage) to
forge a specifically Christian identity. In Feldmeier's view, this is a direct
response to the "non-identity" that results from the social rejection and
persecution associated with becoming a Christian in Asia Minor. As he
puts it succinctly in a later article, "society's rejection of the faithful receives theological explanation."[37] By understanding themselves as resident aliens in the world, believers may take hope in their eschatological
inheritance to come—while at the same time making meaning in the
here-and-now out of a difficult external situation.[38]

Elliott and Feldmeier can be seen as representative of two basic poles to this conversation: a legal (or "literal") interpretation of 1 Peter's resident alien topos and a metaphorical one.[39] Within this general orientation, there is room for a variety of nuances—and the complexities have multiplied within the scholarly debate.[40] But the discussion has for the most part remained oriented along a single axis as defined by these poles. One notable exception to this has been the work of David Balch. Thus without denying the importance of the debate as currently constituted (or the significance of the scholarship that has engaged it), I wish to follow Balch in pointing to a further tension in the text of 1 Peter that may in fact decenter any straightforward opposition between literal and metaphorical interpretations of the resident alien.

As Balch has noted in a now classic debate with Elliott, a certain uncritical dualism between sect and society seems to drive Elliott's literal-legal interpretation of the topos. On Elliott's reading, the addressees of 1 Peter emerge as relatively uncomplicated sectarians, standing in resistance to the surrounding Roman culture as a result of political displacement and social marginalization—all of this summed up in their legal resident alien status. But as Balch points out, other aspects of the text (such as the domestic code in 2.11–3.12) signal a "movement toward peace and harmony with Greco-Roman society."[41] Particularly important is the exhortation of 2.12–14: "Have such good conduct among the Gentiles so that, though they slander you as evildoers, when they see your good works, they may glorify God on the day of visitation. Submit to every human institution on account of the Lord, whether the emperor, as the one who has power, or governors, as those sent by him in order to punish evildoers and commend those who do good" (*tēn anastrophēn hymōn en tois ethnesin echontes kalēn, hina, en hō katalalousin hymōn hōs kakopoiōn ek tōn kalōn ergōn epopteuontes doxasōsin ton theon en hēmera episkopēs. Hypotagēte pasē anthrōpinē ktisei dia ton kyrion, eite basilei hōs hyperechonti, eite hēgemosin hōs di' autou pempomenois eis ekdikēsin kakopoiōn epainon de agathopoiōn*). The text goes on to urge its audience both to fear God and honor the emperor (*ton theon phobeisthe, ton basilea timate,* 2.17) and then offers specific instructions for the behavior of slaves, wives, husbands, and general members of the Christian community (2.18–3.12). In Balch's evaluation, these passages show that 1 Peter " 'enthusiastically accepts' ethical ideas and patterns of conduct that the Roman emperor and his governors praise as 'good.' "[42] He therefore concludes that the text "continues the acculturation process in the hellenistic Jewish diaspora" and argues that the boundaries of Christian communal identity are maintained in terms of the Christ story, not (as Elliott maintains), the *oikos tou theou.*[43]

This analysis highlights a tension in the text that I would argue is crucial for thinking about the role of outsider identity in this epistle (though Balch's concern is primarily with the function of the household code in 1 Peter, not the resident alien topos). Balch's reading shows that whatever the alien topos in 1 Peter may signify in terms of Christian identity, it does not do so entirely over and against the "other" of Roman society. While clearly the designation of Christians as aliens draws some sort of boundary, that boundary is not unimplicated in the norms or values of the culture being figured on the other side of the line.

To build on this point further, 2.11 calls the "resident aliens and sojourners" to be people who "keep free from fleshly desires which wage war against the soul" (*apechesthai tōn sarkikōn epithymiōn haitines strateuontai kata tēs psychēs*). What is non-negotiable for 1 Peter is that these Christians ought to understand themselves in some fundamental way as outsiders. Indeed this outsider status is one of the primary justifications for their existence as a distinct group. But what sort of outsiders? These are not aliens who withdraw from Roman society and Mediterranean urban life for the desert or the caves. Rather, they are aliens who submit to Roman governors and honor the emperor. The text associates them with the soul over and against the flesh, but not in order to encourage a radical social separation or displacement. Instead it mobilizes a socially conventional, philosophical high ground—*psychē* over *sarx*—in order to buttress an apologetic conclusion: "Gentile" non-Christians are unjustified in any rejection of Petrine Christians because these "outsiders" actually live exemplary lives—according to the ethical and cultural standards of Roman society itself.[44]

In this way, the text marks Christian identity as distinctive by figuring Christians as outsiders to the social order, while simultaneously engaging in a paraenetic agenda that serves to reinscribe their place in that social order. While certain early readers of the text may actually have been technical resident aliens within the Roman legal system and others may have been persecuted and marginalized by their surrounding society (or both), we should not allow these possibilities to obscure the important constructive dynamic at work here: 1 Peter's use of the alien topos does not function to place its audience outside the social order in any absolute sense, but rather to situate and inflect its place within it in a particular way—in Moore's terms, a project in articulating "a usable social identity."

Methodological Reflections: The Early Christian Alien and the Sociology of Knowledge

Given this brief analysis of 1 Peter, I contend that the binary opposition between the legal-literal and the metaphorical has restricted the interpretive options for understanding the early Christian alien topos in a problematic way. Debating only whether the topos signifies a legal reality or a metaphorical response to a preexistent social reality (i.e., persecution) too easily obscures the constructive ways in which the topos "creates and shapes the symbolic worlds it professes to evoke and describe" (to borrow a phrase from Elisabeth Schüssler-Fiorenza).[45] It is indisputable that the figure of the Christian as an alien, foreigner, or sojourner proved exceedingly useful to early Christian writers, as evidenced by its appearance in numerous texts of the first and second century. But what this evidence can plausibly tell us needs further interrogation—and more specifically, interrogation in a methodological register not over-determined by the confines of the 1 Peter debate. Both the legal and the metaphorical sides of this debate assume some kind of singular so-ciohistorical situation in which early Christians were outsiders. Thus an "actual" outsider status functions as the primary historical given to which the topos then secondarily responds. All that is at issue in the debate is the precise nature of that status.

The larger question looming in the background is whether (and to what degree) ancient texts can be fruitfully mined for sociohistorical data using the methods of sociology. Elliott builds his position with re-spect to the resident alien topos on the contention that they can. Stating his methodological assumptions explicitly, he calls for an approach that intertwines exegesis and social-scientific method to yield

a sophisticated sociological approach to group formation, the conditions of social organization, the cultivation and expression (including religious expres-sion) of group interests and goals, the conflict of diverse interest groups and their varying ideologies, and the effect of group interaction, both internal and external, upon the composition of biblical literature as well as upon the direc-tion and success of the movements to which the groups belong. In a word, the task yet before exegetes is the interpretation of the biblical literature as products and reflections of a dynamic social process, of socioreligious movements.[46]

Here Elliott relies on a crucial assumption about the viability of mov-ing from literary-theological texts to concrete social data, one that is shared by numerous scholars working in this mode of biblical and early Christian studies.[47] Indeed this assumption similarly undergirds the con-clusions of the metaphorical pole in the 1 Peter debate.

But as Elizabeth Clark has recently argued (with reference to a slightly later period of Christian history), "these social-scientific appropriations [obscure] the fact that scholars of late ancient Christianity deal not with native informants, nor with masses of data amenable to statistical analysis, but with texts—and texts of a highly literary, rhetorical, and ideological nature."[48] Clark's response to this theoretical challenge is not to call for the wholesale abandonment of sociological method in early Christian studies, but rather to suggest "that scholars of ancient Christianity would profit . . . from entering more fully into conversation with those whose business it is to deal with ideology, rhetoric, and textuality."[49]

Contemporary historical work in this vein is often grouped under the loose rubric of "New Historicism" (or in Stephen Greenblatt's more recent phrase, "cultural poetics"), a perspective initially associated (at least primarily) with Greenblatt's circle at the University of California at Berkeley, but conceptually indebted on many levels to Michel Foucault.[50] New Historicism can also be located more broadly within a general turn from social to cultural history.[51] Gabrielle Spiegel concisely summarizes the general contours of this approach as follows: "New Historicists point to the culturally specific nature of texts as products of particular periods and discursive formations, and they view reality—history—as itself mediated by linguistic codes that it is impossible for the critic/historian to bypass. . . . The debt here to Foucault is clear, and as with Foucault, the goal of New Historicist criticism is to demonstrate the power of discourse in shaping the ways in which the dominant ideology of a period creates both institutional and textual embodiments of the cultural constructs governing mental and social life."[52] In the case of the early Christian resident alien, this approach points us to the need for greater attention to the ideological and rhetorical dimensions of the topos as they function in various contexts. It thus resists reconstructing a historical narrative of singular, teleological progression, in which early Christians evolved from being alien outsiders to rulers of the Roman world because of the inherent superiority of their religion. And it proves equally helpful in complicating overly romanticized views of alien status as somehow more faithful to the essence of "true Christianity."

This emphasis on the topos's rhetorical dimensions begs the larger question of historical referents: does a turn to rhetoric *necessarily* take the possibility of sociohistorical assertions (such as those made by Elliott, Feldmeier, et al.) off the table on theoretical grounds? I would argue, no. One could imagine a situation in which a confluence of different types of evidence from the ancient world (inscriptions, Roman legal records, further documentation that definitively situated the early Christian texts in question in their precise social and geographical contexts) might allow us to draw more robust (and even strongly plausible) historical conclusions regarding the relation of the alien topos to the social situation(s) of the early Christians who employed it. In the case of the texts examined in this book, however, this evidence is sadly lacking. But even so, I contend that this lack of supplementary evidence renders more clearly visible the theoretical point I wish to highlight (following Clark and others): that even if we did possess further evidence making social scientific inquiry a more viable project, we would still need to attend to the variable rhetorical dimensions and functions of the topos.

My point then is not to oppose rhetorical analysis to social history in the study of early Christianity, but rather to underscore that the rhetoricity of the first Christians' speech about their alien status has social and historical dimensions that call for analysis. As Foucault famously articulates, "to speak is to *do* something—something other than to express what one thinks. . . . [A] change in the order of discourse does not presuppose 'new ideas,' a little invention and creativity, a different mentality, but transformations in a practice, perhaps also in neighboring practices, and in their common articulation."[53] Following Foucault on this point, I do not wish to analyze early Christian appeals to the figure of the alien in a way that treats the texts as a "transparent medium"[54]—that is, a window through which to view putative social groups behind those texts. Rather, speaking, claiming, or otherwise articulating one's alien status needs to be recognized as itself a type of social practice, one that could be strategically put to use for varying purposes within the larger project of early Christian identity formation.

In this way, sociology is not entirely off the table on the theoretical level. But my more focused interest here is not in "grids and groups, networks, liminality, and 'thick description,'"[55] but rather in the sociology of knowledge and identity. To this end, I find it helpful to build on this broadly Foucaultian orientation with the theoretical insights of the French sociologist, Pierre Bourdieu. Acknowledging the value of Foucault's focus on "the primacy of relations" (and the resultant emphasis on "discourse"), Bourdieu argues for what he calls a "genetic structuralism,"[56] articulated in terms of his materialist vocabulary of field, capital, and *habitus*. A field in this sense "consists of a set of objective, historical relations between positions anchored in certain forms of power (or capital) . . . simultaneously a space of conflict and competition."[57] As with Foucault, the emphasis here is on relations ("To think in terms of field is to think relationally"[58]), but in such a way that *agency* remains of primary importance.

Here Bourdieu applauds his forebear Max Weber for the reintroduction of specialists (religious, in this case) along with "their particular interests, that is, the functions that their activities and products—religious doctrines, juridical corpora, etc.—fulfil for them" into the purview of sociological analysis; however, he wishes to push beyond Weber to the recognition that "intellectual worlds are *microcosms* that have their own structures and their own laws."[59] Bourdieu thus calls for more than the analysis of discourses rolling autonomously *through* history or the analysis of agents acting autonomously *upon* history, but rather for the application of "a relational . . . or structural mode of thought to the social space of producers."[60] He therefore likens a field to a game, or more specifically, a "space of play," in which "Players agree, by the mere fact of playing, and not by way of a 'contract,' that the game is worth playing, that is it 'worth the candle,' and this *collusion* is the very basis of their competition."[61]

Closely connected to this conception of field is Bourdieu's notion of capital, manifest in various forms (economic, social, cultural, symbolic). It is important to note that capital in this sense has a much broader scope than the purely economic, serving instead to designate "what is efficacious in a given field, both as a weapon and as a stake of struggle, that which allows its possessors to wield a power, an influence and thus to *exist*, in the field under consideration, instead of being considered a negligible quantity."[62] Returning to the game analogy then, players play the game within a given field (artistic, religious, economic) by strategically using the various forms of capital at their disposal. As Bourdieu aptly summarizes, "We can picture each player as having in front of her a pile of tokens of different colors, each color corresponding to a given species of capital she holds, so that her *relative force in the game*, her *position* in the space of play, and also her *strategic orientation toward the game* . . . the moves that she makes, more or less risky or cautious, subversive or conservative, depend both on the total number of tokens and on the composition of the piles of tokens she retains, that is, on the volume and structure of her capital."[63]

Thus capital must be considered not only in terms of an overall amount held by each particular "player" but also in terms of the different (and always shifting) distributions of its various kinds among players. Furthermore, capital can be used for more than simply the increase of capital: "players can play to increase or to conserve their capital, their number of tokens, in conformity with the tacit rules of the game and the prerequisites of the reproduction of the game and its stakes; but they can also get in it to transform, partially or completely, the immanent rules of the game."[64] At stake then are not only the particular holdings of any given player but also the very nature of the field itself.

With these two pieces in place, Bourdieu avoids sliding into a purely functionalist or economic determinism by triangulating field and capital with his concept of *habitus*. *Habitus* has been famously articulated by Bourdieu as

systems of durable, transposable dispositions, structured structures predisposed to function as structuring structures, that is, as principles which generate and organize practices and representations that can be objectively adapted to their outcomes without presupposing a conscious aiming at ends or an express mastery of the operations necessary to attain them. Objectively "regulated" and "regular" without being in any way the product of obedience to rules, they can be collectively orchestrated without being the product of the organizing action of a conductor.[65]

This admittedly complex description can perhaps be more simply summarized as "socialized subjectivity,"[66] that is, "the strategy-generating principle enabling agents to cope with unforeseen and ever-changing situations."[67] That is to say, the dispositions that make up a *habitus* yield social practices that are predictable and structured while nonetheless following "a *practical logic*, that of the fuzzy, of the more-or-less, which defines the ordinary relation to the world."[68]

Bourdieu's appeal to *habitus* thereby allows him to avoid a hard and fast dichotomy between individual, autonomous agency on the one hand and social determinism on the other by asserting that "the individual, and even the personal, the subjective, is social, collective . . . because the human mind is *socially* bounded, socially structured."[69] Accordingly field, capital, and *habitus* can only be understood and effectively applied in relation to one another. As Loïc Wacquant notes, "an adequate theory of field, therefore, requires a theory of social agents . . . [while] the theory of habitus is incomplete without a notion of structure that makes room for the organized improvisation of agents."[70]

Now on the whole, Bourdieu's theory is obviously a species of sociological method. It is geared primarily toward the sort of contemporary sociological analysis in which the sociologist can observe the field in question firsthand (as Bourdieu has done in France and Algeria). Thus when it comes to the resident alien topos, the problems of applying social theory to ancient texts still obtain. As noted above, the lack of other kinds of evidence (beyond the literary-theological texts) that could more firmly locate the social situation(s) of those Christians who used the topos renders any straightforward application of Bourdieu's methodology problematic.

What remains helpful, however, is the philosophy of language that is tied to Bourdieu's sociological approach. Here his foundational insight is that "the relations of communication *par excellence*—linguistic exchanges—are also relations of symbolic power in which the power relations between speakers or their respective groups are actualized."[71] Bourdieu argues that utterances are not (except very rarely) only communicative signifiers but also "*signs of wealth*, intended to be evaluated and appreciated, and *signs of authority*, intended to be believed and obeyed. . . . [I]t is rare in everyday life for language to function as a pure instrument of communication."[72] That is to say, language works in the world not simply to communicate but also to *do* things (as most famously noted by J. L. Austin).[73] However, as Bourdieu is quick to note, the potential efficacy of language in this sense can never be effectively analyzed apart from the social and institutional structures that shape, define, and authorize that efficacy in various ways: "The linguistic relation of power is never defined solely by the relation between the linguistic competencies present. And the weight of different agents depends on their symbolic capital, i.e., on the *recognition*, institutionalized or not, that they receive from the group."[74]

In what ways, then, can this general theoretical orientation prove illuminating to an analysis of the resident alien topos in early Christianity? Within the above framework, Bourdieu's insights into the functions of language in any given sociohistorical space are particularly helpful on two counts. First, Bourdieu argues for a construction that he terms the "space of possibles," defined as "a common framework" that cultural producers share, even as this framework is historically conditioned and continually shifting.[75] It is this space of possibles that orients any given field of discourse and cultural contestation "by defining the universe of problems, references, [and] intellectual benchmarks" that are *possible* within that field, even without the explicitly conscious knowledge of the cultural producers involved.[76] Following this logic, then, the range of possible uses and positions for the alien topos in antiquity was not unlimited. Instead the contours of *how* the motif could be deployed need to be understood as a historically conditioned and socially constructed discursive space. Examining the discursive fields of connotation in which the figure of the alien functioned in the Roman world allows us a starting point to map out (at least broadly) the space of its possible uses.

Note also that the space in question was not a static one: rather any space of possibles is continuously being constructed, redefined, and/or subverted by the acts of cultural production and struggle taking place within the field. It is therefore important to recognize that any particular discursive strategies under examination "depend on the state of the legitimate problematic, that is, the space of possibilities inherited from previous struggles, which tends to define the space of possible position takings and thus orient the search for solutions and, as a result, the evolution of production."[77] By situating the resident alien topos in the appropriate intersection of various discursive fields that made its meaningful deployment in antiquity possible at all (such as citizenship, ethnicity, and exile), we can then draw out the valences of its usage and function(s) in a more nuanced manner.

Second, Bourdieu is also helpful in drawing specific attention to the relationship between the symbolic power of language and the work of communal identity formation. This connection serves as a starting point from which to examine the possible sociological import of the rhetorical move to construct the self as "other." Bourdieu argues, "it is in the constitution of groups that the effectiveness of representations is most apparent."[78] Thus representation of oneself and one's group is never a neutral activity; rather, "The categories according to which a group envisages itself, and according to which it represents itself and its specific reality, contribute to the reality of [the] group."[79] However, the constructive role that linguistic (and in this case, specifically textual) representation has in constituting and/or contesting a group's reality is effective only insofar as this constructive process is (in Bourdieu's terminology) *misrecognized.*[80] Representations function with a certain symbolic capital; but the power of that capital to persuade within a field (and thus to shape a vision of reality) requires that people "misrecognize the arbitrariness of its possession and accumulation."[81] Indeed symbolic power—"as a power of constituting the given through utterances, of making people see and believe, of conforming or transforming the vision of the world"—is necessarily "a transformed, i.e. misrecognizable, transfigured and legitimated form of the other forms of power."[82] Therefore the strategic deployment of the alien topos to construct early Christian reality depends on a certain misrecognition of the process at work—a misrecognition that erases the strategies, choices, and power dynamics at play (with respect to individuals and institutions) in order to render Christian "alien status" a *given,* nothing more than a linguistic response to some unitary extralinguistic reality. It is this misrecognition that fueled the power of the topos to shape the field of early Christian identity (and the foundations of what was to become imperial orthodoxy) as forcefully as it did. The spectrum of scholarly interpretations that continue to regard it as reflective of one kind of singular historical reality or another is a testimony to the powerful persistence of this Bourdieuian misrecognition.

Alien Authors and Alien Readers

Another level of complexity emerges when we turn to questions of the ongoing life of these texts in early Christianity. Here I am interested not so much in the history of interpretation (although this remains an avenue for further research), as in the potential impact of the resident alien topos in a variety of contexts and situations in the first two centuries of the Common Era. That is to say, the rhetorical and ideological functions encoded in the topos—understood as themselves a mode of social practice—have implications that go beyond a unitary "author" of each text and that author's intended meaning in appealing to the figure of the alien. Rather, it is also necessary to consider questions of reading, drawing on the insights of contemporary literary theory to explore the multiple possibilities in which the topos might have functioned for early Christian *readers* within an ancient discursive space. This is simply to acknowledge the basic insight expressed by the circle of Mikhail Bakhtin that "any true understanding is dialogic in nature. . . . Therefore there is no reason for saying that meaning belongs to the word as such. In essence, meaning belongs to a word in its position between speakers."[83]

Many discussions in the realm of literary theory in the last fifty years have shifted toward an exclusive focus on the reader at the expense of both author and text. For example, Richard Rorty has argued that "a text just has whatever coherence it happened to acquire during the last roll of the hermeneutic wheel, just as a lump of clay only has whatever coherence it happened to pick up at the last turn of the potter's wheel,"[84] while Stanley Fish maintains, "The fact that it remains easy to think of a reading that most of us would dismiss out of hand does not mean that the text excludes it but that there is as yet no elaborated interpretive procedure for producing that text."[85] In a similar vein, Roland Barthes's notion of the "writerly text" focuses on the reader's active role in the production of meaning. Barthes therefore declares that "the birth of the reader must be at the cost of the death of the author," averring that "To give a text an Author is to impose a limit on that text, to furnish it with a final signified, to close the writing."[86] His purpose is to open up space for polysemy and plurality in interpretation, "a difference which does not stop and which is articulated upon the infinity of texts, of languages, of systems: a difference of which each text is the return."[87]

In fleshing out this project, Barthes uses the vocabulary of "cultural codes," analyzed by Graham Allen as that in which human beings "feel and think and act . . . in the cultural space of the _déjà_, the already spoken, written, read."[88] On one level, this is useful terminology for thinking about the multiple functions and possibilities at the disposal of ancient readers as they interpreted and reinterpreted the resident alien topos as a means to mark modes of otherness.[89] Overall, however, radically reader-centered approaches such as Barthes's reflect an intriguing semiotic possibility, but prove to be less directly helpful for the purposes of this book, given its sociological and historical orientation toward an ancient field of discourse—one that reflects a rich and diverse but nonetheless _limited_ number of possible appropriations and uses of the topos in actual early Christian practice.

Perhaps more helpful is Umberto Eco's argument for "a dialectical link between the _intentio operis_ and _intentio lectoris_."[90] This appeal to "the intention of the text" is an attempt to recognize a "semiotic strategy" within the text itself "conceived in order to produce its model reader" and to put that strategy into dialectical conversation with the interpretive freedoms of actual readers.[91] This conversation can look a variety of ways, sometimes stretching the tension of the dialectic to an excruciatingly taut degree. For example, Eco points out insightfully that "one can read a text conceived as absolutely univocal as if it were infinitely interpretable"—a favorite trick in certain strains of contemporary reading—or on the other hand, "one can read as univocal a text whose author wanted it to be infinitely interpretable (as would be the case of fundamentalists if by chance the Kabbalists were right)."[92] Here Eco's concern is not to maintain a place for an *intentio auctoris* (he himself acknowledges that his approach "makes the notion of an empirical author's intention radically useless"[93]) but rather to preserve some sort of role for the constraints on interpretation implied by the existence of the text itself (the *intentio operis*): "Between the mysterious history of a textual production and the uncontrollable drift of its future readings, the text qua text still represents a comfortable presence, the point to which we can stick."[94]

For this analysis, however, given the lack of information about the empirical authors of *any* of the early Christian texts in question, it is not necessary to drive such a strong wedge between the *intentio auctoris* and the *intentio operis*. For all practical purposes, these two *intentiones* amount to the same thing, because the only access we have to anything like an empirical author is the strategic intentions that we find embedded in the text itself. Thus in appropriating theoretical vocabulary and insights from literary theorists such as Barthes and Eco, I am not ruling out notions of authorial/textual intent entirely; however, I am relativizing them to the extent that I will not look to any particular construction of an author as the final arbiter of the text's meaning. Instead, I will treat each use of the alien topos under analysis as part of a dialogical conversation, taking into account both the text's own strategic intentions and the larger cultural field of early Christian identity formation in the Roman Empire—the result being a necessary acknowledgment that *multiple* interpretive options were possible for early Christian readers who encountered the call to understand themselves in terms of this topos in the first and second centuries.[95]

Thus I maintain that this methodological melding of broadly Foucaultian historicism, Bourdieuian sociology of knowledge, and contemporary literary theory (while admittedly theoretically eclectic) opens a promising avenue for exploring the variegated uses of the early Christian resident alien topos within a historically constituted discursive field. Though not without its limitations, this approach, I suggest, can provide the requisite analytical tools for investigating both the specific texts and the broader questions that Christian appropriations of the alien figure raise. These are questions that play out on a number of levels: what are the implications (both theological and political) of the topos's different possibilities? What rhetorical strategies are embedded in the texts that themselves call for analysis? And in the broader sphere of theology and Christian identity, what are the potential benefits and the drawbacks of invoking the topos in a constructive way? In what ways does claiming alien status function advantageously to shore up a secure communal identity?—and what problematic (and even potentially violent) possibilities might be introduced in the process as these texts are used and re-used in ever-changing contexts? It is my hope that a critical exploration of the shifting figure of the alien in early Christian projects of self-definition will render visible something of what is at stake in different ways of constructing the Christian self as other.

Chapter Overview

Employing Bourdieu's notion of "the space of possibles," Chapter 1 explores the connotative possibilities of the alien topos in Roman antiquity. I begin by examining the discursive "blurriness" between registers of civic and ethnoracial status in which the category of the Roman citizen was situated—that is, the insider par excellence over and against which the alien was defined as outsider. I investigate the tensions and ambivalences that constituted the Roman citizenship as a category of identity, and the ways that these instabilities can be seen most visibly in the complex interplay of disdain and desire that Romans felt for the "others" they encountered in travel and imperial expansion. I then turn to the ways in which Roman philosophers exploited these ambivalences in the late republic and early empire, using them to revalue the trope of exile to positive and even desirable ends. Finally, I survey a selection of examples drawn from Hellenistic philosophy, the Hebrew Bible, its Greek translation, and the writings of Philo, all of which resignify (and thus valorize) the resident alien figure—the beginnings of a discourse that early Christians joined as they thought through their own "alien identity" in response to particular situations and paraenetic needs.

Chapter 2 analyzes the function of the alien topos in the Epistle to the Hebrews. Here I examine the ways Hebrews uses this language of outsider status to construct a lineage of strangers and sojourners for its audience, rooted in a collective memory of Abraham and other great heroes of the faith. I look at the tension between this alien identity and the relatively conventional ethical paraenesis of Hebrews 13, with particular attention to how this traditional paraenetic agenda is rendered in outsider terms through the call to join Jesus *outside* the camp. In this way, I argue, Hebrews constructs a kind of "usable social identity" for its audience, one that maintains both the radical distinctiveness of Christian "marginality" (at least rhetorically) and simultaneously an affirmation of rather conventional Greco-Roman mores.

Chapter 3 turns to a second-century Christian text, the *Epistle to Diognetus*. Like Hebrews, *Diognetus*'s use of the alien topos locates Christian identity very much within the bounds of conventional cultural ideals of the Roman world. But in doing so, the text also makes the argument that Christian alien status is in fact a result of Christians *surpassing* the Romans around them—that is, fulfilling the Romans' own norms better than they do. The text thus resists what it imagines to be a Roman construal of Christian marginality, offering instead an alternative vision that seeks to bolster Christian distinctiveness, to appeal to those outside the Christian community, and to change the shape of the Roman field of identities all at once.

Chapter 4 remains in the second century, considering a rather different use of the alien topos as seen in the *Shepherd of Hermas, Similitudes*. While the text still constructs the Christian self as other (at least implicitly), it does not emphasize alterity as the definitive marker of Christian identity in the way that Hebrews and *Diognetus* do. Christians are in fact foreigners in the logic that *Hermas* sets up. But the text places its rhetorical emphasis on the alien status not of Christians, but of financial practices within the Christian community that it opposes, explicitly marking certain kinds of commitments, assets, and business arrangements as foreign (and therefore evil). It then goes on to produce Christian difference (and thus identity) in another way, advancing a radical economic agenda meant to undercut the commonplaces of affluent Roman life.

Chapter 5 looks at a reversal of the alien topos as found in the *Apocryphon of James*. While using traditional themes and terminology of the topos, the apocryphon in fact dialogically engages and calls into question the basic move seen in each of the previous chapters to valorize Christian marginality in some way. I argue that while *Ap. Jas.* shares with the other texts a commitment to a true city where Christians belong, it does not positively deploy the rhetoric of alien status for the purposes of identity formation. Instead the text playfully reworks the terms of the topos, positing a single city to which Christians very much belong, but where they have unnecessarily made themselves outsiders through their failure to grasp a deeper soteriological point. The text uses this interpretation of the alien-stranger to buttress its particular notion of salvation, one that emphasizes self-motivation and self-realization. Thus Christians are not outsiders but insiders—they only have to realize it and act accordingly. In the context of this soteriological vision, Jesus functions not as a savior but as a teacher, contesting the legitimacy of a Christian identity built around alterity and urging an alternative vision of identity, one predicated upon Christians taking hold of the salvation that is rightfully theirs.

The conclusion briefly explores the potential repercussions of this project for the narrative reconstruction of early Christian history. It then revisits the broader questions of theology and identity raised in this introductory chapter. Here I offer some critical reflections on the theological stakes involved in a rhetorical stance of marginality and the implications of the alien topos's diverse uses in antiquity for contemporary theological reflection.

Translations of early Christian texts under consideration are my own throughout this study. In the case of additional ancient materials, I have occasionally provided my own translation or relied on standard translations (noted in each instance) with recourse to the original languages as needed. Transliterations of Greek, Hebrew, and Coptic script are rendered according to the systems found in the *SBL Handbook of Style*.

Chapter One
Citizens and Aliens

No, those who get on badly in foreign parts continually cry out that one's own country is the greatest of all blessings, while those who get on well, however successful they may be in all else, think that they lack one thing at least, a thing of the greatest importance, in that they do not live in their own country but sojourn (xeniteuein) in a strange land; for thus to sojourn is a reproach!

—traditionally attributed to Lucian of Samosata

What kind of "other" was the resident alien within the various discursive fields of the early Roman Empire? What might a designation of "alien," "sojourner," or "foreigner" have meant to various audiences or readers in this context? In the second century C.E., Lucian of Samosata (or whoever the author of this epigraph may be) could offer a straightforward remark about the reproach of alien status with no need for further argument or explanation, confident that his readers would understand and agree. But what sort of reproach? Was the category of the alien a relatively neutral civic descriptor—in which case the reproach in view may have been tightly circumscribed, bordering on mild? Or—as the pathos of the above declaration would seem to indicate—did this status suggest something more?

If we follow contemporary usage, the term "resident alien" may seem on the face of things to be primarily a political term, signifying a certain kind of civic outsider status (though even here, the force of the negative valence that the term encodes can vary). Yet the easy slippage in antiquity between "resident alien" (*paroikos*) and terms whose connotations cannot be limited to the civic sphere in the narrowly political sense (such as *parepidēmos*, *xenos*, and *allotrios*) points to a more complicated situation.[1] While the appellation "resident alien" could and undoubtedly did (in some circumstances) denote a certain kind of civic/political status, its connotations also inevitably intersected with ancient thinking about foreignness—and thus cultural differences, ethnicity, and race.[2]

This slippage was not unique to the alien topos. In fact, it can in many ways be traced to ambiguities already entailed in Greek and Roman concepts of citizenship. As discussed, the category of the alien is a relational and even parasitic one, an outsider term dependent for its meaning(s) on a corresponding insider term—in this case, the citizen.[3] And ancient notions of the citizen were themselves situated in a discursive "blurriness" between two overlapping registers of identity, the civic and the ethnoracial (insofar as a group of citizens constitute a "people," a notion that spans between both registers).[4] More specifically, the social complexities involved in Rome's rapid territorial expansion rendered this blurriness visible in particular ways—ones that were not culturally neutral, but instead were inflected by the power dynamics of empire. As Denise Buell points out, "[The] slippage between ideas of ethnicity, race, and civic status would have been especially clear to ancient readers in relation to being Roman since Romanness is both a civic identity (linked to the city of Rome) and a broader ethnoracial one (in the context of the Roman Empire)."[5]

Yet within this blurriness, the connotative possibilities for both the alien and the citizen were not infinite. Rather they were determined by a complex interplay of cultural codes—a term I take from Roland Barthes, but further defined by Daniel Boyarin as that which "either conscious or unconscious . . . both constrain[s] and allow[s] the production (not creation) of new texts within the culture; these codes may be identified with the ideology of the culture, which is made up of the assumptions that people in the culture automatically make about what may or may not be true and possible, about what is natural in nature and in history."[6] In view here, then, is what Bourdieu calls the "space of possibles" (as discussed in the previous chapter)—the framework that defines the kinds of discursive positionings that are possible at a particular sociohistorical moment.[7] This is not a static notion, nor one whose contents can ever be nailed down precisely. But Bourdieu draws our attention to the fact that a space of possibles "is what causes producers of a particular period to be both situated and dated."[8]

The task of this chapter then will be to "situate and date" (i.e., to *historicize* in a broad sense) the connotative possibilities for the alien topos in the first two centuries of the Common Era. Here the slippage between the topos's civic and ethnoracial dimensions is of paramount importance, insofar as these two strands are not easily separated or unpacked apart from one another. I will therefore explore the ways in which these categories intertwine, overlap, and blur in ancient Roman thinking (with some reference to its Greek precursors). As we will see, this discursive blurriness carries within it certain instabilities, tensions, and ambivalences that are crucial to recognize in order to map the possible connotations of the alien figure.

These are instabilities that especially come to the fore in ancient discussions of boundary crossing. For Romans, boundaries could be crossed in multiple ways. The boundaries of Rome itself were crossed by foreigners immigrating to the capital city from throughout the Empire. And the Romans themselves crossed boundaries through travel, bringing them into contact with various kinds of cultural and political "others" in the many territories that they conquered or sought to conquer. These encounters, both at home and abroad, called into question any secure borders to Roman identity, foregrounding the need to shore up exactly what made the "Roman self" distinctive and (in the eyes of the Romans) worthy of ruling the world. But they also opened up spaces of ambivalence, different modes of desire, and even possibilities for interrogating the value of Roman citizenship itself. This can be seen with particular force in the contested figure of "the exile," a position that could be lamented, celebrated, or both. And it is in these tensions intrinsic to the very project of erecting boundaries, I will argue, that we need to locate the connotative possibilities for both despising and valorizing the resident alien.

Locating the Roman Citizen

My investigation begins, however, not with the alien but with the citizen—the "other" over and against which the alien is defined. In many ways, "the citizen" (*ho politēs*) functioned as Rome's insider term par excellence during the first centuries of the Empire.[9] While not all citizens were of the same status, citizenship signified a certain minimum threshold on the hierarchical pyramid that ordered the Roman social universe. Roman citizenship was an institution fundamentally oriented around the legal, political, and symbolic privileges of a group of elite men, categorically positioned (at least in the dominant Roman discourse) above such others as slaves, foreigners, and barbarians.[10] But, with that said, it remained a complicated category both conceptually and in its institutional incarnations. Indeed the character, politics, and boundaries of Roman citizenship were not monolithic but varied according to time and place throughout the Empire.

The idea of the citizen had a distinguished cultural pedigree, both in Platonic and Aristotelian reflections on the nature of the ideal citizen and in the history of the classical *polis*.[11] In the context of classical Athens, political functions such as the right to own property, vote, and hold office had been crucial to the institution of citizenship.[12] But among the immediate predecessors to Rome's political ascendancy—the Hellenistic monarchies that emerged in the wake of the classical city-states' demise—citizenship tended to be primarily about certain kinds of honorific status.[13] Greek cities exchanged *isopoliteia* with one another (a kind of mutual reciprocity with respect to citizenship), and also conferred honorary citizenships on individuals. Thus by the first century B.C.E. it had become common for male elites to accrue multiple citizenships, usually to their political and economic advantage.[14]

With Rome's meteoric rise to power came rhetorical and political attempts to change all this by recasting *Roman* citizenship as the apogee of status across the entire Mediterranean world. This process was facilitated by the structural possibilities that existed in the system for non-Romans to join the club. This could happen in a number of ways: first of all, there was the army. Auxiliaries who served twenty-five years or more became citizens (along with their families) upon completion of their service.[15] In addition, individuals could receive Roman citizenship through serving as a magistrate, being formally (i.e., legally) freed from slavery, or being granted it as a recognition or reward for a service provided to the state.[16] But perhaps most important was the complex system by which entire collectives of non-Romans could become citizens of the Republic and later the Empire.

This practice of granting Roman citizenship to whole communities needs to be understood in the context of Rome's rapid expansion. From the fourth to first centuries B.C.E., through a complex historical process, Rome took control of the Italian peninsula, in time uniting Italy politically as a Roman state.[17] As its influence and territorial holdings expanded (eventually stretching throughout the Mediterranean), it also extended the institution of Roman citizenship. Gradually a paradigm emerged in which newly incorporated communities could move up a scale of status toward the acquisition of citizenship. Various grades existed along this scale (*civitas, municipium, colonia,* etc.[18]) and communities could be promoted—through petition or as a reward for military service.[19] As their territorial holdings grew, the Romans made use of this system through the end of the Republic and the first two centuries of the Empire. As late as the reign of Septimius Severus (193–211 C.E.), communities were still applying to move up to a higher status.[20]

Throughout this process, the question of multiple and competing citizenships loomed large—as Roman citizenship became an option, or more often a necessity, for Italian cities (and later for provincial ones), where were one's loyalties to lie? We can see one attempt at an answer to this question (toward a very specific political and ideological end) in Cicero's *De legibus*, proclaiming the unitary nature of the Roman citizenship in the first century B.C.E. Cicero allows that a man may acknowledge his municipality as a homeland or *patria*, but ultimately, the *patria* of Rome always trumps all others: "So we consider both the place where we were born our fatherland and also the city in which we have been adopted [i.e., Rome]. But that fatherland must stand first in our affection in which the name of republic signifies the common citizenship of all of us. For her it is our duty to die, to her to give ourselves entirely, to place on her altar, and, as it were, to dedicate to her service, all that we possess."[21] Here the Roman orator's rhetoric tries to produce the impression of a political reality in which, whatever competing loyalties one may hold, in the final analysis, it is the citizenship of Rome that matters.

Ethnicity, Race, and Civic Status in Antiquity

Yet this vision of a unified and all-encompassing Roman citizenship was not so easily secured—even rhetorically. For one thing, on a conceptual level, Roman citizenship was not an entirely civic category, and thus required shoring up in more than just political terms. That is, as a discursive category for marking insider status, its connotations were not contained or containable solely within the legal-political sphere administered by the institutions of Roman government (in contrast to certain contemporary notions of citizenship, themselves dependent on the rise of modern nation-states). Rather, the discursive purview of Roman citizenship bled beyond the boundaries of the purely civic, overlapping and intertwining with ethnic and racial considerations as well.

The question of "ethnicity" and/or "race" as viable categories in antiquity (rather than anachronistic) is one that has provoked much scholarly conversation. Are one or both of these terms appropriate to apply to an ancient discursive field, or are they simply modern constructs, inextricably implicated in a set of concerns foreign to the ancient world? The classicist Jonathan Hall has argued that "ethnicity" as a category ought not to be seen as either an essentialist given (the primordialist position) nor a purely political maneuver (the functionalist position), but rather "a cultural construct, perpetually renewed and renegotiated through discourse and social praxis . . . [one that is] socially constructed and objectively perceived."[22] In this way, Hall's work attempts to salvage categories such as "ethnicity" and "ethnic identity" as useful and usable vocabulary for thinking about cultural currents, negotiations, and group definitions in the ancient world.

But what about "race"? As Denise Buell points out, for many scholars, " 'race' has fallen out of favor as an analytical category for classical antiquity. The arguments against using race rely on a definition of race as clear, immutable, grounded in biology, and especially indicated by skin color. Thus defined, race (in contrast to 'ethnicity') is deemed irrelevant for antiquity because it is anachronistic."[23] This line of argument tends to focus on the ways in which modern understandings of race emerged out of nineteenth-century biologism. Accordingly, race emerges as a category whose only legitimate application is to the modern era. So Buell

summarizes: "Since this particular formulation does not appear in sur-
viving ancient Mediterranean texts, so the logic goes, one should not
import 'race' into the study of antiquity."[24]

However, Benjamin Isaac has argued in a major new study that while
"the idea of race in its recent form is a by-product of Darwin's work,"
there nonetheless exists in antiquity what he terms "proto-racism," a
strain of prejudice based on "presumed common characteristics . . . that
are considered unalterable, based as they are on factors beyond human
control."[25] According to this argument, ethnic/group prejudice (which
also exists in antiquity) allows for the possibility of change. Proto-racism stands in contrast to this type of prejudice as follows: "According
to ancient thinking, external influences could alter physical and mental characteristics—such as the southern sun which turns white people
into blacks—and these subsequently became stable and were inherited.
Furthermore, if we read that people are superior because they are of
pure lineage, then this is an imagined construct aimed at establishing
superiority on the basis of heredity. Such theories can be qualified as an
early form of racism."[26] For Isaac, the key issue is one of immutability, or
more precisely, the ancient *perception* of immutability with reference to
acquired characteristics that then become fixed.[27] Ethnic identity is perceived as culturally constructed and mutable, while those characteristics
properly categorized as racial are perceived as immutable.

A contrary position on this issue is taken by Denise Buell in her recent work on "ethnic reasoning" in early Christianity.[28] Buell argues that
"neither term [race or ethnicity] has a one-to-one counterpart in antiquity; moreover . . . these terms cannot be neatly distinguished even in
modern parlance."[29] That is to say, "ethnicity" is no less a modern construct implicated in contemporary concerns than "race" is. Furthermore,
Buell challenges the idea that mutability versus immutability can serve
as a viable distinction between the two categories, maintaining instead
that in antiquity, mutability functions as a crucial aspect of all ethnic
and/or racial thinking. She therefore contends that both ethnicity and
race have fixed and fluid elements—and that both of these dynamics
call for critical attention. Following anthropologist Ann Stoler and classicist Irad Malkin, Buell seeks "to resituate scholarly discussions away
from the question of whether or not race/ethnicity is fixed or mutable
to analyses of how discourses of race and ethnicity rely upon the notion
of fixity or primordiality even while they are also always under negotiation and flux."[30] As a result of this theoretical position, Buell uses "race"
and "ethnicity"/"ethnic group" as roughly interchangeable terms, both
of which can be used to translate such slippery Greek words as *ethnos* and
genos.[31] Her purpose in doing so is not to turn the terms into synonyms,
but rather "[to provoke] attention to their inexactness—both in the con-

temporary moment and in their relationship to ancient categories of cultural difference."[32]

Here I propose to follow Buell's approach in not strictly distinguishing between race and ethnicity so as to highlight precisely this inexactness as it was operative in Roman antiquity—a complex interplay of cultural negotiation (fluidity) and appeals to essence (fixity) that cannot be easily mapped onto separate terms. This interplay in all its imprecision has important implications for how we understand the connotative blurriness of Roman citizenship, particularly as Rome's power spread.[33] With the Empire expanding, Romans increasingly had to make sense of their own identity as citizen-insiders; and here a strictly civic/political division between citizens and non-citizens was not enough. Rather ethnoracial logic came to the fore (in both its fluidity and its rhetorical reliance on fixity), proving useful for mapping a complicated field of cultural differences not reducible to civic designations (though still implicated in them). We can see this dynamic most visibly—as well as the ambivalences that it inevitably produced—in Roman discussions of travel.

Encountering the Other: Ancient Travel and Cultural Ambivalence

The most prominent traveler (and by extension, ethnographer) of antiquity lived several centuries before the Roman Empire: Herodotus of Halicarnassus (c.484–c.425 B.C.E.). Through his many and varied encounters with ethnoracial difference, Herodotus constructs colorful narratives of cultural alterity, highlighting the ways the people he writes about invert the normal practices of "other people."[34] As François Hartog has argued, this strategic appeal to a universal norm functions in fact to conceal Herodotus' conflation of universality with Greeks and Greek practices—part of a larger project in which the exotica of otherness serves as a mirror image of a putatively coherent, normative Greek self (an image that works rhetorically to unify a diverse set of family/tribal loyalties and citizenships specific to individual Greek city-states).[35]

But Herodotus' ethnographic project is more complex than just a simple opposition or mirror reflection. This becomes visible (as Hartog argues) in numerous places throughout the narrative, but particularly in his construction of the Scythians, figured as the prototypical nomadic other in contrast to the autochthonous Athenian self.[36] In one example, the Scythian Anacharsis travels the world, and on his way back to Scythia, passes through Cyzicus (a Milesian colony and thus definably *Greek* space). Here he discovers the worship of the Mother of the Gods (Cybele) and vows that "if he came back to his own land safe and sound [i.e., Scythia], he would sacrifice as he saw the Cyzicenes doing and would establish an all-night festival there."[37] When it is discovered that Anacharsis has imported this "Greek" contamination, Saulius the king of Scythia shoots him dead with his bow and arrow. The narrative concludes grimly: "Now when anyone mentions Anacharsis, the Scythians say they do not know any such person—and that is because he went traveling to Greece and adopted foreign customs."[38]

In a second paired story that immediately follows, Herodotus describes Scyles, a king of Scythia with a fascination for all things Greek:

Though Scyles became king of Scythia, he was not pleased with the Scythian manner of life but was far more given to Greek ways, from the training he had had. So this is what he did: as often as he led the army of the Scythians to the city of the Borysthenites—these Borysthenites declare that they are Milesians—he would leave his army in the suburbs but himself go within the walls and shut up the gates. Then he would take off his Scythian clothes and take on Greek clothes and in that shape would go and walk about the marketplace, with no bodyguards or indeed anyone else. They guarded the gates that no Scythian might see him wearing Greek dress. He followed a Greek way of life, and, in especial, he made offerings to the gods in the Greek fashion. When he had spent a month or more like this, he would put on his Scythian clothes and go back.[39]

As the narrative progresses, Scyles even goes so far as to be initiated into the Bacchic rites. When the Scythians see him in a Bacchic frenzy along with other devotees of Dionysus, they are enraged, and Scyles' brother Octamasades beheads the wayward king. The conclusion is similar to what we saw in the case of Anacharsis: "So careful are the Scythians to guard their own customs, and such are the penalties that they impose on those who take to foreign customs over and above their own."[40]

Together these two stories indicate that ethnicity/race is a complicated category for Herodotus. On the one hand, the deities in question here, Cybele and Dionysius, are somewhat surprising choices, given that in their Greek context (and later in their Roman one as well), they are two of the major divinities associated with the category of foreignness and all the ambiguities that surround it.[41] Yet these are the very deities that the Scythians reject as being too "Greek." Why these two, Hartog asks pointedly, rather than a pair of unequivocally Greek deities like Apollo and Hera?[42] In his analysis, these narrative tensions "[hinge] on the interplay between the near and the far."[43] Herodotus's point is not about fixed contents associated with particular ethnic identities like "Greekness," but rather about the importance of boundaries and the transgressive danger associated with crossing them: "truth lies on this side of the frontier, error beyond it."[44] At the same time, this monological situating of truth on "our side" of the boundary is not entirely stable. What lies beyond the frontier is fascinating and alluring, even as it is also dangerous.

In this way, though these extended examples from Herodotus come from significantly before the Roman period, they nonetheless reveal something of the broader discursive significance accorded to travel throughout antiquity: travel offered opportunities to buttress and fortify the ancient self through the contrasts entailed in encounter with the other. But it also opened up the self to problematic desires and perils, conjured inevitably into existence through the crossing of putatively impermeable but in fact tremendously fluid cultural boundaries. As Michel de Certeau puts it evocatively, the traveler's narrative (as a subset of what he terms "spatial stories") "privileges a 'logic of ambiguity' through its accounts of interaction. It 'turns' the frontier into a crossing, and the river into a bridge. It recounts inversions and displacements: the door that closes is precisely what may be opened; the river is what makes passage possible; the tree is what marks the stages of advance; the picket fence is an ensemble of interstices through which one's glances pass."[45]

Romans too were travelers—and as such participants in travel's attendant ambiguities—but their travels took place in a decidedly different sociopolitical context: that of territorial expansion, domination, and empire. Here ethnoracial logic had its uses, not least of which was to reassert the centrality and superiority of the Roman citizenship—in both civic and ethnoracial dimensions. To this end, the Romans availed themselves of arguments going back as far as Aristotle and other Greek thinkers: "The nations inhabiting the cold places and those of Europe are full of spirit but somewhat deficient in intelligence and skill, so that they continue comparatively free, but lacking in political organization and capacity to rule their neighbours. The peoples of Asia on the other hand are intelligent and skilful in temperament, but lack spirit, so that they are in continuous subjection and slavery. But the Greek race participates in both characters, just as it occupies the middle position geographically, for it is both spirited and intelligent."[46] According to this construction, occidental peoples are spirited but mentally deficient; oriental peoples are intelligent but soft and worthy of slavery. Both deserve to be colonized by the ideal who holds the center. As Isaac argues, once this cultural logic was in play, "Roman authors took over these ideas, duly substituting themselves as the ideal rulers."[47]

Thus in one sense it became easy for Romans to fall back on a straightforward distinction between themselves and everybody else, even as "foreigners" from the far reaches of the Mediterranean increasingly came to constitute significant portions of the city of Rome's population. In response to these shifting demographics, Juvenal (60?–after 127 c.e.) sneeringly reports, "The Syrian Orontes has long since poured into the Tiber."[48] Indeed, a vitriolic passage in his sixth satire attacking Phrygians, Egyptians, Jews, and other foreigners present in Rome makes clear the social disdain with which some Romans regarded the foreigner or ethnoracial other, both as a category and in its specific embodiments.[49]

The periodic expulsion of various foreign groups from the city of Rome (attested by numerous Latin authors) points to a similar cultural attitude.[50]

On the frontiers, a similar contempt was easy to cultivate. In his treatise *Germania*, the Roman historian Tacitus (c.56–112 C.E.) clearly looks down on the German tribes for their violence and indolence: "When they are not entering on war, they spend much time in hunting, but more in idleness—creatures who eat and sleep, the best and bravest warriors doing nothing, having handed over the charge of their home, hearth and estate to the women and the old men and the weakest members of the family: for themselves they lounge about, by that curious incongruity of temperament, which makes of the same men such lovers of laziness and haters of quiet."[51] But Tacitus was also no stranger to the ambivalent desires that were the occupational hazard of ancient travelers. He in fact simultaneously applauds the German barbarians' strength, cultural purity, and love of liberty, using a romanticized notion of the foreigner to offer a contrast to contemporary Roman society—one in which the Romans suffer by comparison: "Personally I associate myself with the opinions of those who hold that in the people of Germany there has been given to the world a race unmixed by intermarriage with other races, a peculiar people and pure, like no one but themselves, whence it comes that their physique, so far as can be said with their vast numbers, is identical: fierce blue eyes, red hair, tall frames."[52] In this interplay between disgust for the coarse barbarians and praise of their stalwart, passionate and faithful nature, Tacitus capitalizes on the usefulness of a rhetoric of otherness in order to launch an implicit critique of the Roman self.

Yet a fuller picture of the strategies of Roman identity formation resists a straightforward dualism (however ambivalent) between self and other. Whereas classical Greek thinkers had made ample use of the binary division between the Greek self and the "barbarian," things were not so simple for the Romans.[53] As Hartog argues, "With the arrival of Rome upon the scene, that is to say with the victories of Rome and its legions, the great divide between the Greeks and the Barbarians definitively ceased to be a tenable way of summing up the human race."[54] Instead, new questions emerged: how well would it actually work for the Romans simply to substitute themselves into the Greek half of the binary? Certainly Tacitus availed himself of this conceptual option—and both conquered Greeks and other conquering Romans also made the substitution.[55] But this move proved in many ways to be a conceptually impoverished one, lacking the analytical sophistication needed to secure a stable center to Roman identity as the cultural complexities of the empire rapidly multiplied, continually threatening to spiral out of control. As D. B. Saddington points out, in the context of this continuous imperial expansion, terms such as *barbarus* and *externus* simply could not remain fixed or rigid signifiers but had to function as "sliding terms of reference."[56] Indeed, room had to be made for varying degrees of barbarity,[57] as the Romans engaged in the twin projects of ruling the world and continuing to produce/maintain some sense of "Roman-ness" while the Empire's boundaries swelled.

Another possibility, as Hartog points out, was to break the Greek/barbarian polarity (which situated the Romans—whether literally or symbolically—in a Greek lineage) by repositioning the new imperial power as a third term: "It was all a matter of genealogies. The thesis of Rome's Trojan origin, magnified by Virgil, was to break away from [the binary] view and set up Rome as a third group, from 'the very start.' This was all the more acceptable given that . . . [t]he Trojans may not have been Greeks, but they were certainly not Barbarians either."[58] This strategy necessitated that Romans articulate Roman identity in civic/ethnoracial terms not only in relation to the bewildering diversity of other cultures in the distant provinces (which could still be conveniently lumped under a blanket term like "barbarian") but also with respect to the peculiar position of the Greeks.

On the one hand then, many Romans did exhibit a profound anxiety about the "Greek" as a threat to Roman *virtus*. For example, the ever-malicious Juvenal offers a predictably acerbic comment: "I cannot abide . . . a Rome of Greeks; and yet what fraction of our dregs come from Greece?"[59] But on the other hand, the Romans clearly admired the intellectualism of the Greeks and appropriated their cultural achievements and educational system to be the basis of their own.[60] As Arnaldo Momigliano points out, "The Romans decided to find out about the Greeks, tried to learn the language, accepted Greek gods and reshaped their constitution on lines which some Greeks recognized as akin to their own constitutions."[61] Homi Bhabha captures this dynamic well (with reference to a very different imperial context), characterizing the general productivity of colonial power in terms of "the *productive* ambivalence of the object of colonial discourse—that 'otherness' which is at once an object of desire and derision, an articulation of difference contained within the fantasy of origin and identity."[62]

Tim Whitmarsh has explored the complexity of these Roman attitudes toward Greeks and Greek *paideia*, characterizing them in terms of a double ambivalence:

On the one hand, in terms of cultural definition, Rome used the advent of Greek *paideia* as a narrative stage in Roman history, marking the transition from origins to civilization: this could be presented as either a civilizing or a luxurifying process. On the other hand, in terms of competitive ambition within the Roman hierarchy, the possession of Greek education . . . could be used as a counter in the game of elite self-positioning (and conversely, the accusation of excessive devotion to Greek arts could be used rhetorically to impugn an enemy . . .). At all times, however, Romans were expected to keep in view the military and economic subordination of Greece to Rome.[63]

Here Whitmarsh convincingly argues that the political realities of empire never dropped out of view. While "Greekness" was figured simultaneously (in Bhabha's terms) as "an object of desire and derision" in the project of working out *Roman* identity, the power axis on which these ambivalences played out was one fundamentally oriented by Rome's imperial domination of Greece. Yet the political complexities of the empire (and the elasticity of Roman citizenship within it) ensured that this axis was in many ways not a secure one. As Whitmarsh points out, during the early Empire, "Greeks of the highest socio-economic ranks were . . . increasingly implicated in structures of Roman power: ever larger numbers of elite Greeks acted as intermediaries between their cities and Rome, were awarded Roman citizenship, found their way into the Roman Senate, and attained important offices."[64]

Thus we see that encountering the other raised a variety of questions and complexities for ancient projects of identity that were not easily put to rest. Following in the footsteps of eminent Greek ethnographic explorers such as Herodotus, the Romans also traveled to the far reaches of the Mediterranean world. However, they did so as conquerors, erecting political and symbolic boundaries meant to fortify and stabilize Roman identity within a framework of Roman imperial power. But this stability proved elusive. Gazing through the fences they erected, the Romans discovered that propping up the citizen-self as a secure symbolic center was not such a straightforward project in the face of an unsettling range of civic and ethnoracial differences. Not only were they troubled by conflicting desires regarding those on the other side of their fences, but the fences themselves proved permeable in both directions—a permeability facilitated in fact by the relative ease (on a structural level) with which the Romans themselves incorporated new persons and communities into their citizenship. These ambivalences reflected tensions and instabilities within the discourse of Roman citizenship itself. And while some thinkers sought to cover these over quietly, we will now turn to others who pushed on the instabilities. In the process these authors questioned the value of the Roman citizenship and exploited the possibilities this opened up for refiguring traditionally negative terms associated with the "un-citizen"—such as the exile, the foreigner, and the alien.

Exile and Its Discursive Possibilities

As the ambivalences we have just charted attest, the project of erecting boundaries entails the possibility of (and indeed the potential desire for) crossing them. In the ancient Roman discourse of the civic/ethnoracial insider and its others, these possibilities emerged through various kinds of contact, encapsulating what de Certeau calls the "paradox of the frontier: created by contacts, the points of differentiation between two bodies are also their common points."[65] But for the purposes of locating the figure of the alien (and its possible uses) in its Roman discursive context, one particular way that Roman travelers in the late Republic and early Empire crossed these boundaries calls for further attention: the phenomenon of exile—the displacement of persons from some sort of center (usually identified with a native city or homeland) across political, geographical, and symbolic borders.

Jan Felix Gaertner has recently pointed out that the term "exile" is notoriously difficult to define in its ancient context—due in large part to ancient authors' fluid and somewhat imprecise use of terms such as *fugē* (Greek), *fuga* (Latin), and *exilium*. Thus Gaertner argues, "Whereas the modern derivatives of the Latin word *exilium* imply an involuntary departure, sanctioned by political or judicial authorities, the ancient usage of the corresponding terms . . . [covers] both the expulsion of groups or individuals and their voluntary departure. . . . Moreover, ancient authors often do not distinguish between exile and other forms of displacement: ancient consolatory treatises on exile, for example, often mix mythical and historical exiles with characters that today would be called fugitives . . . or voluntary exiles."[66] Overall, then, the ancient concept of exile seems to have been a capacious one, covering multiple modes of displacement not included in its modern counterpart.

In carving out this discursive space, mythical characters from the ancient Greek past provided both Greek and Roman writers with a stock set of paradigmatic figures to reflect on exile's meaning(s). Stories were told and retold of exemplary figures of exile—Cadmus, Heracles, Jason, Odysseus, Patroclus—to which the Romans added their own more specifically Roman characters, most notably Aeneas. While the tribulations that these heroes endured were not ignored, at the same time, the trope was a flexible one and often focused on the positive results that a temporary exile yielded (such as heroic exploits or the founding of a city).[67] As Hartog shows, in Virgil's *Aeneid*, "To found the city or the Roman race (*Romanam gentem*) will in effect be to resurrect the kingdom of Troy . . . [Aeneas's] exile is transformed into a return."[68]

Around the concept, however, numerous tropes of lament, isolation, and marginality also accrued, building on a tradition already well established in the classical period. Given the centrality of the *polis* for thinkers such as Plato and Aristotle, as Tim Whitmarsh points out, "Exile from the *polis* was, thus, a form of social death, and the horrors of exile are iterated time and again."[69] Such sentiments were expressed freely in the Roman period as well (though most often these are preserved in more complicated treatises that explore both the complaints and consolations of exile—the latter to be discussed in more detail below).[70] For example, during his banishment of 58–57 B.C.E., Cicero—though well aware of more consolatory ways to interpret exile—bemoans his fate multiple times over to his friend Atticus: "I will not mention all that I have lost,— you know it well enough, and it would only open my wound again. But this I do assert that no one has ever lost so much and no one has ever fallen into such a depth of misery. Time too, instead of lightening my grief, can but add to it: for other sorrows lose their sting as time passes, but my sorrow can but grow daily, as I feel my present misery and think on my past happiness. I mourn the loss not only of my wealth and my friends but of my old self. For what am I now?"[71]

Similarly, the second-century C.E. Greek writer Favorinus of Arelate offers a largely traditional catalog of the evils of exile (though his treatise will go on to refute them):

It is not inopportune, in the present circumstances, to list and (as it were) herald [the burdens of exile] by name. First, then, is [. . . love of one's fatherland . . .]. Second is strong affection for one's kin and familiar companionship. Third would no doubt be, what is apparently not granted to most people, enjoyment of wealth, property, and private possessions. Along with this comes what the majority affect to despise, but in truth lust after: an appetite for honours and reputation in one's own land, and, related to it, a horror of ill-repute and a bad name amongst the people. In addition to all these, and (as it were) waiting on the by-line, is the mightiest and most alluring figure: liberty, much coveted, consisting of freedom of action and in the use of property. All of these figures confront the single soul of the sufferer, wanting to humble it, to knock it down, to trip it up, binding it to the point of painful suffocation.[72]

Beyond these Roman and Greek writers, other foreigners who streamed into Rome from the far reaches of the new empire brought with them their own memories of exile and displacement. Most important for our purposes are the reflections of Jews on their situation of dispersal throughout the Greco-Roman world. The potent imagery of Psalm 137 hearkens back to the Babylonian exile of 586 B.C.E.: "By the rivers of Babylon—there we sat down and there we wept when we remembered Zion. On the willows there we hung our harps. For there our captors asked us for songs, and our tormentors asked for mirth, saying, 'Sing us one of the songs of Zion!' How could we sing the LORD's song in a foreign land? If I forget you, O Jerusalem, let my right hand wither!

Let my tongue cling to the roof of my mouth, if I do not remember you, if I do not set Jerusalem above my highest joy."[73] But as Eric Gruen points out, by the time of the Second Temple period, the situation of Jews living outside Palestine was by no means this dire: "Jews abroad had chosen their residence voluntarily and (in many cases) had been there for generations. They had no cause to ache for Jerusalem."[74] Still, the stories of exile and diaspora to be found in the biblical texts provided powerful narrative resources for Jews in the project of maintaining Jewish identity in complex multicultural scenarios. These were resources that for the most part fit nicely within a broader cultural discourse of exile that highlighted the afflictions of the exilic state.

Yet there were also tensions in this discourse—ones that ancient thinkers took advantage of to construe the boundary crossing represented by exile in multiple directions, not all of them negative. As Gaertner shows, in the fifth and fourth centuries B.C.E., exile comes to be seen "as a relative concept that can be applied not only to states banishing individuals but also to individuals dissociating themselves from states, and two more intellectual concepts of exile come to the fore: exile as a condition that provokes a profound change of perspective and offers knowledge and greater insight, and exile as a political, social, even metaphysical metaphor."[75] Gaertner offers a paradigmatic example of each of these shifts from the fifth and further centuries: (1) the Greek historian Thucydides, who, reflecting on his experiences of the Peloponnesian war, claims that "I saw what was being done on both sides, particularly on the Peloponnesian side, because of my exile, and this leisure gave me rather exceptional facilities for looking into things";[76] (2) the Cynic philosopher Diogenes of Sinope. According to Diogenes Laertius, "When someone reproached him with his exile, his reply was, 'Nay, it was through that, you miserable fellow, that I came to be a philosopher.' Again when someone reminded him that the people of Sinope had sentenced him to exile, 'And I them,' said he, 'to home-staying.' "[77]

Roman authors inherited the complexities of this discourse and put it to good use, recycling and refiguring older themes to make sense of their own displacements in new political and cultural contexts.[78] Cicero, for instance, in a somewhat better mood than the one evidenced above, ponders whether exile is in fact really so evil: "In fact, if we now inquire into the real meaning of exile, not the disgrace of the name, how far, pray, does it differ from continual residence abroad? . . . Can exile bring disgrace upon the wise man? . . . 'One's country is wherever one does well.' Socrates, for instance, on being asked to what country he claimed to belong, said, 'To the world'; for he regarded himself as a native and citizen of the whole world."[79]

Seneca the Younger (first century C.E.) makes a comparable philosophical point regarding his own exile: "The very name of exile, by reason of a sort of persuasion and general consent, falls by now upon the ears very harshly, and strikes the hearer as something gloomy and accursed. . . .Therefore, putting aside the verdict of the majority who are swept away by the appearance of things, no matter what ground they have to trust it, let us see what exile is. It is a change of place."[80] Later in the same consolatory treatise, he goes on to argue, "Eager therefore, and erect, let us hasten with dauntless step wherever circumstance directs, let us traverse any lands whatsoever. Inside the world there can be found no place of exile; for nothing that is in inside the world is foreign to mankind."[81]

In this way, Tim Whitmarsh notes, "exile was not simply a tool of imperial repression: it was also appropriated by its victims (and no doubt, by others, too) as a rhetorical resource through which individual agents could articulate their own philosophical status."[82] This was a resource available not only to exiles of solid Roman pedigree but to Greeks and others in various kinds of complicated cultural and political relationships with respect to the hegemony of Rome.[83] Yet the materials examined in this section have one thing in common: the authors all claim to be experiencing exile literally—that is, some sort of physical displacement (whether involuntary or voluntary) from their homeland.[84] However, the trope did not in fact require the movement of bodies across geographical boundaries in order to function as a useful resource for ancient projects of "self-positioning."[85] Indeed, its rhetorical flexibility allowed it to be appropriated as a counter to the citizen-insider, an alternative mode of claiming insider identity, even without the credential of actual geographical displacement.

Valorizing the Resident Alien

The revaluation of terms such as "queer" suggests that speech can be "returned" to its speaker in a different form, that it can be cited against its originary purposes, and perform a reversal of effects. More generally, then, this suggests that the changeable power of such terms marks a kind of discursive performativity that is not a discrete series of speech acts, but a ritual chain of resignifications whose origin and end remain unfixed and unfixable. (Judith Butler)[86]

As we have seen in the case of the exile, tensions and fissures in the ancient discourse of ethnocitizenship allowed for multiple possibilities to realign and refigure outsider terminology in insider terms. While the positioning of "the citizen" as antiquity's fundamental insider term drove the logic of citizenship discourse, that insider valence could be appropriated and directed elsewhere. Therefore a fixed and stable boundary between a valorized Greek or Roman "us" and a despised "them" (whether exile, foreigner, or resident alien) could not really be maintained. Indeed (following Judith Butler above), no discourse, modern or ancient, can entirely control or fix the possibilities for "discursive performativity" or "resignification" of a set of terms within a cultural field. There are always options for thinking, speaking, or acting otherwise—or as Butler quotes J. L. Austin, "There are more ways of outraging speech than contradiction merely."[87]

Furthermore, the possibilities for resignification that we examined in Roman and Greek valorizations of exile did not in fact require a physical state of exile. Insofar as exile could be appropriated metaphorically to designate multiple kinds of outsider status, its connotations remained relatively fluid, thus easily overlapping with other modes of marginality. This fluidity allowed writers in the Hellenistic and early Roman period to collapse subtle distinctions between terms like "exile" and other labels of outsider identity such as "alien" or "sojourner"—especially since all of them were implicated in the ancient discursive blurriness between the civic and the ethnoracial. They could then be collectively refigured to a common end, emerging as a usable topos for the construction of the self *as* other.

Philosophers of the early Roman period (especially middle Platonists) were wise to the rhetorical advantages of this move. We see an illustrative example in the treatise *On Exile* by Plutarch (c.46–120 C.E.). Drawing on Platonic ideals, he depicts the human soul as a sojourner on earth that seeks its true fatherland in heaven:

> But "exile" (*ho phygas*) is a term of reproach. Yes, among fools, who make terms of abuse out of "pauper," "bald," "short," and indeed "foreigner" (*ton xenon*) and "immigrant" (*ton metoikon*). But those who are not carried away by such considerations admire good men, even if they are poor or foreigners or exiles. . . . Empedocles,[88] however, when beginning the presentation of his philosophy, says . . . that not he himself merely, but all of us, beginning with himself, are sojourners here and strangers and exiles (*metanastas entautha kai xenous kai phygadas hēmas ontas*). "For," he says, "no comingling of blood or breath, O mortals, gave our souls their being and beginning; it is the body, earth-born and mortal, that has been fashioned out of these," and as the soul has come hither from elsewhere, he euphemistically calls birth a "journey," using the mildest of terms. But it is truest to say that the soul is an exile and a wanderer (*pheugei kai planatai*), driven forth by divine decrees and laws; and then, as on an island buffeted by the seas, imprisoned within the body "like an oyster in its shell," as Plato says, because it does not remember or recall "what honor and what high felicity" it has left, not leaving Sardis for Athens or Corinth for Lemnos or Scyron, but Heaven and the moon for earth and life on earth.[89]

Here Plutarch performs precisely the move described above: he groups "exile" with other terms of alterity ("foreigner," "immigrant," "sojourner"). Since the physical and legal displacement of exile is not in view in any literal sense, he can easily pass over the subtle (and admittedly unstable) differences in the civic and ethnoracial connotations of each term. Instead he situates them together rhetorically as a single topos, acknowledging the use of exile and foreigner terminology as a general figure of cultural reproach, but then explicitly revaluing it by association with the soul over and against the body. In this way, alterity is valorized, still serving as what Whitmarsh calls "a positive accreditation of philosophical success."[90] But unlike the Greek thinkers analyzed by Whitmarsh, Plutarch lays no claim to physical displacement or marginalized legal status (though these remain in view in his reflections). Rather the accreditation he asserts is grounded in a properly philosophical recognition of identity structured by a body-soul dualism.

A similar rhetorical strategy but to different (and decidedly theological) ends can be found in the Hebrew Bible and the literature of early Judaism. The Hebrew term *ger* (commonly translated as "foreigner," "alien," or "sojourner") appears frequently in the Pentateuch, both on its own and as part of the so-called deuteronomic triad (alien, orphan, widow).[91] In this context, its usage is primarily legal, detailing prescriptions for the behavior and treatment of the alien in Israel.[92] But José Ramírez Kidd has drawn attention to a key shift in the function of the term *ger*, moving from a purely legal usage to a *figura theologica* applied to collective Israelite identity.[93]

According to Kidd's mapping of this shift, Israelite reflections on the alien move from the strictly legal to a new consciousness of displacement and its ramifications, following the Israelites' own experience of the Babylonian exile. Kidd sees two important texts reflecting this process in Deuteronomy: (1) "You shall not abhor an Egyptian, because you were a resident-alien (*ger*) in his land" (23.8b);[94] (2) "You shall love the resident-alien (*ger*) because you were resident-aliens (*gerim*) in the land of Egypt" (10.19). Dating both these motive clauses to after the exile,[95] Kidd concludes, "It was the new awareness of being themselves *gerim* (10.19b), which created a new sensitivity to the non-Jewish *ger*. . . . That is why the command to love the *ger* 10,19a makes reference to Israel's own experience (10.19b): it is an appeal to their collective memory. It was possible to identify with the *ger* because they had been *gerim* themselves."[96]

The next stage in Kidd's development schema is evidenced in three other Hebrew Bible texts: (1) "The land shall not be sold permanently, because the land is mine; for you are resident-aliens and sojourners (*gerim wetoshabim*) in my presence" (Lev 25.23); (2) "For I am a resident-alien (*ger*) with you, a sojourner (*toshab*) like all my fathers" (Ps 39.13b); (3) "For we are resident-aliens (*gerim*) before you and sojourners (*toshabim*), like all our fathers; as a shadow are our days on the earth and there is no hope" (1 Chron 29.15). In all of these texts, Kidd sees a move entirely away from the legal realm to the sphere of metaphor and identity.[97] As he puts it, "This metaphorical use of the term played a fundamental role in Israel's understanding of its fundamental vocation. The Israelites did not only keep alive the memory of their forefathers as *gerim*, but understood their own existence as *peregrinatio*."⁹⁸

For Kidd, the key to this gradual development is Israel's own physical experience of Babylonian exile—and he divides the texts up according to a source-critical framework fundamentally oriented around this point. If Kidd is correct in the post-exilic dating schema that undergirds his textual argument, then we see in these later biblical texts a similar conceptual conflation of the resident alien and sojourner with the figure of the exile, via the memory of Israel's own exile. (Though note that the collapse of these distinctions is only implicit; the texts do not group the categories together in the way that Plutarch does.) However, even if one does not accept Kidd's source-critical reconstruction in all its specificities, his primary point—the emergent use of the *ger* motif in the Hebrew Bible to construct collective Israelite identity—remains illuminating.

When the Hebrew Bible was translated into Greek, this crucial term *ger* was rendered using a variety of Greek terms: primarily *prosēlytos*, but also *paroikos*, *g(e)iōras*, and *xenos*.⁹⁹ Scholars debate whether the noun *prosēlytos* carries the technical sense of conversion in its Septuagint usage (a sense clearly attested later in both Philo and epigraphical evidence) or whether it functions in these texts more or less interchangeably with *paroikos*.¹⁰⁰ But be that as it may, the Septuagint usage of *paroikos* and other related terms of the alien *topos* proved to be fertile ground for the exegetical intersection of Jewish scriptural traditions with the philosophical valorization of the alien motif discussed above. We see evidence of this intersection primarily in the work of Philo of Alexandria, often with a focus on the alien status of the patriarch Abraham.¹⁰¹

For example, in Genesis 23.4 (LXX), Abraham declares himself a resident alien and sojourner among the Hittites (*Paroikos kai parepidēmos egō eimi meth' hymōn*). This proclamation functions for Philo as a site from which to expound dualistically on the value of the soul over the body, through the valorization of sojourner status. He pursues this project in *De confusione linguarum*:

This is why all whom Moses calls wise are represented as sojourners (*paroikountes*). Their souls are never colonists leaving heaven for a new home. Their way is to visit earthly nature as people who travel abroad to see and learn. So when they have stayed awhile in their bodies, and beheld through them all that sense and mortality has to show, they make their way back to the place from which they set out at first. To them the heavenly region, where their citizenship lies, is their native land; the earthly region in which they became sojourners is a foreign country (*patrida men ton ouranion chōron en hō politeuontai, xenēn de ton perigeion en hō parōkēsan nomizousai*). . . . We shall not be surprised, then, to find Abraham, when he rose from the life of death and vanity, saying to the guardians of the dead and stewards of mortality, "I am a stranger and sojourner with you." . . . [T]he wise person does but sojourn in this body which our senses know, as in a strange land, but dwells in and has for their fatherland the virtues known through the mind (*paroikei men hō sophos hōs en xenē sōmati aisthētō, katoikei d' hōs en patridi noētais aretais*), which God "speaks" and which thus are identical with divine words.[102]

We find a comparable argument—but without reference to Abraham—in *De agricultura*:

"We came to sojourn—not to settle there" [cf. LXX, Gen 47.4[103]]. For in reality a wise person's soul ever finds heaven to be their fatherland and earth a foreign country, and regards as their own the dwelling-place of wisdom, and that of the body as outlandish, and looks on themselves as a stranger and sojourner in it (*paroikein, ou katoikein ēlthomen. tō gar onti pasa psychē sophou patrida men ouranon, xenēn de gēn elache kai nomizei ton men sophias oikon idion, ton de sōmatos othneion, hō kai parepidēmein oietai*).[104]

In both cases, Philo emphasizes the formation of individual identity. He conceptualizes the ideal human self (the wise person) as the one who embraces and celebrates sojourner status out of a recognition of the basic (but temporary) duality involved in human existence (the realm of *psychē* and/or *nous* over that of *sōma*). While in many ways similar to the example from Plutarch cited above, the Philonic texts are distinct insofar as they intertwine discursive strands from both philosophy and biblical traditions in the process of revaluing the resident-alien. This is an intersection that will prove highly significant as we turn now to the analysis of early Christian texts and their multiple uses of the alien figure.

Conclusion

The alien topos functioned in the early Roman Empire as part of a rich discursive field, one that blurred both civic and ethnoracial categories of status and identity in its possible connotations. As a prominent "other" of antiquity's most basic insider term (the citizen), the designation "alien" most often suggested a situation of social, political, and cultural marginality, construed primarily as a state of reproach and a cause for mourning. But the ambiguities involved in the production of this civic/ethnoracial other also ensured that the boundary between the citizen and the alien remained permeable in complicated ways. Within this space of ambivalence, multiple options emerged for valorizing the topos—options with powerful implications for the formation of individual and communal cultural identities.

Thus, as early Christians turned to the alien motif as a resource for articulating the shape and meaning of their own identities, they did so as participants in an already complex conversation. Yet at the same time, as Denise Buell points out, practices that could be broadly characterized as "religious" played a major role in the imperial period "to mark and re-define both citizenship and ethnic belonging."[105] As Christians thought through what was to count as particularly *Christian* practice in relation to the enormous variety of social, philosophical, and cultic practices that surrounded them (practices that, from a modern standpoint, we might loosely group as "religious"), they found themselves well placed to take advantage of the rhetorical resources that the alien topos offered. And as we will see, they put this space of possibles to work for them in produc-tive ways, while at the same time changing the very shape of the field by their own positionings of the topos within it.

Chapter Two

Going to Jesus "Outside the Camp": Alien Identity in Hebrews

"Otherness," whether of Scotsmen or lice, is a preeminently political matter.
—Jonathan Z. Smith

Early Christians talked about themselves as aliens and outsiders. Often it was with just a few words or phrases, as in 1 Peter or some of the other examples surveyed in the Introduction. But sometimes the trope was developed more extensively, becoming a major theme in exhortatory treatises and epistles. Among the books that were eventually included in the New Testament canon, the other text besides 1 Peter that makes significant use of the alien topos is the Epistle to the Hebrews. Where 1 Peter offers just a few brief allusions to the topos, Hebrews develops an extensive scriptural lineage of "strangers and sojourners" on which its narrative of salvation history turns. Not only are Abraham, Isaac, and Jacob (as well as other great heroes of the faith) to be understood in terms of their alien status, but so is Jesus—and, by extension, the text calls its readers to understand themselves as marginal aliens through joining Jesus "outside the camp."

But as I will argue, the "marginality" that the text constructs is a complicated affair. Hebrews claims this scriptural lineage, figuring its audience as aliens, in order to mark Christians as different, distinct, and worthy of their own separate identity. However, comparable to what we saw in 1 Peter, the actual practices that it exhorts readers to engage in prove to be quite thoroughly assimilated to the broader cultural values of the Roman world—even though Hebrews skillfully refigures them as visible markers of alien identity. This rhetorical sleight of hand encodes a crucial tension in the text, one that points toward the dangers not so much of difference but of *proximity* in the field of ancient identity construction. How were Christians to mark their identity as *different* in a world in which so many of their values, norms, and ideals for living did not particularly stand out? How were they to differentiate themselves with respect to the array of identities and practices that flourished all around them? Here Hebrews' use of the alien topos functions strategically to invent a specific communal identity for Christians (i.e., a community of aliens) while still allowing for a certain social integration in the larger Roman context. Yet as Bourdieu notes, every move within a social field has the potential to "unmake and remake" that field, to change in some small way both the shape of the field and the rules of the game.[1] Thus even a strategy of differentiation that has practical assimilationist dimensions is still a strategy—and therefore acts within and upon the field of identities to leave it different from before.

Abraham the Alien

The Epistle to the Hebrews has been characterized by Harold Attridge as "the most elegant and sophisticated, and perhaps the most enigmatic, text of first-century Christianity."[2] We have little concrete information about the milieu in which Hebrews was produced: its author is anonymous and its provenance uncertain.[3] It is difficult to date any more specifically than between 60 and 100 C.E.[4] Although commonly referred to as a letter, Hebrews does not open with the standard epistolary format that is seen in other New Testament epistles. (It does, on the other hand, end like a letter, including a benediction and greetings.) Rather, the text characterizes itself as a *logos tēs paraklēseōs* or "word of exhortation" (13.22), probably best understood as a kind of homily.[5] As a word of exhortation, the text has affinities with ancient rhetoric of both the deliberative and epideictic varieties: it attempts throughout to persuade its audience toward a particular course of action (deliberative), while simultaneously focusing on the virtues and achievements of Jesus as a praiseworthy figure (epideictic).[6]

Ernst Käsemann was the first scholar to draw attention to the wandering people of God as a key motif for understanding Hebrews in its entirety: "Faith thus becomes a confident wandering . . . in every age faith's wandering must be a march through a zone of conflict and death, and it is clearly shown in the example of Jesus . . . God's people traverse [this zone] for the sake of the Word."[7] But while helpful in emphasizing the importance of movement and wandering in Hebrews, Käsemann's study pays relatively scant attention to an important sub-theme, the text's use of the alien topos beginning in chapter 11:

By faith Abraham obeyed, when he was called to go forth to a place which he was going to receive as an inheritance; and he went out, not knowing where he was going. By faith he sojourned (*parōkēsen*) in the land of the promise, as in a foreign land, dwelling in tents along with Isaac and Jacob, those fellow-heirs of the same promise. For he was waiting expectantly for the city having foundations whose artisan and builder is God . . . . In faith, all these people died, not having received the promises. But they saw them and greeted them from a distance. And they confessed that they were strangers and sojourners (*xenoi kai parepidēmoi*) on the earth. For those who say such things make it clear that they are seeking a homeland. And if they were reminiscing about that land from which they had departed, they would have had a time to return. But as it stands, they long for a better homeland, that is, a heavenly one. Therefore God is not ashamed to be called their God; for he has prepared a city for them. (Heb 11.8–10, 13–16)

In this pericope, Hebrews carefully constructs the character of Abraham as "the *paroikos* 'par excellence.' "[8] By designating Abraham as one who sojourns (*paroikeō*)—and therefore a *paroikos* or "resident alien"— the text makes a characterization that resonates thematically with biblical traditions and linguistically with the Septuagint.[9] Notably in Genesis 17.8, God explicitly promises to give to Abraham and his descendants the land of Canaan where Abraham currently sojourns as a resident alien (*kai dōsō soi kai tō spermati sou meta se tēn gēn, hēn paroikeis, pasan tēn gēn Chanaan*). Also in 23.4, Abraham exclaims to the Hittites, "I am a resident alien and sojourner among you" (*Paroikos kai parepidēmos egō eimi meth' hymōn*).

But simply appealing to the Septuagint connection does little to illuminate the *function* of Abraham as *paroikos* in the Hebrews pericope.[10] In fact, ancient biblical interpreters inflected the story of Abraham the sojourner in multiple ways; these sometimes included interpretations that explicitly downplayed Abraham's alien status. For example, Philo characterizes Abraham's arrival in the land of promise as "just like having come back from a foreign land to his own country" (*kathaper apo tēs xenēs eis tēn oikeian epaniōn*).[11] Similarly, in *Jewish Antiquities*, Josephus only mentions that Abraham "settled" (*katōkēse*, 1.154; cf. also 1.157) in Canaan.[12] In Reinhard Feldmeier's analysis,

Quite deliberately, then, *living in the land as situation of fulfilled promise is contrasted with the existence as strangers.* The corollary of this is that in its own land Israel is not a sojourner at all, but a full citizen, designated as such by God. This connection is so close that even the foreignness of the patriarchs, so frequently emphasized in the book of Genesis, is suppressed and the text is emended accordingly. . . . Thus Josephus also places down the foreignness of Abraham, and instead emphasizes that he *lived in the land, left it to his descendants, and possessed it.*[13]

Even in an early Christian context, a text such as *1 Clement* uses the Abraham story in a similar way, highlighting the patriarch's faithful obedience (10.1–2, 7) and his future inheritance of the land (10.4), but not his sojourning status at any point during the narrative. Thus it was not an interpretive given for Hebrews 11 to emphasize Abraham as a resident alien. Rather, Hebrews' foregrounding of the topos raises the question of what is at stake in the specific ways that the pericope builds a distinct narrative using the biblical materials at its disposal.

In Hebrews' particular telling of the story, Abraham is an exemplar of faithful submission: having been called, he obeyed and went out by faith, even though he was ignorant of where he was going (*Pistei kaloumenos Abraam hypēkousen exelthein eis topon hon ēmellen lambanein eis klēronomian, kai exēlthen mē epistamenos pou erchetai*, 11.8). The text couches the discussion from the outset not only in terms of faith (the motif that serves as an anaphoric structuring device throughout the chapter[14]) but also in terms of Abraham's obedience. As an act of *hypakoē*, Abraham enters into the new status and identity which the pericope will go on to explicate.

In 11.9, Hebrews begins in earnest the explicit construction of Abraham the alien. Sojourning is what characterizes the patriarch's faithful obedience to God's call: living in the land divinely promised to him as though it were foreign (*Pistei parōkēsen eis gēn tēs epangelias hōs allotrian*). But the sojourning motif has a larger function than simply to describe the particular character of Abraham. Accordingly, Hebrews spreads its net a little wider, designating not only Abraham but also Isaac and Jacob as those who dwelled in tents, evoking imagery of nomadic transience (*en skēnais katoikēsas meta Isaak kai Iakōb*); Isaac and Jacob are included not simply as fellow tent-dwellers but also as fellow-heirs (*tōn synklēronomōn tēs epangelias tēs autēs*). With the addition of these two figures to the motif, the *social* function of the sojourning motif comes into view. The implications are communal, articulating an identity for a multigenerational group of people (Abraham, Isaac, and Jacob), not simply the Abraham figure.[15]

Heroes, Paraenesis, and Identity

On one level, this move to the social dimensions of sojourning is not surprising. Indeed all the heroes in the catalogue of Hebrews 11 have larger communal implications insofar as they function as examples for the text's Christian readers. As David deSilva points out, the example list "is calculated to rouse emulation by praising the figures of the past who have attained honorable memory."[16] Readers of the text are meant to identify with the individuals being listed and emulate their positive character traits. Thus figures such as Abel, Enoch, and Noah all display characteristics of faithfulness. And while Hebrews may not intend that its audience straightforwardly imitate some of the specific actions under discussion (e.g., Abel's sacrifice—see the discussion of cultic practice below), the heroes' general faithfulness serves as a standard for the audience.

We see a similar dynamic at work in another early Christian catalogue of heroes, *1 Clement* 9–13 (c.93–97). Here the text instructs its readers to look intently upon those who have perfectly rendered service to God's magnificent glory (*atenisōmen eis tous teleiōs leitourgēsantas tē megaloprepei doxē autou*, 9.2). *1 Clement* then embarks on an excursion into this process of "looking intently," reminding its readers that Enoch was found righteous in obedience (*hos en hypakoē dikaios heuretheis*, 9.3), Noah faithful through his service (*pistos heuretheis dia tēs leitourgias autou*, 9.4), and Abraham faithful in his obedience (*pistos heurethē en tō auton hypēkoon genesthai*, 10.1). A bit further on, the text informs us that, on account of such virtues as faith, hospitality, and piety, Abraham was given a son (*dia pistin kai philoxenian*, 10.7) and both Lot and Rahab were saved (*dia philoxenian kai eusebeian*, 11.1, 12.1).

These descriptions in *1 Clement* function not just to convey information about each particular character but also to draw out individual paraenetic implications for the text's readers. The text makes this broader thrust explicit in 11.1 with the more general application of Lot's deliverance: "On account of his hospitality and piety, Lot was saved out of Sodom, when the entire region was judged by fire and sulfur; when he did so, the Master made clear that he does not forsake those who hope in him, but consigns to punishment and torment those who have other allegiance" (*Dia philoxenian kai eusebeian Lōt esōthē ek Sodomōn, tēs perichōrou pasēs kritheisēs dia pyros kai theiou, prodēlon poiēsas ho despotēs, hoti tous elpizontas ep' auton ouk enkataleipei, tous de heteroklineis hyparchontas eis kolasin kai aikismon tithēsin*). Here the text marks Lot's example as more generally applicable to those who hope in God, thereby implying that its project of recounting examples is not simply descriptive or of passing narrative interest. These heroes also have contemporary theological and paraenetic relevance for the text's readers.

But the catalogs of heroes in *1 Clement* 9–13 and Hebrews 11 are not identical in their paraenetic maneuverings. The comparison with *1 Clement* makes clear an additional hermeneutical move that Hebrews 11 performs in the Abraham pericope. Both texts set out a series of historical exemplars whose laudable actions are intended for practical appropriation by readers, both individually and communally. But in contrast to *1 Clement* 9–13, Hebrews 11 also places an explicit emphasis on community, constructing a discourse of common identity.[17] Here Pamela Eisenbaum has drawn attention to another function of what she terms "a multi-dimensional hero list": "to explain and legitimate the existence of the community which is being addressed, by grounding the members of that community in a significant genealogical history."[18]

Consequently, the discourse of identity that Hebrews articulates here applies not only to Abraham or to his immediate descendants. Instead the patriarchs function as representatives of a much broader vision of lineage—one that allows for the appropriation of alien status (and also the promise of the eschatological city introduced in 11.10) by readers who will claim this sacred history as their own. Opening up the scope of the alien topos in this way appears to be pivotal, in fact, to the text's purposes in employing it at all. (Note that in order to make this move, the text must interrupt the flow of the narrative by introducing Isaac two verses prior to the announcement of his miraculous birth in 11.11.[19]) As Eisenbaum aptly summarizes, Abraham functions as an ideal example for what the text wants to convey: "separation and marginalization . . . The audience is part of this trajectory by implication."[20] Hebrews confirms and reinforces this conclusion in what follows, a series of interpretive moves that broaden the scope of Abraham's outsider status even further. Thus 11.12 contrasts the one man, Abraham (*henos*), to those begotten by him: "just as the stars of heaven in number and innumerable as the sand along the shore of the sea" (*kathōs ta astra tou ouranou tō plēthei kai hōs hē ammos hē para to cheilos tēs thalassēs hē anarithmētos*). The reference in 11.13 to *houtoi pantes* (or "all these ones") who have died in faith continues this broadening function.[21]

The pericope then moves on to disclose that "all these ones" are those who died without having received the promises. Indeed, they only saw them and greeted them from a distance (*mē labontes tas epangelias alla porrhōthen autas idontes kai aspasamenoi*, 11.13). As Attridge points out, Hebrews has already made the claim in 6.15 that Abraham did in fact obtain a promise (*kai houtōs makrothymēsas epetychen tēs epangelias*).[22] However, this promise refers to the birth of Isaac, a fact acknowledged by Hebrews 11 as well (11.11–12). Instead a different promise is in view, the promise of land as put forth in 11.9. Yet in 11.13, the connotations of the alien topos serve to shift the focus away from a specific piece of territory (Canaan) toward a broader concept of eschatological homeland (*patris*), mentioned explicitly in 11.14: "For those who say such things make it clear that they are seeking a homeland" (*hoi gar toiauta legontes emphanizousin hoti patrida epizētousin*).

But this *patris* is not yet possessed. Rather "all these ones" confess that they are strangers and sojourners on the earth (*kai homologēsantes hoti xenoi kai parepidēmoi eisin epi tēs gēs*, 11.13). Here the deployment of the alien topos turns overtly to a cosmological heaven-earth dualism that will be developed throughout the remainder of the text. While 11.10 has already implicitly moved in this direction by contrasting God's eschatological city to the patriarchs' sojourn (*exedecheto gar tēn tous themelious echousan polin hēs technitēs kai dēmiourgos ho theos*), 11.13 makes the dualism explicit with the phrase *epi tēs gēs*. In contrast, then, to a more ambiguous case like 1 Peter, the strategic thrust of this passage evokes the philosophical trope of the soul's time dwelling in the body as a temporary sojourn (or even exile) away from its heavenly homeland.[23]

This connection to ancient philosophical thought notwithstanding, the precise philological nuance of the terms used here (*xenoi kai parepidēmoi*) remains unclear.[24] But this matters little to the larger interests of the text's rhetorical project. Whatever specific connotations the phrase *xenoi kai parepidēmoi* is meant to carry (scriptural, legal, philosophical, or some combination thereof), the key point is unmistakable: both terms have a powerful outsider valence, one that the text invokes not just to tell a story but to point to a communal identity of marginality that its readers are meant to appropriate. The narrative of strangers and sojourners in Hebrews 11 works "to sanction and sanctify a particular state of things,"[25] offering a scriptural lineage of alterity that encourages and entices readers to situate themselves within it.

Rereading Hebrews in Light of Alien Status

This call to readers to take on an identity of marginality comes toward the end of the epistle. However, it casts a long shadow across the text as a whole, resonating with and even transforming the inflection of earlier paraenesis and identity-constructing moves. Up to this point, one of the ways that Hebrews has focused its paraenetic energy is by contrasting its audience to the Israelites of the exodus—urging them throughout chapters 3 and 4 not to be like the generation whose corpses fell in the wilderness (*ta kōla epesen en tē erēmō*, 3.17). Readers are given strict warnings not to harden their hearts (*mē sklērynēte tas kardias hymōn*, 3.8, 15) and to fear lest anyone seem to have fallen short while the promise of entering God's rest still remains (*Phobēthōmen oun, mēpote kataleipomenēs epangelias eiselthein eis tēn katapausin autou dokē tis ex hymōn hysterēkenai*, 4.1). In 4.11 the text offers a strong thrust of exhortation: "Let us hasten then to enter into that rest, in order that no one might fall in the same pattern of disobedience" (*Spoudasōmen oun eiselthein eis ekeinēn tēn katapausin, hina mē en tō autō tis hypodeigmati pesē tēs apeitheias*). In this way the Israelite wilderness generation serves as a foil against which the text may more effectively urge a different agenda for its readers: to hold fast to their confession (*kratōmen tēs homologias*, 4.14; *katechōmen tēn homologian*, 10.23; cf. also 3.1) and enter God's rest.

The contents of this confession remain historically inaccessible.[26] But even though Hebrews never nails down a precise referent, its use of *homologeō* at 11.13 reverberates back to the earlier references. Here "all these ones" (that is, Abraham, Isaac, and Jacob—and by extension, the readers) *confess* that they are strangers and sojourners on the earth.[27] In this way, I would argue, the resonance with earlier uses of *homologia* in the text allows (and indeed encourages) readers to reimagine the contents of their confession (whatever that may be) in light of their identity as strangers and sojourners on the earth. Therefore, the call to "hold fast" (*kratōmen*, 4.14; *katechōmen*, 10.23) now becomes not simply about dogged perseverance in the face of perceived oppression or continued assent to certain Christological propositions, but also about embracing a certain understanding of social identity—choosing to identify with a community that classifies itself as outsiders. As Craig Koester asserts, Hebrews uses the earlier calls to hold fast in order to "bolster commitments by affirming the confession that gave the group its identity."[28] Consequently, in linking the language of confession to the alien topos, Hebrews employs its carefully engineered articulation of Christians' marginal status as a powerful means of promoting solidarity. The peculiar doubleness of the topos works here toward a compelling end: marginality marks the site of the community's cohesion and strength. Therefore, in confessing this alterity, readers in some sense enact the commitment to the confession called for in earlier passages. Insider status receives robust reinforcement in outsider terms.

In a similar way, Hebrews' deployment of the alien topos also transforms the inflection of its various metaphors of entrance used in earlier parts of the text. By constructing its audience as a community of strangers and sojourners, the text repositions them as a group in relation to these metaphors. Prior to chapter 11, within the metaphorical space set up by chapters 3 and 4, the community stands on the edge of the eschatological Promised Land, and their window of opportunity for entrance into God's rest remains (see 4.1, 6). They are called to approach the throne of grace with boldness (*proserchōmetha oun meta parrēsias tō thronō tēs charitos*, 4.16), possessors of a hope that enters inside the curtain (*eiserchomenēn eis to esōteron tou katapetasmatos*, 6.19). In fact, we learn later, this is no mere hope. The audience has actually *obtained* an entrance into the sanctuary for themselves through the blood of Jesus (*tēn eisodon tōn hagiōn en tō haimati Iēsou*, 10.19).

Yet, ironically, the introduction of the alien topos in chapter 11 refigures these images. "Entrance" must now be understood through solidarity with a community of outsiders. By verbally appropriating a self-designation as strangers and sojourners (*hoi gar toiauta legontes*, 11.14), Abraham, Isaac, and Jacob, along with the community that they represent rhetorically, "make it clear that they seek a homeland" (*emphanizousin hoti patrida epizētousin*, 11.14). The text maintains that this "sojourner status" is one that is voluntarily assumed. Indeed if these people had been reminiscing about the land from which they went out, they would have had opportunity to return (*ei men ekeinēs emnēmoneuon aph' hēs exebēsan, eichon an kairon anakampsai*, 11.15). But the strangers and sojourners do not seek to return.[29] To do so would be to threaten or call into question their status as resident aliens. And it is only as aliens that they will obtain the entrance that they seek: a better homeland, a heavenly one (*kreitton-os . . . epouraniou*, 11.16).

Thus there is a place of "true citizenship" for Christians, a locale in which their insider status is recognized and assured. Hebrews will partially clarify the eschatological details of how they may gain entrance to this heavenly homeland in what follows. But throughout, the rhetorical emphasis remains on the outsider position of Christians in the present moment—insider status defined in alien terms. With this paradox in place, the pericope closes with an appeal designed to reinforce and encourage solidarity: God is not ashamed to be called these people's God, for he has prepared a city for them (*dio ouk epaischynetai autous ho theos theos epikaleisthai autōn; hētoimasen gar autois polin*, 11.16).

A Hermeneutical Turn: Hebrews 13.13 and Ancient Cultic Discourse

Although the overt discussion of aliens and strangers ends here,[30] the motif continues to reverberate as a subtext throughout both the rest of chapter 11 and the remainder of the text. Regarding chapter 11 as a whole, Eisenbaum has convincingly argued that outsiderness is "the most fundamental characteristic of the heroes of Hebrews."[31] This plays out in multiple ways. First of all, the text depicts Moses as a hero who chooses outsider status (*mallon helomenos sunkakoucheisthai tō laō tou theou . . . ton oneidismon tou Christou*, 11.25–26) over the pleasures of a symbolic "citizenship" (the treasures of Egypt, *tōn Aigyptou thēsaurōn*) because he is looking ahead to his reward (*tēn misthapodosian*).[32]

In a similar vein, the finale of Hebrews 11 crescendos to a feverish pitch as it depicts the sufferings of the faithful, culminating in a vivid and evocative description of marginalization: "They went around in sheepskins, in goat skins, in need, afflicted, ill-treated—of these people the world was not worthy—wandering about in deserts and mountains and caves and holes in the ground" (*periēlthon en mēlōtais, en aigeiois dermasin, hysteroumenoi, thlibomenoi, kakouchoumenoi, hōn ouk ēn axios ho kosmos, epi erēmiais planōmenoi kai oresin kai spēlaiois kai tais opais tēs gēs*, 11.37–38). Here again the text reiterates the solidarity of its audience with those who have chosen this outsider status. The heroes of chapter 11 do not achieve their entrance. As the chapter closes, they have not received the promise (*ouk ekomisanto tēn epangelian*, 11.39). The implication for readers is that God's better thing (*kreitton ti*, 11.40) very much depends on them, because without their solidarity, this community of past "strangers and sojourners" will not be made perfect (*hina mē chōris hēmōn teleiōthōsin*, 11.40). To this end, the next chapter opens by exhorting its audience to put aside every impediment and easily besetting sin (*onkon apothemenoi*

panta kai tēn euperistaton hamartian, 12.1), to run the race set before them
(*trechōmen ton prokeimenon hēmin agōna*, 12.1), and to look to Jesus in
order not to grow weary (*aphorōntes eis ton tēs pisteōs archēgon kai teleiōtēn
Iēsoun . . . hina mē kamēte*, 12.2, 3). Only through these steps of identification with those sojourners who have gone before—an increasingly
self-conscious positioning of the Christian self as other—will entrance
be obtained for all.

As chapter 12 continues, Hebrews returns to spatial metaphors, contrasting what the community has not approached—"that which can be
touched, a kindled fire, darkness, gloom, and storm" (*psēlaphōmenō kai
kekaumenō pyri kai gnophō kai zophō kai thyellē*, 12.18)—to what they have
approached: "Mount Zion and a city of the living God, heavenly Jerusalem" (*Siōn orei kai polei theou zōntos, Ierousalēm epouraniō*, 12.22).[33] Here
again the language of entrance is not far from view. But what is the way
of this approach? How does the audience come to the heavenly moun-
tain and the *polis* of the living God? The answer comes only in the final
chapter of the text:

Do not be carried away by various strange teachings; for it is good that the heart
be made firm by grace, not by foods, which have not benefited those who conduct themselves [in this way]. We have an altar from which those who serve in
the tent do not have authority to eat. For the bodies of animals whose blood is
brought into the sanctuary as a sin offering by the high priest are burned outside
the camp. Therefore Jesus also suffered outside the gate in order that he might
sanctify the people through his own blood. *Therefore let us go to him outside the
camp*, bearing his reproach. For here we do not have an enduring city; rather
we seek after that city which is to come. Through him let us always offer up a
sacrifice of praise to God; this is the fruit of lips which confess his name. Do not
neglect well-doing and fellowship; for God is delighted with such sacrifices. (Heb
13.9–16, emphasis mine)[34]

Here Hebrews takes a key hermeneutical turn: the call to go to Jesus
outside the camp, bearing his reproach (*exō tēs parembolēs ton oneidismon
autou pherontes*, 13.13), serves as the overt lens through which all the previous paraenesis of the text is refracted. That is to say, 13.13 functions
hermeneutically to transform the text's paraenesis. How is the audience
to hold fast, approach, and enter? These are metaphors steeped in the
language of insider status—yet they must now be appropriated through
identification with the margins (i.e., by going to Jesus outside the camp).
The text's final word on drawing near does not emphasize joining Jesus
in the heavenly sanctuary (9.24) but rather joining him in identification
with alterity and reproach. It is the strangers and sojourners who will
experience entrance into the city that is to come.

At the same time, however, this crucial hermeneutical move takes
place in a specific context—a larger discussion that makes extensive use

of cultic imagery (13.9–16). Here the text plays with biblical categories associated with the Levitical cult, drawing a strong contrast between Levitical cultic practice and the sacrifice of Jesus. This practice is invoked explicitly in 13.11: "For the bodies of animals whose blood is brought into the sanctuary as a sin offering by the high priest are burned outside the camp" (*hōn gar eispheretai zōōn to haima peri hamartias eis ta hagia dia tou archiereōs, toutōn ta sōmata katakaietai exō tēs parembolēs*). Attridge characterizes this verse as a "generalizing paraphrase" of the portion of the Yom Kippur ritual described in Leviticus 16.27–28[35]: "So the young bull of the sin offering and the goat of the sin offering, whose blood was brought in to be an appeasement in the sanctuary, will be brought outside the camp and they will be burned in the fire, even their skin and their meat and their dung. The one who burns them will wash his clothes and bathe his body with water and after these things, he will come into the camp" (LXX: *kai ton moschon ton peri tēs hamartias kai ton chimaron ton peri tēs hamartias, hōn to haima eisēnechthē exilasasthai en tō hagiō, exoisousin auta exō tēs parembolēs kai katakausousin auta en pyri, kai ta dermata autōn kai ta krea autōn kai tēn kopron autōn; ho de katakaiōn auta plynei ta himatia kai lousetai to sōma autou hydati kai meta tauta eiseleusetai eis tēn parembolēn*).

Helmut Koester's work on Hebrews 13 clearly demonstrates the way in which this textual contrast operates:

Leviticus: Whoever performs the burning *outside the camp is unclean.*
Hebrews: Jesus suffered *outside the gate* in order to *sanctify* the people.
Leviticus: After being *sanctified* he may *enter the camp* again.
Hebrews: Let us *go out* to him *outside the camp* to bear his *reproach.*[36]

Formulated in this way, we can see how Hebrews reworks elements of the Levitical tradition to highlight the *cleansing* function of Jesus' sacrifice, thereby shifting the role of the space *exō tēs parembolēs*. This reading of the Levitical mandate transforms *exō tēs parembolēs*. "Outside the camp" was once a place that created a need for cleansing—a cleansing that was necessary before one could return inside. But it is now the site of the sacrifice that actually brings about the people's purification.

Scholars have understood the significance of this reinterpretation of Levitical tradition in a number of ways. One option is to read this passage as an allegory, privileging otherworldliness (i.e., soul over body) in the tradition of Philo.[37] For example, James Moffatt argues that this text "makes a broad appeal for an unworldly religious fellowship, such as is alone in keeping with the *charis* of God in Jesus our Lord."[38] Another major alternative is to interpret the appeal to join Jesus *exō tēs parembolēs* as a call to leave Judaism. According to this argument, as F. F. Bruce maintains, "the 'camp' stands for the established fellowship and ordinances of Judaism. To abandon them, with all their sacred associations inherited from remote antiquity, was a hard thing, but it was a necessary thing."[39]

Koester argues against both these interpretive trajectories, suggesting that the contrast is not Philonic or anti-Jewish but rather an "anticultic antithesis": "And since the refuge in sacred places and cultic performances is abolished for those people who stay 'outside the camp' with Jesus, the sacrifices of God are rather thanksgiving and charity (Hebrews 13.15–16)."[40] In view then, for Koester, is a polemic against the ongoing appropriateness of cultic practice for Christians. As Attridge observes, some sort of cultic dining has most likely inspired the connection between strange teachings and food in 13.9 (*didachais poikilais kai xenais mē parapheresthe; kalon gar chariti bebaiousthai tēn kardian, ou brōmasin en hois ouk ōphelēthēsan hoi peripatountes*).[41] This would certainly seem then to be sound textual support for Koester's position. He may therefore be correct that the contrast being articulated in 13.9–16 places its primary emphasis on the generally anti-cultic rather than the specifically anti-Jewish or the otherworldly.

But with that said, I would maintain that this interpretive solution does not necessarily exhaust the potential function of cultic discourse in Hebrews. For as we think about possible readers and audiences for Hebrews in the late first century, we need to analyze the semiotic strategy of 13.9–16 not only in light of the text's intended emphasis (whether Philonic otherworldliness, anti-Judaism, or "anti-cultic antithesis"), but also in terms of the larger fields of connotation/contestation at play in the Roman Empire—fields in which various readers might locate this particular appeal to cultic discourse as it could be put to work for the larger purposes of early Christian identity formation.[42] As Roland Barthes argues, texts should not be seen "as mere 'messages,' or even as 'statements' (that is, finished products, whose destiny would be sealed as soon as they were uttered), but as perpetual productions, enunciations, through which the subject continues to struggle; this subject is no doubt that of the author, but also that of the reader."[43] Barthes's point raises an important question then with respect to the discursive fields in which ancient readers moved: what sorts of work could discussions of cult and cultic practice do in ancient projects of identity construction?

Thinking with Cults: Magna Mater as Example

Here an analogous example from Roman antiquity proves illustrative. Cultic practice and discourse were ubiquitous in the Roman world, as Robin Lane Fox notes, "intertwined with every group, each level of a city's social existence."[44] Particularly relevant for my purposes, however, is the discourse surrounding cults labeled as "foreign"—that is, in some way exterior with respect to a perceived normative center of so-called "Roman-ness" across the empire. On the one hand, the marker stones of the *pomerium* (the sacred boundary of the city of Rome) provided a physical boundary that helped to construct and maintain a "definitional myth": foreign cultic practice could not take place inside the city's sacred boundary.[45] Yet on the other hand, the temple of Magna Mater, a cult that represented the quintessentially "foreign," could be incorporated within the *pomerium* such that its priests—the exotic, castrated *galli*—became, in Mary Beard's apt phrase, "the Roman emperor's closest neighbors" on the Palatine Hill.[46]

In trying to understand the relationship between cult and outsider status with reference to Magna Mater (and foreign cults more generally), scholars have typically posited two possible solutions: either the Romans gradually domesticated foreign cults (thereby eradicating their foreignness), or they were simply ignorant of the truly foreign nature of these cults prior to incorporation.[47] In response to this dichotomy, Beard argues convincingly that these conflicting aspects of discourse surrounding Roman attitudes toward "foreign" cults (evidenced by both archeological remains and texts) should not be reduced to either option, but instead understood in terms of unresolved tension. Thus she sees foreign cultic discourse as a rhetorical site for struggles of identity formation—in this case, "the nature of 'Roman-ness': on what it was to be Roman and on what could count as Roman religious experience [during the first centuries of the Common Era]—in the context of a huge and ethnically diverse empire."[48]

What does this have to do with Hebrews 13.9–16? My purpose here is not to compare Magna Mater (or any other so-called "mystery religion") to early Christianity or to draw an explicit parallel between the insider/outsider boundary of the *pomerium* and the placing of Jesus and Hebrews readers on the rhetorical outside of an insider/outsider boundary (Heb 13.13).[49] Instead, I am interested in a particular discursive intersection in antiquity that both Hebrews and discussions of Magna Mater have in common: the interplay between cultic discourse and foreign status as a site for thinking through questions of identity. More specifically, I wish to highlight the way Beard's creative approach to a scholarly dichotomy that posits gradual domestication or ignorance of a cult's foreign nature as the *only* two interpretive options proves illuminating to the binary opposition between the literal anti-Jewish/anti-cultic antithesis and allegorical Philonic otherworldliness so often used to interpret Hebrews 13.9–16. That is to say, we do not necessarily have to read the contrast in this passage between the Levitical cult and the sacrifice of Jesus as either definitively anti-cultic *or* definitively allegorical/symbolic (with respect to the soul in the world) and nothing more. The example of Magna

Mater points toward the possibility that something more complex may be at work.

Indeed, Hebrews picks up the same two motifs which Beard highlights with reference to Magna Mater—cultic discourse and outsider status—and uses their intersection in a different way. Whereas Roman literary elites looked to the outsider cult of Cybele as a rhetorical site for working out the nature of "Roman-ness," leaving the issue of the cult's foreignness in unresolved tension, Hebrews 13 takes a definitive stand on the issue of outsider status, calling its audience actively to take on an alien or "foreign" identity by going to Jesus outside the camp; at the same time, it allows the question of cultic practice to remain in an unresolved tension. On the one hand then, the text seems to offer an objection to cultic regulations connected to food in 13.9. It also makes the move to metaphorize "sacrifices" in 13.15–16. On the other hand, however, the text gives an ambiguous but nonetheless decidedly positive characterization of the Christians' altar (*thysiastērion*) in 13.10.[50] Thus cultic discourse in this passage functions as a rhetorical site for working out a certain notion of "Christian-ness"—a conception of early Christian identity whose accent falls on embracing outsider status, rather than a clear and unambiguous stance on a certain type of Christian cultic practice (or lack thereof).

In this way, the appeal to cultic imagery in Hebrews 13.9–16 does not necessarily function solely to allegorize or polemicize against cultic practice. Rather it places the text's critical project of identity formation in a larger connotative cultural context, one that would not have been limited to the Jewish scriptures for any given early Christian readers (despite the fact that 13.9–16 relies heavily on the language and categories of Levitical tradition found in the biblical tradition as mediated through the LXX). As noted above, cultic practice and discourse were to be found everywhere in the ancient Mediterranean. Due to this ubiquity across the Roman Empire, as Mary Beard points out, "religion was, and remained, good to think with."[51] Thus the intersection of ancient discourses on cult and foreign/alien/outsider status provided a site for diverse groups—not only elites interacting with Magna Mater in Rome but also early Christians—to construct and solidify boundaries of communal identity amidst the disorienting heterogeneity of the Roman world.

In Hebrews 13.9–16, then, we see the culmination of a project of identity construction that enters this larger conversation (at least from the reference point of ancient readers), while still making use of rhetoric and images associated with the Levitical tradition. The result is a movement of identity to the periphery—a movement that readers appropriate through embracing a self-identification of alien status. How does one go to Jesus outside the camp? Hebrews is ready to answer: by claiming an identity of communal "otherness" (with respect not simply to "Judaism" but in relation to the much broader diversity and fluidity of religious identities available in Roman antiquity), and then reinterpreting and implementing the exhortations of the text from that position of constructed marginality.

A "Usable Social Identity": Radical Rhetoric and Traditional Norms

These exhortations that Hebrews calls its readers to reinterpret in light of their alien status include more than just the paraenetic metaphors discussed above (urging the audience to enter and draw near). Also in view are the very concrete directives found in 13.1–7. In this way, the call to go "outside the camp" does not simply orient the readers toward an otherworldly city; rather the concern extends to matters of tangible everyday life. Seemingly traditional directives—exhortations to hospitality, care for prisoners, marital purity, finances, and imitating community leadership—are transformed by this call. That is to say, these directives (read in the light of 13.13) serve to constitute communal behavior in such a way as to reinforce the audience's radical sense of itself at the margins of society, while at the same time advocating a not particularly radical course of conduct—certainly not one that undermines broader social stability in any significant way. As Helmut Koester points out, "for Hebrews, 'outside the camp' is identical with the worldliness of the world itself."[52]

The specific practices outlined in the chapter mark out this space of worldliness. Readers are exhorted to care for those internal to the community through *philadelphia* (13.1). Yet they are to look outward as well: hospitality to strangers (*tēs philoxenias mē epilanthanesthe, dia tautēs gar elathon tines xenisantes angelous*, 13.2) not only recalls the possibility of angelic/divine visitation[53] but also opens a bridge between this community of strangers and the larger world. Here a return to language echoing the alien topos (i.e., various cognates of *xenos*) strengthens the link to the outside—this time designating not the Christian self, but rather the external other who should be treated hospitably.

Chapter 13's paraenesis continues with a call to identification with those in prison and undergoing torture (*mimnēskesthe tōn desmiōn hōs syndedemenoi, tōn kakouchoumenōn hōs kai autoi ontes en sōmati*, 13.3), connecting the audience to circumstances of extreme marginalization. And it may well be that some early readers of Hebrews found themselves facing the imminent threat of physical imprisonment. Nevertheless, what I wish to highlight here is the rhetorical function of the connection being made—one not dependent on any such threat. Rather, the text works here to form communal identity through an imaginative association with the social margins. The exhortation to remember *as if* in prison or being tortured calls readers to envision the communal Christian self in solidarity with these circumstances, while not actually advocating any particularly subversive action.

Similarly, the call to marital purity (*Timios ho gamos en pasin kai hē koitē amiantos, pornous gar kai moichous krinei ho theos*, 13.4), or contentment with one's material possessions (*Aphilargyros ho tropos, arkoumenoi tois parousin*, 13.5), or remembrance and imitation of one's leaders (*Mnēmoneuete tōn hēgoumenōn hymōn, hoitines elalēsan hymin ton logon tou theou, hōn anatheōrountes tēn ekbasin tēs anastrophēs mimeisthe tēn pistin*, 13.7) can hardly be characterized as especially radical with respect to traditional Roman norms of this period. Some have argued that the exhortations to sexual fidelity in 13.4 are a means by which Christians differentiated themselves from Roman society, basing this argument on an appeal to the laxity of Roman standards.[54] But many Jewish, Greek, and Roman moralists promoted comparable values (in forms no more rhetorical than what we see in Hebrews), thereby problematizing a construal of 13.4 in terms of the radically different nature of early Christian sexual morality. In general then, the various paraenetic directives of 13.1–9 seem to fall loosely under the kind of common wisdom and values found in Greco-Roman, Jewish, and early Christian moralists.[55]

Thus nothing in these exhortations indicates radical or subversive engagement with the surrounding society. It is not that socially subversive options for communal life and practice (or what Denise Buell calls "alternative forms of embeddedness"[56]) did not exist in antiquity.[57] But as Wayne Meeks points out, "[these] specific admonitions . . . pertain to life not in some desert retreat but in an urban congregation."[58] Indeed what we see here (borrowing again a helpful phrase from Laurence Moore) is the production of a *usable social identity*,[59] one that the text generates through its interlacing of the alien topos with traditional social paraenesis. The dynamic operative here is similar to what we saw in 1 Peter, but articulated much more thoroughly. Readers are to join Jesus in alterity, performing their alien status not through radical practices of differentiation but through behaving more or less like everybody else. In this way, Hebrews situates Christian identity in a carefully balanced tension between alien status and a relatively conventional ethical vision.

Does this tell us anything about the earliest audience(s) for Hebrews? Scholars have hazarded many guesses, arguing backward from Hebrews' rhetoric of alienation to various conclusions: for example, the audience was a faction of displaced Jewish priests,[60] or a community suffering severe social ostracism (see 10.32–34),[61] or a group of people forced to redefine their own anxiety in light of a failed parousia.[62] Any of these remain real historical possibilities. I do not wish to aver that Christian difference did not exist or to preclude the possibility that *some* early Christian readers of Hebrews suffered something like the social rejection described in Hebrews 10.32–34. But lacking further supplementary evidence, the textual data alone cannot settle the question.

My interest here moves in a different direction, looking to the tensions that the text enacts rhetorically in its use of the alien topos to articulate Christian identity. As I argued in the introduction, these are rhetorical tensions that would call for analysis, *even if we did possess further evidence* for locating the sociohistorical "reality" of the first readers' alien status as it existed behind the text. As Foucault eloquently argues, the goal of such a project is not "to neutralize discourse, to make it the sign of something else, and to pierce through its density in order to reach what remains silently anterior to it, but on the contrary to maintain it in its consistency, to make it emerge in its own complexity."[63] And complexities do emerge in the tensions that constitute and crosscut Hebrews' use of the alien topos.

As we have seen, the text situates its practical vision of alien identity in assimilationist terms, calling Christian distinctiveness into being rhetorically while relying (in part) on a sort of misrecognition or sleight of hand—one whereby joining Jesus in alterity outside the camp boils down in practice to a rather unremarkable paraenetic program.[64] Yet the move to claim the name "alien" in this way has multiple discursive effects. As Bourdieu notes, "by structuring the perception which social agents have of the social world, the act of naming helps to establish the structure of this world. . . . There is no social agent who does not aspire, as far as his circumstances permit, to have the power to name and to create the world through naming."[65] Accordingly, by naming Christians as aliens, Hebrews stakes a claim to their discrete identity in the world. It does so through providing the narrative resources of a scriptural lineage, thereby allowing Christians to assert their marginality (and thus their difference) even as they seek to conform in multiple ways to the norms of the Roman world around them.

But this is not necessarily all. Such a strategy of differentiation—the power to speak one's difference into existence—may itself work to resist the shape of the social world as currently constituted. As Judith Perkins puts this succinctly, "the basis for Christianity's difference is located precisely in its talk."[66] And as ancient readers of Hebrews elaborated and reiterated their alien identity over time, the power of this narrative to form Christian selves may well have functioned (in Bourdieu's terms) as "an act of social magic that can create difference *ex nihilo* . . . [managing] to produce discontinuity out of continuity."[67] At the very least, it did not leave the field of possible Roman identities unchanged. The community of Christian aliens envisioned by Hebrews may not have been out to turn the Roman social order upside down. But in claiming a space of existence for this imagined community, Hebrews makes its mark—a mark that is in some way necessarily resistant (even as it simultaneously seeks certain kinds of assimilation) to the field of identities that preceded it. As I have argued, the status of the alien is always necessarily a *relational* one. Thus in asking Christians to see themselves as valorized outsiders, Hebrews implicitly asks others to see them that way as well.

Conclusion

This chapter has sought to analyze the complex ways in which Hebrews' use of the alien topos functioned as a practice in its own right, one whose effects could be felt in the discursive field of ancient identities, both Christian and otherwise. Whether or not it responds to some external factor such as legal status, persecution, or even the failed parousia, the topos nevertheless performs a specific rhetorical function with respect to the project of early Christian identity formation: it carves out a place for conceptualizing and maintaining a distinctive Christian insider status within the vast cultural field of cultic identities in the Roman empire, while at the same time leaving the issue of actual cultic practice in unresolved tension. Hebrews does this by appealing to a scriptural lineage, one in which a rhetoric of alterity figures Abraham and other great heroes of the faith as aliens. Readers are to join this lineage, employing the paraenetic metaphor of going to Jesus "outside the camp" as a way to reread the rest of the text's paraenesis in terms of their alien status. This includes not just the text's many metaphors of entering and drawing near, but also concrete directives for communal behavior—directives that largely situate Christians' practical norms and values within broader Roman social ideals in a conventional way. In this way, Hebrews promotes and reinforces its audience's understanding of its own distinctiveness within Roman society, while at the same time maintaining a connection to biblical tradition and an affirmation of traditional mores.

Consequently, the text's strategic use of the alien topos constructs a particular kind of rhetorically shaped "usable social identity." Its assimilationist tendencies may lend themselves on a practical level to producing Christians not so different from others around them (at least in the ancient Roman context)—even as the refiguring of those tendencies through the language of alienation works to articulate a viable and distinct Christian identity. But, as I have noted, in laying claim to a valorized space of marginality, this strategy of differentiation does enact a resistance of sorts, seeking to choose the terms on which others recognize the place of Christians within the field of ancient identities. And a similar strategy could also be put to more overtly resistant ends—speaking back to the Roman social order through appropriating its own conventional terms—as we will see in a second-century text, the *Epistle to Diognetus*.

Chapter Three

Outsiders by Virtue of Outdoing: The *Epistle to Diognetus*

In the second century, the designation of the Christian as alien and so-journer remained a useful (and indeed prevalent) category for forging and negotiating identity. Scholarship on the topos has tended to treat second-century materials primarily in terms of their relationship to the earlier canonical sources (1 Peter, Hebrews).[1] But Christians in the second century had their own reasons for turning to the alien topos, reasons not primarily (or at least not entirely) determined by earlier texts. Rather, the alien topos proved helpful for these Christians in advancing their own projects of identity formation, bound up as they were in particular interests and paraenetic needs. We see evidence of one such project in the *Epistle to Diognetus*. This is a text that—like Hebrews—puts the trope of alien status to work in order to situate Christian identity very much within the Roman social order. But it also inflects the topos in a particular way, deploying it as part of a larger argument in order to resist explicitly a certain (Roman) construction of that social order and way of thinking about Christians' place within it.

The *Epistle to Diognetus* is an anonymous apologetic treatise of the later second century preserved in a single thirteenth- or fourteenth-century manuscript (*Codex Argentoratensis Graecus* 9).[2] The codex was housed in Strassburg until it was destroyed by fire in 1870 during the Franco-Prussian War. Multiple transcriptions of the text made prior to the manuscript's destruction mean that *Diognetus* is still extant today (albeit with some textual problems).[3] Most scholars agree that the text is composite, with chapters 11–12 being a secondary addition.[4] The text is written in excellent Greek, characterized by Bart Ehrman as "one of the true literary gems of early Christianity."[5] Although labeled an epistle, *Diognetus* is not in fact a letter but rather a *logos protreptikos* or "speech of exhortation," defined by Helmut Koester as "a literary genre designed as an invitation to a philosophical way of life, directed to all those who were willing to engage in the search for true philosophy and make it the rule for their conduct of life."[6] Thus its paraenetic passages are not overtly directed to Christian insiders (in contrast to what we have seen in 1 Peter and Hebrews). Indeed the text makes extensive use of the third person in its portrayal of Christian life and identity, as well as in its polemics against Jews and Greeks/non-Christians. In fact, chapters 5 and 6 of *Diognetus* (the relevant portions of the text for study of the alien topos) are written entirely in the third person.

Nevertheless, *Diognetus*'s third person rehearsal of Christian identity still has direct implications for how early Christians thought about themselves. As David Aune argues, "it is probable that both apologetic and protreptic literature played an important internal role in providing self-definition for the group within which it arose."[7] Making a similar point, Robert Grant contends that "an apologist's efforts are likely to produce significant changes in the way the minority [group] looks at itself. As he tries to present its ideas as persuasively as possible, the persuasion is likely to convert the converted and modify their ideas at least in form."[8] While this analysis of *Diognetus* 5–6 hopes to show that the rhetorical dynamics at play are significantly more complex than simply "converting the converted," the basic point that both Aune and Grant make remains apposite: even though not addressed to Christians directly, the text's use of the alien topos has important implications for thinking about varieties of Christian identity in the second century.

Turning now to the text itself, we see an extensive development of the Christian self as other in these two chapters:

5.1. For Christians are not distinguished from other people by means of country nor language nor customs. **2.** For nowhere do they dwell in their own cities, nor use a peculiar language nor practice a peculiar way of life. **3.** Indeed this teaching of theirs has not been discovered by any thought and reflection on the part of inquisitive people, nor do they engage in human doctrine, as some do. **4.** But while dwelling in both Greek and barbarian cities, as each one's lot is cast, and adhering to the local customs in both dress and diet and the rest of life, they show forth the remarkable and confessedly paradoxical character of their own citizenship (*politeias*). **5.** They live in their own homelands, but as resident aliens (*paroikoi*); they participate in all things as citizens (*politai*), but endure all things as strangers (*xenoi*). Every foreign country (*xenē*) is their homeland but every homeland is a foreign country. **6.** They marry like everyone else, they have children; but they do not expose those they have given birth to. **7.** They set a common table, but not a common bed. **8.** They happen to be in the flesh, but do not live according to the flesh. **9.** They spend time on earth, but they have their citizenship (*politeuontai*) in heaven. **10.** They are obedient to the established laws, but they outdo the laws in their own lives. **11.** They love everyone, but are persecuted by everyone. **12.** They are not well known, but are pronounced guilty. They are put to death, but they are made alive. **13.** They are extremely poor, but they make many rich. They lack all things but they abound in everything. **14.** They are dishonored, but they are glorified in their dishonor. They are slandered, but they are vindicated. **15.** They are reviled, but they bless. They are insulted, but they show honor. **16.** When they do good, they are punished as evil-doers; when they are punished, they rejoice as those who are made alive. **17**. They are opposed by Jews as aliens (*allophyloi*), and they are persecuted by Greeks, and those who hate them are not able to say what the reason for their hatred is.

6.1. To put it succinctly, what the soul is in the body, this is what Christians are in the world. **2**. The soul is spread throughout all the parts of the body, and Christians are spread through the cities of the world. **3**. The soul lives in the body, but it does not belong to the body; and Christians live in the world, but do not belong to the world. **4**. The soul, being invisible, is confined in the body, which is visible; and Christians are known, seeing as they exist throughout the world, but their worship remains invisible. **5**. The flesh, though not being wronged, hates the soul and is hostile towards it, because it is prevented from indulging its pleasures; and the world, though not being wronged, hates Christians because they oppose its pleasures. **6**. The soul loves the flesh which hates it, and also the body parts; and Christians love those who hate them. **7**. The soul is shut up in the body, but it itself holds the body together; and Christians are confined in the world as in prison, but they themselves hold the world together. **8**. The soul which is immortal dwells in a mortal habitation; and Christians sojourn (*paroikousin*) among perishable things, while looking forward to the incorruptibility which is in heaven. **9**. The soul, when treated badly with respect to food and drink, grows better; and Christians, when they are punished, day by day multiply all the more. **10**. God has appointed them to such a position, which it is not right for them to avoid.

Here *Diognetus* deploys the alien topos in a way that is on several levels comparable to what we have seen in Hebrews. The text constructs a communal identity for Christians using the language of aliens (*paroikoi*, 5.5; *allophyloi*, 5.17), strangers/foreigners (*xenoi*, *xenē*, 5.5), sojourning (*paroikousin*, 6.8), and citizenship (*politeias*, 5.4; *politai*, 5.5; *politeuontai*, 5.9). Furthermore, it affirms kinds of mores similar to those found in Hebrews 13. But whereas in Hebrews the tension between radical outsider identity and Roman cultural norms is left implicit (hinging around the call to go to Jesus outside the camp), *Diognetus* attempts to work out this relationship rhetorically, building a careful argument about the role of Christians with respect to the Roman social order. The result is a vision of identity in which Christians are socially integrated (and indeed exemplary) members of Roman society. In fact, *Diognetus* avers, their alien status is actually a function of the degree to which they outstrip the Romans in their ability to fulfill Roman norms. But the implications of this position are not serenely assimilationist. Rather, *Diognetus*'s stance is an agonistic one, appealing to Roman ethical and cultural ideals as a platform upon which to valorize Christian alien identity and thus oppose its relegation to a site of reproach among the hierarchies of status and power that structure Roman society.

Christians as a New Race

Diognetus 5 begins by emphasizing all the ways that Christians are *not* in fact different from anyone else (*Christianoi gar oute gē oute phōnē oute ethesi diakekrimenoi tōn loipōn eisin anthrōpōn*, 5.1).[9] Rather than highlighting an eschatological city where Christians actually belong, the focus in 5.2 is on the cities here and now where Christians live just like anyone else (*oute gar pou poleis idias katoikousin*).[10] As such, they do not "use a peculiar language nor practice a peculiar way of life" (*oute dialektō tini parēllagmenē chrōntai oute bion parasēmon askousin*). So do Christians in fact stand out as a distinct group? On one level, yes—so much so that in the opening lines of the treatise, the text designates them as a "new race" (*kainon touto genos*, 1.1).[11] But this appellation sits in a curious tension with the accentuation of nondifference in *Diognetus* 5.1–2. As Enrico Norelli argues, "even though the Christians are a *genos*, they are not distinguished by the characteristic features of the *genos*."[12] Differences in dialect or "peculiar way[s] of life" do not mark them as a people—though the text maintains their distinct ethnoracial status all the same.

This ethnoracial dimension becomes clear in *Diognetus* 5–6, as the passage continues. After noting that Christian teaching is not the product of any human inquiry or doctrine (5.3), the text locates Christian identity in an attempt to unsettle the traditional *Hellēnes/barbaroi* dichotomy (5.4). This move in some sense parallels a common rhetorical stance in early Christian thinking (one that Denise Buell has noted in both Clement of Alexandria and Justin Martyr) which "positions Greeks and barbarians as eligible to become members of another people, the Christians."[13] But in *Diognetus*'s case, rather than emphasizing a tripartite distinction among races/peoples, the text instead relativizes the importance of the traditional bipartite ethnic framework (Greek/barbarian).[14] It makes the point that its protagonists in fact dwell in both kinds of cities (*poleis hellēnidas te kai barbarous*) and adhere to "local customs in both dress and diet and the rest of life" (*tois enchōriois ethesin . . . en te esthēti kai diaitē kai tō loipō biō*). Still they nevertheless manage to "show forth the remarkable and confessedly paradoxical character of their own citizenship" (*thaumastēn kai homologoumenōs paradoxon endeiknyntai tēn katastasin tēs heautōn politeias*).

In this way, *Diognetus*'s rhetorical construction of early Christians as a new *genos* or "third race" significantly intersects its use of the alien topos. As Buell shows, we see plainly operative in the text the ancient discursive blurriness between ethnoracial and civic categories (as discussed in Chapter One): "This text initially links Christians with a race (*genos*), but when we ask what this means, we find the notion of citizenship at the center. For the *Epistle to Diognetus*, this defining feature makes it possible to portray Christianness in at least partially universalizing terms—as an identity that, like other forms of citizenship, is potentially accessible to all free male people, something that sets Christians apart yet allows them to otherwise 'fit' into the status quo."[15] Here the rhetorical slide between ethnoracial and civic status allows the text to portray Christians as a *genos* that can be joined, setting the groundwork for figuring them as resident aliens and strangers (categories that rely on a similar blurriness between civic and ethnoracial spheres).

But as Buell also observes, in marking out Christians as a "people," *Diognetus* makes clear that it rejects dress, diet, and other commonplaces of cultural life as legitimate indicators of this distinct (and ethnoracially inflected) citizenship.[16] This exacerbates the rhetorical tension within which the text situates Christian identity. If the most commonly legible ways of defining a people in the ancient world are to be rejected, then exactly how does the "showing forth" that the text speaks of in 5.4 occur? While 5.1, 2, and 4a emphasize that Christians are no different from anybody else, 4b adamantly maintains their distinct citizenship. *Diognetus* 5.5 goes on to elaborate that this alternate citizenship is best understood (from the standpoint of Greek and barbarian cities) in terms of the alien status it produces for its members: "They live in their own homelands, but as resident aliens; they participate in all things as citizens, and endure all things as strangers. Every foreign country is their homeland and every homeland is a foreign country" (*patridas oikousin idias, all' hōs paroikoi; metechousi pantōn hōs politai, kai panth' hypomenousin hōs xenoi; pasa xenē patris estin autōn, kai pasa patris xenē*). Yet it remains unclear how this alien identity manifests itself within the broader social order.

Reinhard Feldmeier analyzes this tension in terms of an internal/external polarity: "Externally, Christians are in no respect different (according to *Diognetus* 5:1ff.) from other people; they do not live in different cities, and do not lead remarkable lives. They are, however, marked by a special inner attitude to all these things."[17] For Feldmeier therefore, the alien status that 5.5 articulates should be read in terms of this "special inner attitude."[18] While this is not an unreasonable reading on his part, at the same time, it is worth noting that nothing in 5.5 explicitly signals an interiorizing dynamic. Instead the text goes on to emphasize *exteriority*—specific practices whereby Christians not only comply with all the social requirements of insiders to the Roman society, but actually surpass those requirements.[19]

Infanticide as Ethical Barometer

In a notably different way from Hebrews 13 (which simply lists its traditional paraenetic concerns), *Diognetus* 5 expounds on practical matters using an explicitly contrastive framework. The first topic at hand is marriage and childbearing: Christians marry and have children like good members of Roman society, but—unlike the Romans, so the text implies—they do not expose those children (*all' ou rhiptousi ta gennōmena*, 5.6).[20] What are we to make of this comparison? Ancient literature commonly mentions the exposure of unwanted infants, though the frequency of the practice probably differed throughout the Empire at various times and places.[21] But as John Boswell makes clear in his masterful study on the issue, "Roman moral and legal views of abandonment appear to have been quite indulgent. Neither law nor public opinion posed any barrier to parents exposing or giving children away through the fourth century."[22]

If this is the case, then why does *Diognetus* seem to assume that not exposing children is an ethically superior position? In fact, ancient rhetorical attitudes towards exposure were not completely univocal or unambiguous. For example, the Stoic Epictetus (c.55–c.135) offers the following argument against Epicurus's exhortation, "Let us not bring up children":

> But a sheep does not abandon its own offspring nor a wolf; and yet does a man abandon his? What do you wish us to do? Would you have us be foolish as sheep? But even they do not desert their offspring. Would you have us be fierce as wolves? But even they do not desert their offspring. Come now, who follows your advice when he sees his child fallen on the ground and crying? Why, in my opinion, your mother and father, even if they had divined that you were going to say such things, would not have exposed you![23]

Similarly, Aelian (late second–early third century) describes an ancient law in Thebes that forbade the exposure of children, which he characterizes as "just and at the same time extremely humane."[24]

We also see a strong censure of exposure practices in early Jewish literature. Philo's *Special Laws* makes perhaps the most graphic description:

> Others take them to be exposed in some desert place, hoping, they themselves say, that they may be saved, but leaving them in actual truth to suffer the most distressing fate. For all the beasts that feed on human flesh visit the spot and feast unhindered on the infants, a fine banquet provided by their sole guardians, those who above all others should keep them safe, their fathers and mothers. Carnivorous birds, too, come flying down and gobble up the fragments . . . But suppose some passing travelers, stirred by humane feeling, take pity and compassion on the castaways and in consequence raise them up, give them food and drink, and do not shrink from paying all the other attentions which they need, what do we think of such highly charitable actions? Do we not consider that those who brought them into the world stand condemned when strangers play the part of parents, and parents do not behave with even the kindness of strangers?[25]

Pseudo-Phocylides (sometime between 200 B.C.E. and 150 C.E.) makes a comparable point more succinctly: "Nor, having given birth, should [a woman] expose [her child] to dogs and vultures as prey."[26]

These texts, while vociferous in their protest, reflect a minority opinion in Roman antiquity. As Boswell reminds us, "Most ancient moral writers evince indifference toward or acceptance of abandonment."[27] But the fact that the minority opinion exists at all—and more important, that it exists outside Christian texts—is crucial to the specific rhetorical move that *Diognetus* makes here. Indeed, to the extent that the text is speaking to outsiders, it seems to count on the preexistence of a cultural perspective which views exposure as a negative or at least less than ideal practice. Thus *Diognetus* 5.6 makes no case against exposure. It simply assumes its inferior status, and then appropriates its avoidance as a means of marking of a distinctively *Christian* identity conceptualized in terms of practice.[28] This is a strategy the text will replicate as it further elaborates identity in contrastive terms.

Christians Versus Romans

Accordingly, the remainder of *Diognetus* 5 develops this framework in which Christian practice is contrasted to that of a stereotyped Roman social order. Thus, in 5.7, Christians fulfill expected norms of hospitality (*trapezan koinēn paratithentai*), but never at the expense of sexual purity (*all' ou koitēn*).[29] Here Henry Meecham draws a parallel to the paraenesis in Hebrews 13, arguing that like *Diognetus,* "the writer of Heb. xiii 2–4 enjoins hospitality (*philoxenia*), but insists that the marriage-bed be undefiled (*hē koitē amiantos*)."[30] While Meecham is correct that both texts deal with the topics of hospitality and sexual purity in close proximity to one another, his analysis misses what is distinctive about the move *Diognetus* makes here. Unlike *Diognetus,* Hebrews 13.2–4 does not explicitly link hospitality with purity concerns. Furthermore, Hebrews shows no interest in comparing Christian hospitality to other ways of being hospitable that it sees as problematic, whereas for *Diognetus,* the contrast is the point. Hospitality is brought up only in order to value a specifically *Christian* hospitality as that which maintains a level of sexual purity that is beyond reproach.[31]

Diognetus 5.8 continues this same dynamic, appealing to an *en sarki / kata sarka* contrast: Christians live *in* the flesh like everyone else but they do not live *according to* the flesh (*en sarki tynchanousin, all' ou kata sarka zōsin*). Here many commentators have insisted upon a strictly Pauline sense of these terms, noting the verbal correspondence between *Diognetus* 5.8 and 2 Corinthians 10.3: "For though we walk in the flesh, we do not wage war according to the flesh" (*en sarki gar peripatountes ou kata sarka strateuometha*). Certainly it is the case that any second-century reader familiar with 2 Corinthians could have easily understood *Diognetus* 5.8 with respect to these two Pauline uses (i.e., material and ethical) of *sarx*. But as Norelli points out, "the context . . . is significantly different from that of Paul in 2 Cor 10.3, which treats the struggle of the apostle against the sophists opposing the knowledge of God: here it treats the ethic of the associated life."[32] In addition, elsewhere (Romans 8.4, 12–13), Paul sets the ethical use of *kata sarka* in opposition to *kata pneuma*, a very different sort of contrast from what we see in *Diognetus* 5.8.

In any event, while the hypothesis that early Christians read these phrases intertextually with Paul is plausible, the rhetoric of the text in fact draws a much simpler contrast: like the surrounding society, Christians are "enfleshed." Yet, similar to the ideal of those who pursue the true philosophical life,[33] they stand one step above all this. Thus they are not mired in life according to the flesh. The larger point remains the same whatever the connotations of *kata sarka* might be for any given second-century reader: perhaps "sin" in a Pauline sense, but just as possibly, an inappropriate attachment to material pursuits, or a lack of (Stoic) self-consciousness[34]—or indeed some combination of the above. Here I again draw attention to Eco's theoretical notion of the *intentio operis*—a semiotic strategy within the text that attempts to produce its model reader(s).[35] The point then is that *Diognetus*'s semiotic strategy is in this case far less specific than one aimed overtly at constraining its readers' interpretive options within the parameters of the Pauline connection (if for example, the text were to cite Paul or Romans/2 Corinthians explicitly, with reference to *kata sarka*—not thereby removing the need for interpretation, but rather shifting its locus to the contested ground of Pauline theology).

In this way, the text's strategy allows for an intertextual reading with Paul (and perhaps specifically alludes to it for Christian insiders), but leaves space for a broader spectrum of potential interpretations. Indeed, the precise referents of *en sarki/kata sarka* are only of secondary importance. The emphasis here is on the overall contrast *Diognetus* constructs (from 5.6 and following) between two complementary but nevertheless hierarchized ways of life. 5.9 reinforces this contrast, effectively summing up the larger point of the previous three verses, while adding a turn to an overtly cosmological dualism: "They spend time on earth, but they have their citizenship in heaven" (*epi gēs diatribousin, all' en ouranō politeuontai*).[36]

What does all this mean in terms of practical effect (at least on the level of the text's rhetorical stance)? 5.10 makes *Diognetus*'s conclusion explicit: Christians are "obedient to the established laws, but they outdo the laws in their own lives" (*peithontai tois hōrismenois nomois, kai tois idiois biois nikōsi tous nomous*). In this way, a comparative framework produces a vision of Christians as obedient and even exemplary members of Roman society. As Norelli argues, the dichotomy that the text sets up between Christians and non-Christians is not a strictly oppositional one: "Rather, it deals with the condition of a new ethic . . . that does not pit itself against the civil laws, but follows the same sense and goes beyond them, one which can only benefit the state."[37] Indeed, the outsider status in question is actually being defined as a *function* of the way that Christians live. Even though in 5.9 the self-as-other seems to be defined eschatologically by an appeal to heavenly citizenship, the emphasis in the text's apologetic (and implicitly paraenetic) present is on a kind of *über*-compliance to the norms of the given social context. In the logic of *Diognetus*'s argument, then, Christians take on their communal identity as *paroikoi* and *xenoi* by virtue of *surpassing* these traditional Roman norms—an outsider status predicated (somewhat paradoxically) on the case that Christians play the insiders' game even better than they do.

On one level, this strategy may seem to replicate the use in Hebrews of a traditional or assimilationist paraenetic agenda. That is to say, *Diognetus* holds up obedience to *Roman* laws and norms as a standard around which to think through the value of *Christian* identity and practice. But this conformist strategy does not imply an entirely "friendly" stance to the Roman social order—as the text's framework of comparison and contrast makes clear.[38] Rather this mode of contrastive framing is, in Elizabeth Castelli's phrase, "profoundly polemical."[39] *Diognetus* draws on Roman norms to introduce a powerfully agonistic element into its construction of Christian alien identity. While the dominant cultural logic of the Empire provides the terms on which *Diognetus* makes its defense, that defense nevertheless attempts to speak back to the Roman other with a strong claim for the superiority of Christian peoplehood. As Judith Perkins has argued, "Christian discourse challenged the discourse of power being constructed in other texts of the period"—that is, texts that extolled the virtues of Roman rule and the Roman people.[40] While I would nuance Perkins's formulation to acknowledge that not all early Christian discourse necessarily presented this sort of challenge, in the case of *Diognetus* we see a text that quite forthrightly appropriates certain ideals of Roman discourse in order to confront that discourse.

The contrast *Diognetus* draws between Christians and everyone else (*pantes*, 5.6) proves in fact to be a powerful launching point for a stinging indictment of the very social order whose cultural logic the text's argument relies on. In view is the injustice of Roman society's (perceived) rejection and persecution of Christians. By defining Christians as outsiders (at least on the level of practice) in terms of how they actually uphold Roman values better than the Romans themselves, *Diognetus* is well positioned to offer a further set of forceful contrasts aimed at exposing how unmerited and unreasonable the social rejection of Christians is:

They love everyone, but are persecuted by everyone. They are not well known, but pronounced guilty. They are put to death, but they are made alive. They are extremely poor, but they make many rich. They lack all things but they abound in everything. They are dishonored, but they are glorified in their dishonor. They are slandered, but they are vindicated. They are reviled, but they bless. They are insulted, but they show honor. When they do good, they are punished as evil-doers. When they are punished, they rejoice as those who are made alive. They are opposed by Jews as aliens, and they are persecuted by Greeks, and those who hate them are not able to say what the reason for their hatred is. (5.11–17)

Many commentators have drawn attention to the affinities between this text and the so-called catalogues of suffering (or *peristasis* catalogues[41]) of the Pauline corpus, most notably 1 Corinthians 4.10–13, 2 Corinthians 4.7–12, and 2 Corinthians 6.4–10.[42] This connection is helpful insofar as it illuminates the extensive use of ancient rhetorical conventions employed in the *Diognetus* passage in terms of their function within a particular genre. As Norelli observes, the use of homoioteleuton (rhymed endings of clauses—in this case the repeated use of verbs ending in *-ontai/-ountai*, and *-ōsi[n]/-ousi[n]*) accents the presentation of the oppositions.[43] In addition, 5.11–17 is part of a larger series of asyndetic clauses (clauses not connected by particles or conjunctions) that extends from 5.5 through 5.15.[44] Overall seventeen antitheses are presented in rapid-fire succession, with the second part of each antithesis connected to the first either by *alla* or *kai*.[45] The rhetorical effect is, in Lausberg's apt phrase, "that of pathos-reinforcing intensification."[46]

In 5.16, the style and tempo of the rhetoric shifts,[47] and *Diognetus* returns in 5.17 to language explicitly associated with the alien topos (rather than a general state of marginality). It avers that the Christians are attacked (*polemountai*) by Jews as *allophyloi*, a term new to this discussion but one that carries connotations of alien and foreign status (i.e., often "gentile" in early Jewish literature[48]). Whereas *Diognetus* 5 has previously used the Greek/barbarian polarity in order to emphasize the non-difference of Christians from either (5.4), it here turns to the familiar binary of Jew and Greek seen earlier in the treatise (cf. 1.1, 3.2–3). Thus 5.17 sets up Christians as a third term in this binary ethnic framework, in order to underscore again the injustice of the ways in which their opponents (irrespective of ethnocultural affiliation) regard them. In this context, it seems likely that the use of such a distinctive term as *allophylos* (rather than *paroikos* or *xenos*; cf. 5.5) functions not to valorize the Christian self as other, so much as to continue this carefully constructed argument "underlining the irrationality of the general antagonism toward Christians."[49] The text makes this point explicit in 17b: "those who hate them are not able to say what the reason for their hatred is" (*kai tēn aitian tēs echthras eipein hoi misountes ouk echousin*).

The Soul in the Body and Aliens in the World

Diognetus 5–6 then climaxes with an extensive comparison (or *synkrisis*[50]) between the role of the soul (*psychē*) in the body (*sōma*) and Christians in the world (6.1–10). This famous analogy has been extensively analyzed by scholars of early Christianity and variously located with respect to different schools of ancient philosophy.[51] Most likely, however, it is not necessary to situate the text definitively within one school over and against all others. In terms of how philosophical traditions actually functioned on the ground in the second century, it seems quite possible to read the notion of the soul spread/dispersed throughout the body (*espartai kata pantōn tōn tou sōmatos melōn hē psychē*, 6.2) against an anthropological backdrop which draws loosely upon aspects of Stoic thought (an understanding of the *psychē* as " 'extended' throughout the entire organism . . . literally continuous with the body's matter," yet still in some sense retaining primacy[52]), while at the same time acknowledging the close affinities of this entire section with a Platonic understanding of the soul-body relation (particularly as articulated in the *Phaedo*).[53] Thus the invisibility (*aoratos*) of the soul (6.4) is found in *Phaedo* 79b, while the idea of Christians imprisoned in the world in the same way that the soul is shut up in the body (*enkekleistai men hē psychē tō sōmati . . . kai Christianoi katechontai men hōs en phroura tō kosmō*, 6.7; cf. also *hē psychē . . . phroureitai tō sōmati*, 6.4) has close parallels with the *Phaedo* model.[54]

In terms of the rhetorical deployment of the alien topos in *Diognetus*, however, this extended analogue between Christians and the soul serves to reinforce a vision of the Christian self as other by consistently emphasizing the otherness of the soul with respect to the body/flesh.[55] Thus according to 6.3, "the soul lives in the body, but it does not belong to the body; and Christians live in the world but do not belong to the world" (*oikei men en tō sōmati psychē, ouk esti de ek tou sōmatos; kai Christianoi en kosmō oikousin, ouk eisi de ek tou kosmou*).[56] Furthermore, as the soul is invisible while the body is visible (6.4), so "Christians are known, seeing as they exist throughout the world, but their worship remains invisible" (*kai Christianoi ginōskontai men ontes en tō kosmō, aoratos de autōn hē theosebeia menei*).[57] As Norelli notes, the parallelism is defective—it is not Christians who are invisible (the conclusion which would be required according to the logic of the ongoing analogy with the soul) but their *theosebeia*.[58] Nevertheless, the point still works on the rhetorical level to emphasize the outsider status of the Christian communal self by virtue of its analogical connection to the soul.

Additional comparisons serve to bolster this larger point as well: the soul loves the flesh which hates it, while Christians love those who hate them (6.6); the soul is shut up/imprisoned in the body as are Christians in the world (6.4, 6.7); the immortal soul dwells in a mortal habitation, as Christians sojourn (*paroikousin*) among perishable things, looking forward to heavenly incorruptibility (6.8);[59] when the soul is deprived of material sustenance (i.e., a kind of outsider status), it thrives, while when Christians suffer punishment and marginalization, they multiply all the more (6.9).

At the same time, the analogy also subtly buttresses in a number of ways the text's argument that Christian outsider status is intimately tied to fulfilling and outdoing the established standards of Roman norms. For example, while 6.8 references the incorruptibility which is in heaven (*tēn en ouranois aphtharsian*), this is not characterized explicitly in terms of a heavenly *city* (see discussion of 5.2 above). Rather, the only cities in view in the analogy are those in which Christians are spread throughout the world (6.2), presumably living out their lives as model members of Roman society. As Judith Lieu insightfully notes, "If identity-formation is a process of differentiation, the social identity of the Christians here appears remarkably opaque . . . . [T]he analogy the author develops between Christians in the world and the soul within the body only reinforces the opacity: it implies symbiosis and invisibility, not differentiation."[60]

But if Christian identity emerges in *Diognetus*'s vision as opaque, that opaqueness stands itself as a kind of indictment—an accusation directed against Roman injustice. Thus *Diognetus* testifies that Christians have done no wrong to the world that hates them (6.5). What about Christian opposition to the world's pleasures? This is a delicate issue for a line of argument based on maintaining the basic consonance of Christian life and praxis with Roman mores. Yet here the logic of the analogy neatly allows the text to solve the difficulty. By appealing to a thoroughly respectable philosophical dualism (at least by Roman standards), one which eschews the pleasures of the flesh in favor of the higher status and pursuits of the soul (*misei tēn psychēn hē sarx kai polemei mēden adikoumenē, dioti tais hēdonais kōluetai chrēsthai; misei kai Christianous ho kosmos mēden adikoumenos, hoti tais hēdonais antitassontai*, 6.5), *Diognetus* justifies Christians' opposition to worldly pleasures. The text devalues *tais hēdonais* on philosophically reputable grounds that Romans could easily agree with (i.e., the primacy of *psychē* over *sarx*) and then links any Christian opposition to the social order with the restraining influence (*kōluetai*) exercised by the soul, rather than foregrounding the intrinsic evil of that order. In this way, *Diognetus* maintains its overall apologetic emphasis on the harmonious relationship between Christian practice and Roman norms, while simultaneously appropriating that consonance to protest *Roman* positioning of Christian identity.

In response, *Diognetus* offers its own resistant vision of where Christians are truly situated with respect to "the world" (here effectively equivalent to Roman society). Having become resident aliens by virtue of conforming to Roman norms even better than the Romans do, Christians in fact prove to be of absolutely vital importance for the social order. Thus, *Diognetus* contends, as the soul holds the body together, so Christians also hold the world together (*hē psychē . . . synechei de autē to sōma . . . kai Christianoi . . . autoi de synechousi ton kosmon*, 6.7). The verb used to make this point, *synechō*, has, according to Helmut Koester, a basic meaning of " 'to hold together' so that something is maintained in good order."[61] As such, it is frequently used in ancient philosophical discourse with reference to the function of some positive entity (the deity, the world soul, virtue) to maintain the cosmos. In the same way, for *Diognetus*, Christians function to sustain the social order, becoming, in Norelli's phrase, "the guarantors of the order of the world."[62]

In making this claim, the text implicitly asks its readers to refigure their understanding of where Christians should be placed within Roman hierarchies of cultural status. On the one hand, Christians have a distinct identity: strangers and resident aliens. But on the other hand, because they have taken on this outsider identity through their fulfillment of insider norms par excellence, the social order actually depends on them to hold together. This valorizing reversal of the Christian alien functions as a significant challenge to the Roman status quo, even as its logic depends on the norms of that status quo. The result is to render starkly evident the injustice of Christians' rejection by Roman society.

Consequently, the move *Diognetus* makes in 6.7 extends the rhetorical scope of the larger argument. Indeed, the text's protest to Roman society using Roman cultural standards roots itself not only in the evidence from practice appealed to in chapter 5, but also in a profound and philosophically weighty analogy based on the metaphysical structure of human anthropology. Thus the stakes are high. The concluding verse of this section, 6.10, only raises them higher, grounding the chapter's analogical framework explicitly in the *divine* will, and indirectly (i.e., remaining in the third person rather than switching over to paraenetic direct address) exhorting Christians to continued perseverance: "God has appointed them to such a position, which it is not right for them to avoid" (*eis tosautēn autous taxin etheto ho theos, hēn ou themiton autois paraitēsasthai*).[63]

Conclusion

In conclusion, then, the *Epistle to Diognetus* deploys the traditional resident alien topos in a trajectory similar to that which we see in Hebrews, juxtaposing a rhetoric of radical outsider identity with an affirmation of traditional cultural standards in order to create a usable social iden tity for Christians in the Roman world. But whereas Hebrews lets these two elements stand in an unexamined tension, *Diognetus* maps out a detailed and specific course, one in which the topos functions to construct a culturally integrated but nonetheless distinctive identity. The result is an argument for Christian identity in which Christians assume their alien status by not only complying with the norms of their surrounding cultural context, but in fact excelling in them above and beyond social expectations.

This distinctiveness, though framed in assimilationist terms, is not a particularly irenic project. Instead *Diognetus* throws itself into a rhetorical stance of struggle with the dominant Roman social order, relying on its claim that Christians surpass Romans in their capacity to live up to Roman ideals in order to undercut a Roman vision of Christian marginality in the world. By valorizing Christian alien status in these terms, *Diognetus* 5–6 engages in a three-pronged rhetorical project. While articulating a distinct (but nonetheless usable) social identity for Christians through the language of alterity, it simultaneously offers a protreptic invitation to outsiders and offers a challenge to the prevailing discourse. *Diognetus* thus doubly positions itself in an ancient discursive field of competing philosophical and/or religious stances and ways of life. Within this broader field of Roman cultural identities, its use of the alien topos functions as part of a skillful protreptic appeal, a strategic means of conveying "an invitation to enter upon a truly philosophical or religious life, a defense of the qualities and virtues of such a life, and a description of the basic philosophical concepts by which it should be guided."[64] But it also seeks overtly to resist (and thereby change) the shape of the field in which possible ancient identities were formed.

Indeed as Bourdieu argues, "Symbolic power . . . is a power of 'world-making.' "[65] In this case, *Diognetus* endeavors to "make" the world on multiple fronts, presenting Christian alien status to those outside the fold in a mode meant to be both inviting and resistant. It thereby attempts to hold its own on the competitive playing field of ancient cultural pluralism. As we will see in the next chapter, this is a very different project from that which another second-century text, the *Shepherd of Hermas*, undertakes in its use of the alien topos. Thus an additional example from the second century will highlight the degree to which differing goals, interests, and paraenetic concerns shaped the variable ways in which early Christians strategically put the language of the self as other to use.

Chapter Four

Foreign Countries and Alien Assets in the *Shepherd of Hermas*

Given the flexibility of alien and foreign status as a trope, early Christians found further uses for it in addition to labeling themselves. As I have argued, the claim to alien status is a relational one, drawing a boundary that defines an outside in relation to an inside. In the traditional valorization of the alien topos (as seen in 1 Peter, Hebrews, and *Diognetus*), outsider and insider terms get reversed, so that, by claiming the name "alien," Christians mark their insider status with a revalued language of alterity. But because of this relational dynamic, small differences in emphasis could produce variant effects. We see a noteworthy example of this in another second-century text, *The Shepherd of Hermas*.

Along with the above texts, *Hermas* also articulates Christian identity in the terms of the alien topos, setting up a vision of two cities: the one where Christians currently dwell "as in a foreign country" and their true city which is far away. But unlike these texts, *Hermas*'s articulation of Christian marginality never actually labels Christians explicitly as "strangers," "sojourners," or "resident aliens." While the comparison that the text sets up between two cities does function logically to situate the audience as aliens, *Hermas* does not expend its rhetorical energy interpellating them as such. Instead, it unleashes a polemic against the uses of wealth in the Christian community. Here the text impugns a particular social locale—and its attendant business dealings and financial commitments—by figuring them in terms of their foreignness. In this way *Hermas* deploys the doubleness of the topos to a distinct end (and one different from what we have seen thus far): it retains the valorization of Christian alien identity, while simultaneously bringing the *negative* connotations of the rhetoric of foreignness to the fore in order to demonize one way of life in the hopes that Christians will pursue another.

The Slaves of God

The *Shepherd of Hermas* is a tripartite work usually classified as an early Christian apocalypse.[1] Scholars generally situate it in Rome in the early to mid-second century.[2] The text's three sections are comprised of five visions, twelve mandates, and ten parables (or similitudes). This triple division, as well as manuscript evidence, has led scholars to posit numerous theories mapping out the composite nature of the text, its hypothetical sources, and multiple authors.[3] But these are questions of secondary importance for the purposes of this study. With respect to the alien topos, the key portion of *Hermas* is *Similitude* 1, an extended treatise on the nature of Christian identity:

1. He spoke to me, saying, "You know that you, the slaves of God, dwell in a foreign country; for your city is far from this city. If then you know your city in which you are going to dwell, why do you make arrangements for lands, expensive furnishings, buildings, and worthless living quarters? 2. Accordingly, the one who makes arrangements for these things in this city is not able to return to his or her own city. 3. O foolish, double-minded, and miserable person, do you not grasp that all these things are foreign and are under the authority of another? For the lord of this city will say: 'I do not want you to dwell in my city; instead go out from this city, because you do not use my laws.' 4. So you who have lands and houses and many other possessions, when you are thrown out by him, what will you do with your land and your house and the rest of it, which you have prepared for yourself? For the lord of this region justly says to you, 'Either use my laws or depart from my country.' 5. What then are you going to do, seeing as you have a law in your own city? On account of your lands and the rest of your possessions, will you totally deny your law and walk in the law of this city? Take care lest it be harmful to deny your law; for if you wish to return to your city, you will not be accepted back, because you have denied the law of your city, and you will be shut out of it. 6. So take care therefore; as one dwelling in a foreign country, make no more arrangements for yourself than an adequate sufficiency. Also be prepared, in order that, when the master of this city wants to throw you out for opposing his law, you will go out from his city and depart to your own city and use your own law without hindrance, being joyful. 7. Take care then, you who are subject to the Lord and have him in your heart. Do the works of God, remembering his commandments and the promises that he made, and trust him that he will bring them about if his commandments are kept. 8. So instead of lands, purchase oppressed souls (as each one is able to), and look after widows and orphans and do not neglect them. So spend your wealth and all your furnishings that you have received from God on lands and houses such as this. 9. For on account of this, the Master has made you rich, in order that you should carry out these services [ministries?] for him. It is much better to buy these sorts of lands, possessions, and houses, which you [sing.] will find in your city when you go home to it. 10. This wealth is honorable and joyful, not having grief nor fear, but rather joy. Thus do not deal in the wealth of foreigners. For it is harmful for you, the slaves of God. 11. But deal in your own wealth, in which you can rejoice, and do not counterfeit nor touch that which is alien nor desire it. For it is evil to desire things that are alien. So do your own work and you will be saved."

Who does this parable call Christians to be? How are they to articulate their individual and communal identity? The traditional language of the alien topos is scattered throughout the passage—terms such as *xenos*, *allotrios, ethnos,* and *polis.* And while words associated in other texts with sojourning such as *paroikos* or *parepidēmos* (and their cognates) do not appear, the text still employs something like the sojourning concept in its clear reference to the Christian *hōs epi xenēs katoikōn* (1.6). Unlike the emphases in 1 Peter, Hebrews, or *Diognetus,* however, *Hermas* expends very little rhetorical effort explicitly stressing the Christian's position as a *xenos,* in the world or otherwise. Rather, it appeals to another common trope of marginality in the ancient world. Who are Christians? The text makes this clear in its opening line: the slaves of God (*hoi douloi tou theou*).

This is a markedly different approach to the use of the alien topos from Hebrews' explicit identification of its audience as *xenoi kai parepidēmoi,* going to Jesus outside the camp, or *Diognetus*'s argument that its readers are *paroikoi* and *xenoi,* with a *politeia* that is "confessedly strange" (*homologoumenōs paradoxon . . . tēn katastasin*).[4] Instead, *Hermas* mobilizes a designation of Christian identity rooted in an alternate register of alterity: the slave—always by definition a non-citizen but in a different way from the resident alien/foreigner. Whereas the resident alien is a relative designation (insofar as the resident alien of one city is presumably the citizen of another), the slave is not. The slave is, by definition, not free and not a citizen—i.e., under another's ownership.

But not all owners were equal within the complex status hierarchies of the Roman world. Thus the position of being owned as a slave could be variably refigured and deployed (like the alien topos) to a spectrum of figurative ends, not all of them negative. As Dale Martin has shown, slavery in Roman society was a complicated (and in many ways ambiguous) institution, and subsequently the category of the slave could—in certain situations—have a positive inflection. In this way, Martin argues, "the wealth, position, and disposition of the owner were directly relevant for ascertaining a slave's own position in society and for predicting his or her future. The slave of a shoemaker likely had little status, but the slave of a local power broker or of a respected aristocrat could in turn hold considerable power and respect."[5] Therefore, like the alien topos, the trope of the Christian as slave was easily available for valorization in theological reflection, quickly becoming a positive and traditional insider designation: Christians are the slaves of the ultimate power broker, God himself.[6]

In this passage, *Hermas* in fact relies on the insider valence of the "slaves of God" metaphor. The text maintains that "you, the slaves of God, dwell in a foreign country; for your city is far from this city" (*hoti epi xenēs katoikeite hymeis hoi douloi tou theou; hē gar polis hymōn makran estin apo tēs poleōs tautēs,* 1.1). Here it mixes metaphors drawn from distinct topoi (the Christian as slave, the Christian as resident alien). To some degree the topoi overlap insofar as they both generally evoke positions of alterity in ancient thinking about status. But at the same time, the metaphors do not mesh together seamlessly, because slaves are not, strictly speaking, citizens of *any* city. Why combine the tropes in this way then? By positioning Christians as slaves *of God*, the text situates their proper allegiance elsewhere than the current city. And for *Hermas*, this is a good thing—the center-point around which Christian identity ought to be defined. Being a slave of God is therefore an insider status, one that *Hermas* will build upon in order to deploy the alien topos with a significantly different emphasis from what we have seen in other texts.

A Tale of Two Cities

Accordingly, with this insider designation (i.e., slaves of God) in place, *Hermas* shows little concern to emphasize alien alterity as the definitive marker of what it means to be Christian. This does not mean that the slaves of God in question are not in fact also some sort of sojourners or resident aliens. Indeed, they are those who dwell in a foreign country. But whereas Hebrews and *Diognetus* go to great lengths to fill out the contours of this alien status as a usable identity, *Hermas* capitalizes on the *relational* nature of the alien topos (expressed well by Jonathan Z. Smith's aforementioned emphasis on otherness as "a relativistic category" and "a term of interaction").[7] Consequently it places the *xenos* designation on the *country* where Christians currently dwell, rather than the fundamental identity of Christians themselves.[8]

This does not mean that *Hermas* eschews understanding Christian identity in self-as-other terms. Indeed, the basic cultural logic of the valorized resident alien is still operative in the passage. The text places the problematic city ("this city"/*tēs poleōs tautēs*) at the spatial and temporal center of the action—that is, where the audience is here and now, and where the paraenetic exhortation will have its application. While "this city" may be in a foreign country, it is nevertheless the central reference point. The city where the audience truly belongs is *makran*, moved to the spatial periphery of the image-world that the text is constructing. Thus Christian identity, in its connection to this far-off *polis*, remains associated with the margins (i.e., the self-as-other). Because the dichotomy set up between these two cities allows either city to be seen as foreign from the perspective of the other one, *Hermas*'s centering thrust on "this city" logically ensures an implicit self-as-other positioning to the text's vision of legitimate Christian identity.

But with that said, *Hermas*'s rhetorical center of gravity is different. Unlike the texts examined up to this point, *Hermas* does not accentuate its readers' alien status. Though they are undeniably aliens, the association is understated, receiving little direct attention throughout the course of *Similitude* 1. This is a different way to use the topos from what we have seen thus far—and not surprisingly, the text uses it to a different end. Alterity does not function here primarily to formulate Christian identity, so much as to articulate an oppositional relationship in which emphasis is placed on the foreignness of the *problematic* other ("this city" and every-thing associated with it) rather than the *self*-as-other. As for the two cities, the text does not specify their exact referents. While "this city" may refer to Rome, or more generally to the present world order,[9] *Hermas* tells us little about the character or content of the far-off city. It is obviously in some sense to be associated with Christian identity and community. Fur-thermore, it seems to be loosely eschatological, insofar as it will be dwelt in sometime in the future (*en hē mellete katoikein*, 1.1). Overall though, the parable offers very little detail. Quite probably the semiotic strategy of the text here actually relies upon the intertextual interpretive prac-tices of its potential readers, leaving space for hermeneutical syntheses that draw upon the imagery and resonances of other familiar eschato-logical cities to fill in the gap.[10]

In any event, from *Hermas*'s point of view, the content (eschatologi-cal or otherwise) of *hē polis hymōn* is assumed. At the very least, the di-chotomy between the two cities functions as sufficient leverage to launch into the main thrust of the text's paraenetic argument: "If then you know your city in which you are going to dwell, why do you make arrangements for lands, expensive furnishings, buildings, and worthless living quar-ters?" (1.1) As Carolyn Osiek notes, "The emphasis of the argument is not on the evil of this city but on the *contingency* of Christians' existence in it and the greater allegiance they owe to the other city which is their own."[11] We have seen similar intersections of the alien topos and issues of contingency, impermanence, and eschatology in both Hebrews and *Diognetus.*[12] Here, though, *Hermas* uses the provisional position of the Christian in "this city" to launch a line of argument with a focused and streamlined economic concern—one that is expressed initially in 1.1 in terms of lands, furnishings, buildings, and living quarters, but that will be developed throughout the course of *Similitude* 1.

The next line in 1.2 reinforces this basic point: "the one who makes arrangements for these things in this city is not able to return to his or her own city" (*tauta oun ho hetoimazōn eis tautēn tēn polin ou dynatai epanakampsai eis tēn idian polin*). The pursuit of real estate, wealth, and expensive trappings actually precludes Christians from returning to the city where they will no longer live as *xenoi* (again, the direct designation of Christians as *xenoi* is only implicit). Here a textual problem suggests interesting possibilities regarding the strength of this preclusion. The verb *dynatai* is attested by the fifteenth-century Codex Athous, the most complete Greek text of *Hermas* still extant. The alternative reading *pros-doka* is attested by a quotation of *Hermas* in Antiochus of St. Sabbas, seventh century.[13] This reading is also confirmed by *cogitat* ("be inclined") in both extant Latin versions (second and fourth–fifth century) and "wish to" in the fourth century Ethiopic.[14] Joly, Osiek, and Snyder all argue for *prosdoka* as the original reading. Thus Osiek translates 1.2, "The one who sets up these things in this city does not expect to return to one's own city."[15] In her view, this reading is a better match for the author's larger intent in this passage.

Be that as it may, discerning the "original reading" is of less importance to this analysis. Rather, for the purposes of exploring the functions of the alien topos in *Hermas*, both readings are valuable insofar as they illustrate shifting emphases in agency that variously nuance the thrust of *Similitude* 1's paraenesis. *Dynatai* places the emphasis on the Christian's lack of agency, at least beyond a certain point: too many economic commitments and assets in the problematic realm of "this city" will lead to a point beyond which it is impossible to come back. Here the text's point is not so much to weigh in on the impossibility of post-baptismal repentance with respect to economic sin, as to encourage and motivate the audience rhetorically to ensure that they do not find themselves in this position before it is too late. Elsewhere in *Hermas*, the question of post-baptismal sin and the allowance of a "second repentance" are key issues.[16] But in this passage, they do not seem to be directly in view. The purpose is to warn and inspire the audience to action, not to discourage.[17]

On the other hand, reading *prosdoka* instead of *dynatai* in 1.2 softens the harsh edge of this warning. Here the one who pursues improper assets does not expect or anticipate return to the proper city—a result that is simply to be expected from those who have directed their attention towards wealth in ways that *Hermas* considers reprehensible. This alternative reading fits nicely with the negative characterization of this hypothetical person as double-minded (*dipsyche*) in 1.3, a common refrain throughout *Hermas*.[18] Being divided in one's pursuits has natural (and unfortunate) consequences. Thus the audience ought to do all in its power to avoid this doublemindedness, in an effort to ensure their eventual return to their rightful city. Still, the emphasis of the argument implies the audience's continued agency and ability to make the correct moral choice. If there is a day looming out there beyond which it is too late to return, it is not used as a paraenetic motivator.

While this distinction may seem small, the two variant readings nonetheless illustrate how specific rhetorical choices can shift and nuance the ways that a text's paraenetic strategy actually works—that is, how it functions to persuade with respect to (in Bourdieu's formulation) "the categories according to which a group envisages itself, and according to which it represents itself and its specific reality, [which in turn] contribute to the reality of this group."[19] Representing the group as free moral agents and exhorting them to pursue a single-minded directive is a different rhetorical project from exhorting that same directive while representing the group as those whose days of agency are potentially numbered. Certainly the final paraenetic goal is the same in both cases. But the varying rhetorical strategies do different kinds of work along the way with respect to the contours and nuances of the identity in question (i.e., free moral agents, at least for the foreseeable future? those who stand before an impending point of no return?). Different kinds of rhetorical practices produce different kinds of effects. Thus both readings have value for thinking about the ways in which the use of the alien topos worked to construct, shape, and authorize certain kinds of early Christian identity.

Nevertheless, in the case of both readings, the larger rhetorical goal remains clear—an unequivocal condemnation of the financial entanglements in question: "O foolish, double-minded and miserable person, do you not grasp that all these things are foreign and are under the authority of another?" (*aphron kai dipsyche kai talaipōre anthrōpe, ou noeis, hoti tauta panta allotria eisi kai hyp' exousian heterou eisin*, 1.3).[20] Recent scholarship on *Hermas* has drawn attention to the strong emphasis placed on financial concerns and the proper use of wealth throughout the text.[21] Here the text advances this larger rhetorical concern by developing the figural terms of the alien topos: the lands, investments, and buildings that it inveighs against are *allotria* and *hyp' exousian heterou*. Note, however, that the rhetorical strategy remains consistent. *Hermas* uses the topos not to emphasize the alien status of the Christian but to disparage those economic commitments that the Christian should reject.

Christians and the Lord of "This City"

Similitude 1 then moves to a discussion of the lord of the city (i.e., "this city," not the proper city to which the Christians will one day return) and what his inevitable reaction will be to the kind of *dipsychia* that *Hermas* warns against (1.3–4). Here James Jeffers states unequivocally that *ho kyrios tēs poleōs tautēs* represents the Roman emperor, as part of *Hermas*'s attempt to "[advocate] hostility towards the world's systems, not imitation of them."[22] Osiek more helpfully reminds us that "whether the master of the city is thought to be the Roman emperor, the devil, or someone else is irrelevant, since we are here dealing with a parable and not an allegory."[23] As she argues elsewhere, "a strict correspondence of every character need not be found. In the story world, cities have rulers and laws, which lend themselves easily to the flow of the story."[24] Of course

Osiek's point, while well taken, does not preclude the possibility that
early Christian readers could have filled in this interpretive gap as well
(see discussion of the two cities above)—and indeed they most probably
did. The unspecified lord of the city could easily be read either as one
of the options listed above, or as any particular figure of Roman urban
authority with whom readers were familiar. Any of these hermeneutical
alternatives potentially add to the parable's overall rhetorical power. The
lack of specificity renders the parable more generally usable.[25]

Regardless of the lord's identity, however, his presence introduces a
quandary: he insists that the Christians leave his city because they do not
use his laws (*ou thelō se katoikein eis tēn polin mou, all' exelthe ek tēs poleōs
tautēs, hoti tois nomois mou ou chrasai*, 1.3). As Martin Leutzsch argues, the
model in view here is not a classical Greek *polis* but a Hellenistic mon-
archy.[26] This model came into prominence in the Greek-speaking world
after the death of Alexander the Great (323 B.C.E.), often incorporating
"forms of king-worship . . . based on the idea of the king as saviour and
benefactor, or new founder of the city."[27] In this context, as Dio Chrysostom (c.40–120 C.E.) avers, "the law is the decree of the king."[28] Indeed,
as he elaborates further elsewhere, "So then, a 'city' is said to be a group
of people dwelling in the same place, governed by law. . . . Just as the one
who does not have reason is not a person, so neither is a group of people
who is not observant of law actually a city."[29] Thus, in the logic of this
model, *Hermas*'s lord of the city is perfectly within his rights in demand-
ing that the Christians depart. (Indeed, the text acknowledges as much
with its characterization of this ultimatum as *dikaiōs* in 1.4.)

Following this setup, the text poses a pointed question to the audience
in 1.5: what then are you going to do? (*su oun ti melleis poiein*) Christians
already have a law in their own city (*echōn nomon en tē sē polei*). Will the
audience deny this law of theirs simply for the sake of fields and other
possessions, and then walk in the law of the other city? (*heneken tōn agrōn
sou kai tēs loipēs hyparxeōs ton nomon sou pantos aparnēse kai poreusē tō nomō
tēs poleōs tautēs*) The question hangs in the air, a false conclusion vaguely
reminiscent of the diatribe style.[30] But just in case the point is not clear,
Hermas makes the answer to the question explicit: "Take care lest it be
harmful (*asymphoron*[31]) to deny your law; for if you wish to return to
your city, you will not be accepted back, because you have denied the
law of your city, and you will be shut out of it" (*blepe mē asymphoron estin
aparnēsai ton nomon sou; ean gar epanakampsai thelēsēs eis tēn polin sou, ou mē
paradechthēsē, hoti apērnēsō ton nomon tēs poleōs sou, kai ekkleisthēsē ap' autēs*
1.5). That is to say, "denying your law" is harmful (also translated "unprofitable") because it leads to exclusion from the city. Whatever agency
and free moral choice might have been allowed by the textual variant of
1.2, this apparently does not extend far enough to cover *arnēsis*.[32]

"An Adequate Sufficiency"

This five-verse buildup at last brings readers to the concrete paraenetic payoff: "So take care therefore; as one dwelling in a foreign country, make no more arrangements for yourself than an adequate sufficiency" (*blepe oun su; hōs epi xenēs katoikōn mēden pleon hetoimaze seautō ei mē tēn autarkeian tēn arketēn soi*, 1.6). Here again the text invokes the language of foreignness to emphasize the alterity of the place in which Christians currently dwell. But more importantly, it makes its economic directive clear: Christian identity can only be considered legitimate when tied to a particular kind of financial practice, pithily summed up as having no more than "an adequate sufficiency."[33] The message for readers of *Hermas* is therefore unambiguous. In the logic of the parable, Christians will inevitably face expulsion because they are not citizens of "this city" and in fact actually oppose (*antitaxamenon*) its laws (1.6). Yet if they remain prepared, when the expulsion comes, they will be able to depart to their true city joyfully and without hindrance.[34] Therefore, the audience must keep the mandates of the Lord (*tō kyriō*, in this case unambiguously referring to God) and trust in his promises. In return for obedience to the mandates, he will fulfill those promises (1.7).

Verses 8–9 go on to outline the specifically Christian parameters of this "adequate sufficiency," in particular the knotty problem of what to do with material wealth rather than investing it in property, housing, or business ventures. Here *Hermas*'s answer is to purchase oppressed souls (*agorazete psychas thlibomenas*, 1.8). What does this mean? The text does not specify.[35] At the very least, it includes the care of widows and orphans (1.8), a traditional designation of charity.[36] Thus Christian beneficence to needy members of the community replaces involvement and investment in the commonplaces of Roman economic life. But with respect to Roman economic dealings, something more radical may be in view as well. In light of the text's implicit contrast between Christians as slaves of God and other forms of enslavement (such as legal enslavement to nondivine owners), this call to *purchase* souls may have a more literal inflection, soliciting wealthy readers to pull their resources out of more conventional commitments and use them to purchase enslaved members of the Christian community instead.[37]

Whatever sorts of "purchases" are in view, however, 1.9 makes clear that these services/ministries (*tas diakonias*) for the Lord are actually a far better kind of "lands, possessions, and houses" to acquire. They are in fact acquisitions that Christians will find waiting for them in their rightful city when they return home to it (*poly beltion esti toioutous agrous agorazein kai ktēmata kai oikous, hous heurēseis en tē polei sou, hotan epidēmēsēs eis autēn*). The potential for this kind of acquisition even turns out to be the very reason that the Lord has made some Christians wealthy in the first place (1.9).[38] And while the specific positive content of these "purchases" remains ambiguous, the practices that such purchases *replace* are extremely clear: the possession of lands, houses, and other assets.

As the parable concludes, then, vv. 10–11 underscore its very focused paraenesis by a final nod to the alien *topos*. To some degree the focus has shifted: the discussion now centers on the character of the wealth (*polyteleia*) that awaits Christians in the city that is *makran* (see 1.1). Nevertheless, the logic of center and periphery established at the outset of the parable still holds. The wealth of the Lord's city may be honorable and joyful (*kalē kai hilara*), but its function is more motivational than descriptive; the spatial and temporal sphere of central concern remains "this city."[39] Thus *Hermas* cautions that Christians are not to deal in the wealth of foreigners (*tōn ethnōn*)—that is to say, the economic assets, investments, and ventures of the Roman socioeconomic order that surrounds them and that is (from the text's perspective) irredeemably implicated in the wrong city.

The parable closes by reaffirming its initial insider designation of Christian identity: the readers are the slaves of God (*hymin tois doulois tou theou*). While the *logic* of the argument has positioned them as resident aliens sojourning in a city not their own, the rhetorical *emphasis* remains here (i.e., the identity register of the figurative slave). *Hermas* expends no rhetorical energy following through on its own logic in order to label Christians in terms of their alien status. Instead, v. 11 follows the parable's general tendency, calling upon the audience not to counterfeit nor touch nor desire that which is alien (*kai mē paracharassete mēde tou allotriou hapsēsthe mēde epithymeite autou; ponēron gar estin allotriōn epithymein*)— i.e., the wealth of foreigners (1.10).[40] Here we see again the consistent emphasis of the text to polemicize against the alien nature of everything it opposes. The wrong country, the wrong city, the wrong kind of assets, and the wrong business arrangements are all explicitly marked using the terminology and rhetoric of the alien *topos*. Meanwhile *Hermas*'s readers are to pursue their own work (i.e., that which belongs to the Lord's city) and so be saved (*to de son ergon ergazou, kai sōthēsē*, 1.11).

Investing Otherwise

In this way, throughout the parable, a consistent pattern holds true. Whereas 1 Peter, Hebrews, and *Diognetus* all explicitly highlight the foreign/alien nature of Christian identity, *Hermas* deploys the topos differently in pursuit of a variant effect. The text uses the rhetoric of foreignness not so much to highlight a valorized outsider identity as to cast a social location and a set of economic practices which it finds objec-

tionable in a marginal and distasteful light. As discussed above, because
the alien topos is predicated on a relational logic, the Christian self still
emerges in the parable as a marginal (but valorized) outsider in relation
to the center point of the present city. Yet the rhetorical emphasis of the
text stresses not the self as other, but rather *the other* as other.

Here *Hermas* pursues a somewhat different strategy from those of
the texts already examined. While it may still construct its audience as
outsiders who belong in another city, the paraenesis is a long way from
affirming traditional Roman norms (even in a subversive or resistant
sense). Instead, the text's paraenetic stance is starkly oppositional, using
the rhetoric of alien status in an attempt to create some very real social
difference. *Hermas* envisions a world in which the slaves of God withdraw
from the economic assets and attachments of the Roman social order
and invest otherwise. What it means to invest otherwise, however, the
text leaves suggestively (but also frustratingly) open.

In Reinhard Feldmeier's estimation, this move constitutes "[a] radical
break with this world, the rejection of the acquisition of everything that
goes beyond the essentials of life."[41] On Feldmeier's reading, what *Hermas* has in mind then is a kind of voluntary poverty and communalism of
a sort not unknown in the ancient world (and not limited to Christians).
For example, Seneca (d. 65 c.e.) argues passionately for the incompatibility of riches with the philosophical life:

If you wish to have time for the soul, it behooves you either to be a poor person,
or similar to a poor person. Study is not able to be beneficial without care for
frugality; and frugality is voluntary poverty. Therefore, get rid of those excuses:
"I do not yet have as much as is sufficient. When I attain to that highest point,
then I will give myself entirely to philosophy." . . . [But] how much greater is
that which is promised: perpetual freedom, fear of neither human nor god any
more! And indeed even for the hungry person, it must come to this. Armies have
endured the lack of all things, they have lived on the roots of plants, and borne
hunger by means of things too detestable to say. All these things they endured
for a kingdom—even more extraordinary, a kingdom not their own. Will anyone
hesitate to bear poverty, in order to free the soul from insanities? Therefore,
one must not accumulate first. Even so, one may attain to philosophy without
traveling-money.[42]

But at the same time, the project put forward here is one of philosophical idealism. For the aristocratic Seneca, it most likely functioned as a
type of intellectual exercise, a logical outworking of the metaphysical tenets of Stoicism. In view is the application of these tenets to ideal models
of ethical practice and "the wise person" (*sapiens*).[43] As Pierluigi Donini
notes, "it seems that [the Stoics] made a realistic concession to good
sense when they admitted that a wise man was nowhere to be found,
and that maybe only one or two ever existed in the whole of human

history."[44] Donini therefore concludes that "[mainstream Stoicism] was never a philosophy of sacrifice and self-denial. That explains its success among the Roman aristocracy, a class not consisting solely of generous benefactors."[45] Indeed, one could hold up the ideal of voluntary poverty and detachment from material goods without having any intention of actually divesting oneself of one's own assets.

Actually putting these ideas into practice in Roman cities and towns, on the other hand, had radical and potentially subversive dimensions. Therefore, the kind of economic vision advocated by *Hermas* stands in a certain contrast to the idealized reflections of Stoic philosophy. As James Francis helpfully articulates in his study of pagan asceticism in the second century, "The sort of asceticism advocated by the Stoics . . . with its emphasis on ethics and the internal dynamics of the individual psyche, was constituted precisely to allow individuals to better perform their traditional social roles and functions. Indeed, it elevated these conventions to the level of moral obligations. Physical asceticism, however, tended to do just the opposite. In manifestly rejecting such institutions as property and marriage, radical ascetics placed themselves in opposition to accepted values and thereby posed a threat to the social order."[46]

Thus the rhetorical difference that *Hermas* enacts in this parable seeks to bring into being an actual difference with respect to the conventions of the Roman social order. And as already noted, *Hermas*'s discursive bite may run deeper than just the pursuit of voluntary poverty. We lack further evidence to know what "purchasing oppressed souls" actually entailed. But the text openly envisions an alternative economic strategy for the "slaves of God." And it is feasible that this involved not an ascetic withdrawal so much as a subversive reimagining of Christian investment strategies. Accordingly, *Hermas* may seek not just the "adequate sufficiency" of voluntary poverty, but also the deployment of Christian wealth (through practices such as purchasing slaves or supporting those of lower status) to ends that both fortify an alternative community and work against the hegemony of a Roman socioeconomic field mired in "lands, expensive furnishings, buildings, and worthless living quarters."

Conclusion

The use of the resident alien topos that we see in the *Shepherd of Hermas, Similitude* 1 can therefore be best understood as a strategic move, bolstered by what Bourdieu would call an excellent "feel for the game . . . one which works outside conscious control or discourse."[47] Unlike 1 Peter, Hebrews, or *Diognetus*, the text advocates a socially radical paraenetic agenda, constructing Christian difference in terms of a transfer of economic allegiance from the material goods, assets, and properties that defined affluent Roman life to a set of alternative (and potentially subversive) economic practices. In pursuing this project, *Hermas* turns to the symbolic power of the alien topos as a resource just as useful for *devaluing* particular economic practices as for formulating Christian insider identity in valorized outsider terms.[48] As Bourdieu observes, "One's choice of words, especially in polemical exchanges, is not innocent."[49] In articulating its vision of an alternative Christian economic praxis, *Hermas*'s emphasis on the alien nature of the city, the country, and the economic commitments that it censures proves to be good paraenetic strategy.

It thus takes its place in the emerging early Christian discourse of the self as other. And as we have seen through the analysis of 1 Peter, Hebrews, *Diognetus*, and now *Hermas*, this was a fertile and variegated discourse of identity in the first two centuries of Christianity. In the words of Michel de Certeau, "the discourse that makes people believe is the one that . . . opens up clearings; it 'allows' a certain play within a system of defined spaces. It 'authorizes' the production of an area of freeplay (*Spielraum*) on a checkerboard that analyzes and classifies identities. It makes places habitable."[50] In the foregoing analysis, I have tried to show the textual traces of this "room to move" in actual rhetorical practice as it took place on a checkerboard of possible positionings for Christian identity in the first and second centuries. Together these texts offer us a glimpse into a space of play, not only through their shared rhetorical and cultural terrain, but even more so through the spaces between them—the distinctive ways that each one shapes the trope of the Christian resident alien according to the particularities of a given context and set of concerns.

But as Bourdieu reminds us, "belonging to a group is something you build up, negotiate and bargain over, and play for."[51] Consequently, it is not surprising that the basic rhetorical strategy these texts share (constructing the Christian self as an alien "other" in some way, shape, or form) did not go uncontested in the second century. Turning now to the *Apocryphon of James* (an early Christian text from Nag Hammadi), I will examine the entrance of another voice into this conversation. This is one that engages head-on the figure of the alien/stranger and its relationship to identity. But as we will see, the apocryphon actually calls into question the basic legitimacy of the topos as a register for identity, thereby taking a stance both distinctive and dialogical within this cultural field of play.

Chapter Five

Strangers and Soteriology in the *Apocryphon of James*

> *Indeed, any concrete discourse (utterance) . . . is entangled, shot through with shared thoughts, points of view, alien value judgments and accents. The word, directed toward its object, enters a dialogically agitated and tension-filled environment of alien words, value judgments and accents, weaves in and out of complex interrelationships, merges with some, recoils from others, intersects with yet a third group: and all this may crucially shape discourse, may leave a trace in all its semantic layers, may complicate its expression and influence its entire stylistic profile.*
>
> —*Mikhail Bakhtin*

Not all early Christians thought that speaking about themselves as aliens was a good thing. While numerous texts of the first and second centuries were making exactly this move (as evidenced by our analysis thus far), this was not the only conceptual option available to Christians as they thought about their identity and what its legitimate relationship ought to be to the rhetoric of alienation. Thus there were (perhaps not surprisingly) voices of protest to the increasingly common strategy of constructing the Christian self as other. These voices were not separate or outside the contested discourse of formative Christian identity, but instead entered this "dialogically agitated and tension-filled environment" (to borrow Bakhtin's phrase) in order to make a different kind of claim, one that rejected the valorized alien as a valid trope for identity.

One example that has come down to us is the *Apocryphon of James*. Given its Nag Hammadi provenance, this is a text that has too often been cordoned off both from broader explorations of early Christian identity and from discussions of the alien topos more specifically. Yet *Ap. Jas.* belongs in these conversations. When it comes to the topos, the text contains several familiar themes: Jesus calls James and Peter to compare themselves to strangers, he articulates a vision of soteriology in which Christians possess a distinct city, and he reflects on the relationship of strangers to that city. But these common themes of the topos are put to a very different end from anything we have seen so far.

Unlike 1 Peter, Hebrews, *Diognetus*, or *Hermas*, the apocryphon never makes the move to valorize alien status for the purposes of identity formation. In fact, it explicitly rejects this valorization, instead articulating Christian identity in terms of a particular soteriological agenda—one in which James, Peter, and other disciples must take hold of their salvation for themselves. As such, the text strategically figures the move to claim an alien identity as a mistake, metaphorically equating alien status with a failure to understand salvation correctly. But this reversal is itself a way of deploying the alien topos—and one that must be considered dialogically in relation to the valorization that the text rejects. Indeed the intensity of *Ap. Jas.*'s discursive bite only becomes fully legible in the context of the topos's other (more common) uses in early Christian texts. Thus the apocryphon actually plays off these other positions (though not necessarily the specific texts we have examined) for the very power of its point.

Dialogue and Authority in *Ap. Jas.*

The *Apocryphon of James* is a Subachmimic Coptic text translated from a Greek original and preserved in Codex I (the Jung Codex) of the Nag Hammadi corpus.[1] The text is of unknown provenance and offers us few clues regarding its social or historical location. No other early Christian literature mentions it, and it does not even specify which James it takes as its protagonist.[2] In the most extensive English language study of the text to date, Ron Cameron has argued on form-critical grounds for a dating in the middle of the second century.[3] But on the whole, as Pheme Perkins concludes, *Ap. Jas.* is "notoriously difficult to locate within the spectrum of early Christianity."[4]

The bulk of the text can be classified as a post-resurrection dialogue between Jesus and two of his disciples, James and Peter.[5] What difference does the genre of post-resurrection conversation make? Perkins suggests that this setting for a dialogic exchange is an important way in which texts such as *Ap. Jas.* ground their authority to argue for a particular theological position. As she construes this, "the frequency with which Gnostics set their dialogues into a post-resurrection appearance of Jesus suggests that they considered that a distinct type of dialogue. . . . Such dialogues sought to establish the claim of Christian Gnosticism to be the true intention of the revelation of Jesus."[6] Here Perkins makes an important point about the general function of a post-resurrection dialogue to establish and convey authoritative teaching. At the same time, she herself acknowledges that *Ap. Jas.* "lacks specifically Gnostic theologoumena" (though she continues to treat it in the category of a "Gnostic dialogue").[7] Furthermore, recent scholarship has thoroughly problematized the very category of "Gnosticism" (understood as a reified movement distinct from a supposedly more original orthodox Christianity).[8] Thus, while Perkins's general point about post-resurrection dialogues remains helpful, it seems more appropriate to consider *Ap. Jas.* under the general umbrella of early Christian texts—rather than as a Gnostic text in conflict with Christian orthodoxy.

In this particular post-resurrection dialogue, the main action picks up 550 days after the resurrection event. Jesus appears to his twelve disciples (who are sitting around, putting the Savior's words into books) and engages them in a dialogue with a focus on soteriology: how to enter the kingdom of the heavens (*tmntᵉrro nᵉmpēue*, 2.30). From the outset, his attitude alternates between invitation/exhortation and reproach. Thus Jesus opens with an invitation, pointedly telling the disciples, "I will go to the place from which I came. If you want to come with me, come!" (*tinabōk aptopos ᵉntahiei ᵉmmeu špe tetᵉnouōše eei nᵉmmēei amētᵉn*, 2.25–26) In response his followers modestly defer to the Savior's authority: "If you command us, we come" (*špe kᵉr keleue nen tᵉnnēou*, 2.27–28).

But Jesus is not pleased with this seemingly pious reply. Apparently, his command is not the point. According to J. van der Vliet, "whether or not [the disciples] will enter the Kingdom of Heavens does not depend on an order from his part, but on their own inner preparation alone."[9] Indeed Jesus says as much to the disciples themselves: "No one will ever enter into the kingdom of the heavens when I command them, but rather because you yourselves are full" (*mn laaue anēhe nabōk ahou[n] atmntᵉrro nᵉmpēue; eeišan[r] keleuei nef alla abal je tetᵉnmēh ᵉntōtᵉn*, 2.30–33). He then follows up by taking James and Peter aside in order to fill them (2.34–35). The two disciples dutifully obey the Savior, stepping aside with him in order to be filled.

Unfortunately, at this point a number of large lacunae in the text make it impossible to determine what immediately follows. However, when the text resumes a few lines later, the tone has shifted to that of reproach. Now Jesus is harshly rebuking his two disciples, exhorting them to be ashamed (*šipe če*, 3.11). He points out that they have seen the Son of Man (presumably in this context, the title refers to Jesus himself), spoken with him, and listened to him. Yet Jesus does not see this in a positive light: "Woe to those who have seen the Son of Man. Blessed will be those who have not seen the man [i.e., the Son of Man under discussion[10]], and those who have not mixed with him and those who have not spoken with him and those who have not listened to anything from him" (*ouaei ᵉnnentahneu apšēr[e ᵉmpr]ōme senašōpe ᵉmmakarios ᵉnči neteᵉmpouneu aprōme auō neteᵉmpoutōh nᵉmmef auō neteᵉmpoušeje nᵉmmef auō neteᵉmpousōtᵉm alaaue ᵉntootᵉf*, 3.17–26). He then proceeds—after acknowledging that he

healed the disciples—to disparage that healing, pronouncing woe on
those who have found rest from their sickness and blessing on those who
have known this rest before ever being sick. It is this latter group that
receives the kingdom of God (3.25–35).[11] The implication seems to be
that the path to fullness and the kingdom involves knowing relief *on one's
own* prior to sickness—not relying on Jesus for relief.

Consequently, whatever else the Savior's command to "become full"
may mean, it at the very least implies the importance of the disciples'
own efforts.[12] Yet at the same time, the disciples only receive this information through the teaching of Jesus. Paradoxically, then, despite Jesus'
denigration of those who listen to the Son of Man, he remains necessary
for salvation. In a sense, Jesus is reinscribing his own authority, even as
he subverts it. His role, however, is as a teacher, not an agent of atonement or intercession. The text thereby shifts its emphasis (and with it the
center of gravity for theological authority) to the content of the teaching
rather than the person of Jesus. Given this focus, the dialogue does not
in fact afford James and Peter a great deal of speaking time. Their role is
to object, ask questions, and make requests—all with a view to clarifying
further the substance of Jesus' teaching.[13] *Ap. Jas.* occasionally informs us
about their state of mind (for instance, rejoicing or distressed; see 11.7ff,
12.18), but these disclosures are always with a view to Jesus' reaction as
it segues to his next point. In this way, the dialogue serves as a vehicle to
advance the argument for *Ap. Jas.*'s particular conception of salvation.

Propelling Oneself Toward Salvation

The apocryphon's use of the alien topos can only be understood in the
context of this specific soteriological vision, and I will therefore examine
it here in some detail. Salvation for *Ap. Jas.* is about effort—and about
Christians taking hold of what already belongs to them rather than relying on some external agent. This process of claiming one's rightful
status among those who are saved has numerous dimensions, but one of
the most important is the role of suffering and death. Jesus is clear that
James and Peter are to despise death and yet at the same time to seek it
as a means of attaining life/salvation (5.31, 6.7). As he tells them, "Remember my cross and my death and you will live" (*ari pmeeue* ͨ*mpastauros
auō pamou auō tet*ͨ*nnaōn*ͨ*h,* 5.33–35). A few lines later, after James propels
the dialogue forward by objecting to the mention of the cross and death
(5.35–6.1), Jesus is even more explicit: "Truly I say to you, no one will
be saved unless they believe in my cross. For the ones who have believed
in my cross, theirs is the kingdom of God. Thus become seekers after
death" (*hamēn tijou* ͨ*mmas nēt*ͨ*n je m*ͨ*n laaue naoujeei eimēti* ͨ*nsepist[eue]
apast(au)ros nenta[h]pisteue [ga]r apast(au)ros tōou te tm*ͨ*ntero* ͨ*mppnoute šōpe*

če eret^enšine ^ensa pmou, 6.2–8).

Here the cross would seem to be of paramount importance. But in the context of the text's larger soteriological argument, these exhortations to remember and believe in Jesus' cross/death are not made with a view to their atoning significance.[14] Instead they ought to be understood in terms of the general orientation of *Ap. Jas.* toward the necessity of suffering and martyrdom. As Karen King summarizes, "the Lord insists that he did suffer and that his disciples must likewise suffer and die if they wish to be saved."[15] Indeed as the disciples seek death, it will teach them about election (6.12–13). The point is that not sparing the flesh (5.21) confirms and reveals a disciple's state of chosenness; salvation is self-propelled, perfectly realized in those who seek death (6.9–10).[16]

The text continues throughout to place an emphasis on this role of one's own effort in salvation. According to David Brakke, "As the teacher gives of himself, so the students must work at their salvation."[17] Thus Jesus tells James and Peter, "Hurry to be saved, not being exhorted, but rather be eager on your own accord; and if it is possible, precede even me" (*čepē atret^enoujeei eusapsp en ^emmōt^en alla ^entōt^en ourat ouaet tēne auō ^ešpe ou^en čam ari šar^ep araei hōōt*, 7.10–15). Such zeal will result in the Father's love (*teei gar te thhe eterepiōt nam^erre tēne*, 7.16). This possibility of reaching the kingdom of the heavens even before Jesus himself radically undermines any notion of dependence on Jesus as a direct salvific agent (such as a mediator, high priest, or atoning sacrifice)—while at the same time reinforcing James's and Peter's dependence on him as the purveyor of this information.

The Jesus of *Ap. Jas.* is even playfully ironic in the various ways that he reinforces this point. For example, toward the end of the dialogue, he tells his disciples, "Woe to those on account of whom I was sent down to this place" (*ouaei ^enneei ^en[ta]hout^ennaout apit^en apeeim[a] etbētou*, 13.9–11). Certainly this statement offers an acknowledgment of the belief that Jesus was in fact sent down for the sake of people. Yet the disclosure is ironic in the sense that it functions not to *validate* that belief but to pronounce woe. Jesus then sets in stark contrast the blessed ones who are coming up to the Father (13.8–13). The implication is that ascent does not take place through dependence on a Jesus who was sent down for the sake of humanity. Rather, it is of one's own accord. The fact that one only comes to know this truth through the teaching of Jesus is part of the rich irony of the text. (Note also that this irony is somewhat mitigated by the aforementioned shift in emphasis from the *person* of the teacher to the *contents* of the teaching—thus equalizing Jesus' role as teacher and opening up the potential for others besides him to fill it, as we will see below.)

Of course salvation is not as simple as sheer realization and will power. It is also crucial that those who will be saved preach the gospel. That is to say, ascent requires the enlightenment of others. Even Jesus himself is not exempt from this requirement. As Karen King elaborates, "[people] cannot ascend to God without first bringing others along with them . . . Here there is a definite reciprocity: on the one hand, they are to be 'the cause of life in many'; on the other hand, 'we would be [saved] for their sakes.'"[18] Thus Jesus, after explaining all these things to James and Peter, is able to ascend (*neei tinajoou ᵉnnēt̄ᵉn ša pima tinou de eeinabōk ahrēi aptopos ᵉntahiei ᵉmmaf*, 14.19–22; also *neei ᵉntarefjoou afbōk*, 15.5–6). The two disciples begin to follow him up but the others call them back (15.6–34). It seems that James and Peter also have a role to play as teachers, bringing this knowledge of salvation to those who need it. The two then begin to inform the rest of the disciples, telling them about Jesus' ascent, his promise of life, and the coming of children after them who will need love. On account of these children, the disciples will be saved (15.34–16.2)—presumably in the sense that the disciples will teach the children and therefore be able to ascend.

This idea receives further elucidation in the text's postscript. Here James asserts, "This is the way in which I will be able to be saved, since those ones will be enlightened through me by my faith and through another which is better than mine" (*teei gar te the etinaš oujeei hōs erenet̄ᵉm-meu naji ouaein ᵉnhrēi ᵉnhēt h̄ᵉn tapistis auō ᵉnhrēi h̄ᵉn keoueie essat̄ᵖ atōei*, 16.14–18). According to Brakke, at this point James "assumes a role similar to that of Jesus: it is through James that the readers of this work will be 'enlightened,' and yet James prays that they will enjoy a faith 'better' than his."[19] Salvation therefore descends in a pyramidal fashion, allowing ascent for each new level as those who constitute that level teach the truth to those beneath them; at the same time it is possible for those below to surpass their teachers.

Overall, the text's dialogue format both enhances and propels the explication of this basic soteriological agenda. As Brakke points out, throughout *Ap. Jas.*, "the disciples, including James and Peter, oscillate between understanding and lack of comprehension."[20] This basic problematic drives the aforementioned alternation between encouragement and rebuke that we see in the speech of Jesus. In this way, the teacher's many exhortations to his two disciples can all be classified as a part of his desire for James and Peter to "get it" in a more sustained way than simply momentary flashes of comprehension. Therefore, when James and Peter rejoice prematurely, Jesus censures them harshly (11.6ff). Yet when they are downcast at the harshness of the message, he offers them encouragement: "On account of this I speak to you in order that you might know yourselves" (*etbe peei tijou ᵉmmas ᵉnnēt̄ᵉn jekas eretnasouōn tēne*, 12.20–22)—that is, know your true identity as those who must take hold of their own salvation.

In general, there is a certain semiotic instability to Jesus' speech that operates strategically throughout the dialogue. That is to say, the functions of various terminology and sayings do not remain fixed but shift according to the shifting position of James and Peter (overly confident, confused, discouraged, frustrated) with respect to the central soteriological point that Jesus wishes them to grasp. A case in point is the changing role of Jesus' rebuke: in a moment of encouragement, Jesus exhorts James and Peter to receive censure from him and therefore save themselves (*ji jpio abal hitoot auō ᵉntetᵉntouje tēne*, 11.3–4). In this context, rebuke leads to salvation because it opens up the potential for James and Peter to understand that they can indeed save themselves.

Yet a few pages later, Peter explodes in frustration: "Sometimes you urge us on toward the kingdom of the heavens. Other times still you turn us out. Lord, sometimes you persuade and draw us into the faith and you promise us life. Other times still you push us out from the kingdom of the heavens" (*hᵉnsap men kᵉr protrepe ᵉmman ahoun atmᵉntᵉrro ᵉnmpēue henkesap an ksto ᵉmman abal pjaeis hᵉnsap men kᵉr pithe auō ksōk ᵉmman ahoun atpistis auō kšpōp nen ᵉmpōnᵉh hnkesap an khbarbᵉr ᵉmman abal ᵉntmᵉntero ᵉnmpēue*, 13.27–36). At this point, the two perplexed disciples receive a decidedly different message from Jesus: "But you, through faith and knowledge, have received life. Therefore despise the rejection when you hear it, but when you hear the promise, rejoice greatly" (*ᵉntōtᵉn ᵉnde ᵉnhrēi hᵉn tpistis [mn] psaune hatetᵉnji arōtn ᵉmpōnᵉh eri kataphroni če ᵉmpts[t]o abal eretᵉnšansōtᵉm ara[f] ᵉntetᵉnsōtᵉm ᵉnde apešpōp telēl ᵉmmōtᵉn ᵉnhouo*, 14.8–13). Here I would argue that (given Peter's protest about Jesus' conflicting messages) the rejection that James and Peter are called to despise is that which *Jesus* has been delivering throughout the text. The two disciples stand on the verge of finally grasping the text's elusive soteriology of self-motivation / realization, one so powerful that it ends up even subverting the authority of their teacher's rebuke. Once James and Peter understand their true position in the schema of salvation, they no longer need rejection or rebuke to teach them anything. They ought to despise these because they can.

In places this semiotic playfulness is even strong enough to figure Jesus as a kind of trickster. For example, at the end of an extended speech, Jesus tells James and Peter that he will petition (intercede?) on their behalf before the Father (*tisapsᵉp harōtᵉn hatᵉm piōt*, 11.4–5). How should this be understood in light of the overwhelmingly strong thrust of the text's soteriology as a whole? Any attempt at harmonization seems unlikely. It is more plausible (given the use of irony and shifting meanings in this text) that the statement sets up a kind of trap for the disciples, one that they thoroughly fall into. When they rejoice at *these* words (in contrast to their gloom at the previous words), James and Peter reveal their continued failure to grasp their teacher's message (11.6–7). Had they truly understood (and thus eluded the trap), they would have rejoiced at the earlier words (11.8–10). By choosing to rejoice at the words which imply the wrong kind of soteriology, they provoke the extended outpouring of reproach that follows (11.10ff).

"Compare yourselves to strangers": Alienation in *Ap. Jas.*

It is within this passage that we find Jesus' explicit exhortation to James and Peter to compare themselves to strangers (11.17–18). The text uses the Coptic word *šᵉmmo*, most appropriately rendered as *stranger, foreigner,* or *alien* (Crum 565b). But *Ap. Jas.* is a Coptic translation of a Greek original—and Crum notes that *šᵉmmo* can translate the Greek *allogenēs, allotrios, geiōras* (*sojourner*), *xenos* or *prosēlutos*.[21] In other words, what we see here is another early Christian deployment of the alien topos. As such, it is neither helpful nor tenable to posit a single, unitary meaning for a term like *šᵉmmo*, given that it marks a category that is by definition relational and relativistic rather than essentialized. Instead I wish to consider the function of the term in *Ap. Jas.* in relation to the ancient field of possibilities for the alien topos already examined.

As noted, *Ap. Jas.*'s use of the topos occurs in the context of Jesus' lengthy rebuke to his two disciples:

And when we heard these things, we became happy, for we had been gloomy about those things which we spoke of previously. When he saw us rejoicing, he said, "Woe to you, O ones who are in want of a paraclete. Woe to you, O ones who have need of grace. Blessed will be the ones who have spoken freely and have acquired grace for themselves. Liken yourselves to strangers. What is their way in relation to your city? Why are you disturbed when you alone cast yourselves out and are far from your city? What is the matter with you[22] that you alone abandon your dwelling place, preparing it for the ones who wish to dwell in it? O exiles and fugitives, woe to you because you will be caught. Or perhaps you think that the Father is a lover of humanity or is won over by prayers[23] or grants favor to one for the sake of someone else or puts up with one who asks? (11.6–34)

Here Jesus has seen his two disciples rejoicing inappropriately and is not happy about it. He therefore once again resorts to pronouncing woe. The implication is that James and Peter should not need either a paraclete or grace from any external source. This admonition is quite consistent with the overall soteriology of the text as observed thus far: blessed are those who have acquired grace for themselves (*ahoujpo neu ᵉmphmat ouaetou*).

In this context, then, Jesus' call to James and Peter to compare themselves to strangers (*tᵉntᵉn tēne ahᵉnšᵉmmaei*) is not a good thing. The function of the comparison is reproach, not a more positive deployment for the purposes of claiming an alien identity. Indeed the questions that follow only serve to sharpen the rebuke: what is the way of [strangers] in relation to your city? (*eušoop ᵉnneš ᵉnhe ᵉnnahrᵉn tetᵉnpolis*). That is to say, what is the mode and status of strangers in your city? The answer that the text implies is not a positive one. Strangers live as outsiders with respect to the city, a position that the disciples have placed themselves in unnecessarily through their stubborn inability to grasp the deeper soteriological point—that is, that they already belong to the true city and need only assert that identity for themselves.

Jesus then continues to berate the disciples, asking, "Why are you disturbed when you alone cast yourselves out and are far from your city? What is the matter with you that you alone abandon your dwelling place, preparing it for the ones who wish to dwell in it?" (*etbe eu tetᵉnštᵉrtarᵉt eretᵉn-nouje ᵉmmōtᵉn abal ouaet tēne auō tetᵉnouaeie atetᵉnpolis ahrōtᵉn petᵉmma ᵉnšōpe tetᵉnkōe ᵉmmaf abal ouaet tēne eretᵉnsabte ᵉmmaf ᵉnnetouōše aouēh ᵉnhētᵉf*). Here the text figures the two disciples as having unnecessarily cast themselves out of their true city—a metaphor for their soteriological misunderstanding. Evidently James and Peter have no one to blame but themselves for their current predicament, because they have in fact placed themselves in this undesirable position. In order to reinforce this point, Jesus takes a few more shots at aspects of the wrong soteriology, asking ironically if James and Peter think that the Father can be won over by prayers, petitions, or substitutionary atonement (*ē ešafᵉr kharize ᵉnoueei ha oueei*).

Here *Ap. Jas.* puts a deeply negative coding of the alien topos into play, akin to traditional Roman thinking about the evils of exile and the reproach of sojourning (see Chapter One). The text invokes the category of "the stranger" not to exploit its valorized possibilities but rather to conjure up the specter of the "un-citizen" with all its potentially negative valences. In spite of the more positive uses to which philosophers, Christians, and others were putting the trope, this way of thinking was still alive and well among Romans in the second century.[24] For example, Dio Chrysostom (c. 40–120)—who elsewhere valorizes exile—tells us that many choose death over life after losing the rights and status of their citizenship.[25]

Similarly, outside the discursive realm of literal citizenship, the alien topos could perform an equally negative rhetorical function. Thus the *Meditations* of the Stoic emperor Marcus Aurelius (second century) argues, "If the one who does not recognize the things which are in the cosmos is an alien (*xenos*) in the cosmos, no less an alien is the one who does not recognize the things which are taking place [in it]. He is an exile (*phygas*), the one who flees from civic reason . . . the one who splits off his own soul from that soul of rational things which is one."[26] Here the emperor uses the rhetoric of alienation in a figurative sense, bringing it to bear as part of a forceful polemic against those who do not pursue his conception of the unitary rational life.

In a comparable way, *Ap. Jas.* turns to the figure of the alien-stranger as a powerful image of reproach. While this move may not have been so unusual from the standpoint of traditional Roman discourse, it diverges sharply from what we have observed in other early Christian texts. To recap briefly, Hebrews uses the alien topos to construct a biblical lineage of strangers and sojourners for its audience, rooted in a collective memory of Abraham and other great heroes of the faith. By then consolidating its paraenetic agenda around the call to join Jesus *outside* the camp, the text promotes and reinforces its audience's particular understanding of their own distinctiveness as outsiders who belong in a better city, while at the same time maintaining an affirmation of traditional Roman social ideals. The *Epistle to Diognetus* uses the topos both to forge a culturally integrated Christian identity and to challenge Roman ways of thinking about Christians via an argument that Christians are "aliens" by virtue of surpassing Roman norms. Finally, the *Shepherd of Hermas, Similitudes* invokes the topos not so much to emphasize valorized outsider identity as to polemicize against certain kinds of economic practices and commitments. But, with the other texts, it still assumes and upholds the bedrock legitimacy of the move to construct the Christian self as other.

Ap. Jas. shares with these three texts a common vision that Christians have a particular city to which they belong. Yet it diverges from them with respect to its adamant refusal to valorize alien identity as a way of understanding the Christian self. In this respect, *Hermas, Similitude* 1.1–3 provides an especially useful point of comparison: "You know that you, the slaves of God, dwell in a foreign country; for your city is far from this city. If then you know your city in which you are going to dwell, why do you make arrangements for lands, expensive furnishings, buildings, and worthless living quarters? Accordingly, the one who makes arrangements for these things in this city is not able to return to his or her own city. O foolish, double-minded, and miserable person, do you not grasp that all these things are foreign and are under the authority of another?"

Here both texts share a commitment to a kind of true city. But *Hermas* codes the alien identity of the "slaves of God" dwelling in a foreign place (*hoti epi xenēs katoikeite hymeis*) in an undeniably positive light, a contrast to what we see in *Ap. Jas.* While the Jesus of the apocryphon asks James and Peter (and by extension, the audience) why they abandon their rightful place in the city (11.25–26), *Hermas* instead questions why its audience *fortifies* their place in the present city, by implication denying their alien status at the expense of their own true city (*tēn idian polin*). Furthermore, both texts offer a harsh evaluation of the respective actions under discussion (cf. *Ap. Jas.* 11.27–29 to the exhortation to the *aphron kai dipsyche kai talaipōre anthrōpe* in *Hermas* 1.3), but their contrasting orientations toward the legitimacy of constructing the self as other means that the respective polemics serve different purposes.

In *Hermas*, the text's censure of an orientation toward the wrong city fortifies an understanding of Christian identity as alien. But *Ap. Jas.* does not posit two cities (a temporal city/camp against which Christians define themselves as outsiders, and an eschatological city defined as the goal toward which true insiders travel). Rather, the text appeals to a single city as a metaphor for salvation, thereby articulating proper Christian identity in terms of its soteriological agenda rather than in terms of alien status. This city is a place in which those who do in fact belong as true insiders are instead unnecessarily casting themselves outside as strangers by not recognizing and taking hold of their insider status. At the same time, however, the power of the argument in part relies on the text's playful reversal of the topos's terms.

Conclusion: *Ap. Jas.*, the Alien Topos, and Early Christian Discourse

In *Ap. Jas.* then, we see a deployment of the alien-stranger topos that functions very differently from what is typical of other early Christian paraenesis. While still maintaining the primacy of a distinct city as an image around which Christian identity may legitimately be figured, the text rejects positioning identity at the margins (i.e., the self as other) and instead locates it in realizing and taking hold of one's true insider status. Given the consonance between the text's soteriological stance and this particular deployment of the topos, this intersection of strangers and soteriology proves not only an appropriate fit, but a rhetorically powerful one at that.

But does this contrast between the use of the alien topos in *Ap. Jas.* and other Christian texts tell us anything about the textual relationship between the apocryphon and these other examples from early Christian literature? Could we argue, for instance, that *Ap. Jas.* is aware of one or more of these other texts and is specifically and self-consciously making an allusion, albeit a polemical one? As we have seen, certain "mirror-image" parallels between *Ap. Jas.* and *Hermas* in particular are striking. Yet they do not seem striking enough to posit an attempt, on the part of *Ap. Jas.*'s semiotic strategy (returning to Eco's literary-critical terms), to activate *Hermas* as a specific intertext for readers (or vice versa, if one moves in the opposite direction).[27]

Nor do we have sufficient textual evidence to justify a sociological model of "communities in conflict." Within such a model, both *Ap. Jas.* and *Hermas* (or any of the other texts in question) would represent distinct and reified Christian communities, each having produced their respective texts to reflect a historical conflict over appropriate images of early Christian identity, and their relationship to both soteriology and the language of alienation. But as Frederick Wisse helpfully points out, "It is as difficult to disprove that specific communities were the real referents of early Christian literary texts as it is to prove it. The problem is that for the historian to proceed with any confidence, a community referent must be more than a mere possibility. . . . [T]here are simply too many contingencies that bear on the composition of literary texts to allow inferring indirect evidence from them about the historical situation in which they were written."[28]

This is not to imply, however, that *Ap. Jas.*'s use of the alien topos is an anomaly occurring in lonely isolation. Indeed, I would argue that the text is well aware of the basic move to valorize the topos that occurs in texts like Hebrews, *Diognetus*, and *Hermas*—if only for the fact that the irony of James and Peter's comparison to strangers does not "work" to anywhere near the same degree without the more customary Christian uses of the topos in view. Thus I would maintain that the call to James and Peter to compare themselves to strangers does indeed function polemically (and therefore dialogically). Yet what is being rejected or contested is not a community represented by a specific text (or set of texts), but rather a set of claims regarding alterity and its relevance for how Christians ought to think about themselves. By turning the alien topos on its head, *Ap. Jas.* offers a different vision of identity (as constituted by soteriology)—one in which Christians take hold of their insider status through claiming and working out the salvation that legitimately belongs to them.

Therefore the apocryphon's use of the topos emerges as part of an internal conversation within formative Christianity about the proper role and use of the self-as-other trope as a way to express what it means to be Christian. As Bakhtin insightfully notes, "The living utterance, having taken meaning and shape at a particular historical moment in a socially specific environment, cannot fail to brush up against thousands of living dialogic threads, woven by socio-ideological consciousness around the given object of an utterance; it cannot fail to become an active participant in social dialogue. After all, the utterance arises out of this dialogue as a continuation of it and as a rejoinder to it—it does not approach the object from the sidelines."[29] In this case, certainly, *Ap. Jas.* does not approach the question of Christian identity from the sidelines. It cannot afford to: for both the text and its audience(s), the very notion of salvation is at stake. By appealing then to a category of otherness with so much resonance in early Christianity, the apocryphon draws on a powerful and effective rhetorical resource for making its soteriological point.

Conclusion

In an important article, Rowan Greer characterizes early Christianity in terms of what he calls "the marvelous paradox of Christians as alien citizens."[1] That is, Christians are paradoxically "both involved in and disengaged from society."[2] Greer surveys the practical outworking of this paradox in both pre-Nicene writers (*Diognetus*, Tertullian of Carthage, Clement of Alexandria) and later authors of the fourth-century imperial church (Eusebius of Caesarea, Lactantius, John Chrysostom, Augustine). His conclusion is that, in each instance, "the paradox of alien citizenship can never be put into practice on a social scale. All the figures I have discussed state the paradox as an ideal; but in trying to actualize it, they break it." Thus the balance between alien and citizen proves too tenuous to maintain, and Christian thinkers slide into either "seeing only the alien character of the Christian life" or "changing the message of Christianity from one of deliverance to one of ordering and sanctifying the world."[3]

While Greer's study is a sound and helpful one in many ways, my approach to the conundrum of the Christian "alien citizen" has been somewhat different. Where Greer sees a fragile balance to be preserved (one that seems always doomed to failure), I have followed Bonnie Honing in approaching "foreignness as a topic, a question, rather than a problem. What does it mean? What sort of work does it do in cultural politics?"[4] And more specifically, what work did a claim to one's own foreignness do in an ancient field of cultural and religious identity for a nascent but growing movement struggling to make sense of its own boundaries?

The answer has not been simple or singular; and my analysis has stressed not a string of broken paradoxes but rather a rich and versatile discourse of emerging identity. But even as we have explored the multiple ways in which early Christians spoke their alien status and the different ends to which they spoke it, questions still remain regarding the larger implications of this analysis—questions that touch down in a complex interplay of historiographical, theological, and ethical concerns spanning both the ancient and the modern. Elizabeth Castelli and Hal Taussig capture something of this complexity in their challenge to the field of biblical and early Christian studies to reimagine the academic study of Christian origins with the imagery of painting like Picasso: "Those poised to paint the cubist portrait of Christian origins ought well to ask the difficult questions, for whom or for what do I perform this work? whose interests are served and whose interests blocked by this scholarship? what institutional and personal relations are affected by this mural-painting, and in what ways?"[5]

While I cannot fully answer these pointed questions here, I will in conclusion investigate briefly two separate but interrelated areas of inquiry for which the diverse uses of the Christian alien topos in antiquity have some relevance—and which both touch upon the concerns that Castelli and Taussig raise. The first is historiographical, returning to questions raised in the introduction around the problem of historical method, the transparency of textual data, and the role of rhetoricity. In short, what difference should the diversity we have observed make for how we narrate the historical beginnings of Christianity? My second area of interest is more explicitly theological, returning to questions of the topos's broader implications that I raised in the introduction but have deferred from any direct analysis until now. Here I wish to interrogate, however briefly, what is at stake theologically and ethically in contemporary deployments of the Christian self as other—in the context of how the complexities entailed in the ancient discourse of identity bear upon this question within current theological reflection.

Aliens and Strangers? Reassessing the Landscape of Early Christian History

I begin, then, with historiography: given the variegated uses of the alien topos that we have seen in individual early Christian texts, it seems necessary to ask what this implies for the reconstruction of early Christian history. Throughout this analysis, I have argued that early Christian claims to alien status cannot be treated as a transparent window through which historians can unproblematically view the social situation of those who made such claims. Instead of trying to move behind the text directly, then, I have opted to approach its rhetoricity as a sociohistorical practice in its own right. In this way, I have sought to explore the different kinds of rhetorical work that the topos performed in early Christian thought, examining the multiple, historically rooted, and socially inflected ways in which Christians employed it to articulate identity. But where does this emphasis on rhetorical function leave us in terms of telling the story of the first centuries of Christianity? As Karen King points out (following Paul Ricoeur), "individuals and communities will continue to represent truth, meaning and identity in narrative."[6] And in these projects to nar-

rate the history of Christianity, the rhetorical data of Christians' self-designation as aliens and strangers will inevitably figure. So what does the
topos tell us and where ought it to fit in a historical narrative?

We find an example of one common historiographical approach to
the question of early Christian alienation in Martin Hengel's assessment
of the Pauline mission to the Gentiles: "[The] freedom following from
the 'detachment' achieved by the believer . . . gave the small 'sect' of
Christians the strength to bear all the insults, oppression and persecution from the Roman state authorities which came during the first three
centuries and to overcome them. . . . Paul already found the basis for
this detachment in the presence of salvation: 'For our citizenship is in
heaven' (Phil. 3.20). . . . [Christians] had to limit themselves to the construction of a community ethics within an unfriendly, indeed hostile
world, sustained by true love and humanity—but at the same time quite
'transitory.'"[7] In this reconstruction, Hengel situates the first Christians
over and against a surrounding Roman society that he describes as "hostile" and "unfriendly," provoking Christians with "insults, oppression and
persecution." This characterization of "the world" and its attitude functions in Hengel's analysis as a straightforward sociohistorical fact.

But, on the other hand, it is almost a truism in the study of early Christianity today to maintain that Roman persecution of Christians was not
systematic and indeed only sporadic and localized in nature until the
mid-third century C.E.[8] From this perspective, it is possible to construe
the sociohistorical situation of these same early Pauline Christians rather
differently, as we see in the work of Wayne Meeks: "The Pauline groups'
strong and intimate sense of belonging, their special beliefs and norms,
their perception of their own discreteness from 'the world,' did not lead
them to withdraw into the desert, like the Essenes of Qumran. They remained in the cities, and their members continued to go about their ordinary lives in the streets and neighborhoods, the shops and agora. Paul
and the other leaders did not merely permit this continued interaction
as something inevitable; in several instances they positively encouraged
it."[9] Here Meeks's emphasis is on a certain kind of social integration
rather than a difference that provokes persecution and oppression. So
how ought we to evaluate these two differing emphases regarding the
relationship of early Christians to their surrounding culture? More specifically, what light can be shed on this question by a close analysis of the
different uses of the resident-alien topos?

Rather than seeking to harmonize these two accounts or somehow
adjudicate between them, I wish instead to begin with Hayden White's
intentionally provocative claim that historical narratives are in fact (what
he calls) "verbal fictions, the contents of which are as much *invented* as
found."[10] Many historians have understandably bristled at White's char-

acterization of their work as "fiction," and indeed, using such an incendiary term to characterize historical work seems to overstate the point unnecessarily. But White's basic and quite helpful insight is simply that "no given set of casually recorded historical events can in itself constitute a story; the most it might offer to the historian are story *elements*. The events are *made* into a story by the suppression or subordination of certain of them and the highlighting of others"—a process White calls *emplotment*.[11]

Acknowledging this dynamic as part of the historian's task does not require the conclusion that emplotment is a completely relative or ideologically driven process, or that all plots provide equally good explanations of the data (as might seem to be implied by White's most radical statements). Different types and amounts of data can lead to greater or lesser confidence in various "plots" on the part of the historian. In the case of the early Christian alien topos, as I have already stressed, were further evidence to come to light regarding the social and/or legal status of these texts' audiences (additional extant texts, inscriptions, archaeological remains), it might well bolster an argument for certain plots over others.

Yet White's basic insight still holds, insofar as the historian examining the alien-stranger topos has choices to make about the relative importance or explanatory force of various aspects of the textual data. To narrativize the relevant data is to plot its constituent elements in some type of relationship to one another. Turning back to our two historiographical examples, Hengel's reconstruction privileges rhetorical data in which Christians do indeed designate themselves as outsiders. By reading this data as transparent (i.e., in direct correspondence to a purported situation in the "real world"), he constructs a narrative that emphasizes society's oppression and persecution of the early Christians. For Hengel, then, the rhetorical dimension of the language of alienation is more or less ignored, allowing his narrative to move smoothly from the rhetoric of the texts to the sociohistorical "reality" of a uniform marginal status that Christians suffered under the oppression of Rome.

Meeks's approach, on the other hand, privileges a different set of rhetorical data—that which exhorts early Pauline Christians to behave according to conventional Greco-Roman norms. Yet at the same time, Meeks does not lose sight of the rhetoric of Christian difference. As he extrapolates from these two sets of textual data to a reconstruction of the historical situation, the result is a narrative in which "the Pauline groups suffered some tension between [the new mode] of socialization, which opposes the normal structures of the macrosociety, and the old structures. The latter are not completely escapable, for the Christians continue to live in the city and to interact with its institutions, and besides, they still carry some of its structures in their minds and in the houses where they meet."[12] In this way, Meeks's reconstruction privileges the rhetoric of integration (household codes, exhortations to conventional morality, etc.) over the rhetoric of alien/outsider status, but incorporates both into his narrative in a derhetoricized fashion, using their simultaneous presence in the texts to construct a sociohistorical tension between old and new forms of socialization.

In response to both of these positions, I would argue for an approach to narrating the history of early Christianity (and the use of the alien topos more specifically) that does not seek to erase the rhetorical choices and strategies being deployed in the extant texts by construing them only as transparent signs of something else (i.e., straightforward social data). These are rhetorical strategies that seek to *do* something: both to stake a claim within the ancient field of cultural and religious identity and to influence early Christian lives in their practical dimensions. As such, they are strategies that require analysis. Here I seek to follow the methodological call made most recently by Elizabeth Clark to attend more fully to the textuality of early Christian writings, acknowledging that "[these works] invite a different kind of reading from the cultural phenomena explored as 'texts' by interpretive anthropologists and from the forms of speech analyzed by contextualists."[13]

In this way, while we ought to continue to recognize that *some* early Christians were certainly persecuted and most likely deployed the alien topos to speak meaningfully to their situation, this does not necessitate Hengel's more wide-ranging conclusion that the singular and all-inclusive purpose of this way of speaking was to yield detachment so that sectarian Christians could bear persecution. On the other hand, Meeks's reconstruction is helpful in that it attends (unlike Hengel's) to the presence of both the alien topos *and* exhortations to acculturation in early Christian texts. But with that said, it is not necessary to subscribe uncritically to his further conclusion that the tensions between the two reflect nothing more than the sociohistorical unavoidability of "old structures" (i.e., pre-Christian) of socialization.

Rather, in light of the diversity that we have observed in the varying functions and deployments of the Christian alien topos in the first and second centuries, it is precisely this type of de-rhetoricizing move seen in both Hengel and Meeks that the textual data cannot support. The uses of the topos in Christian discourse of the first two centuries are simply too wide-ranging to sustain confidently any generalized historical assertion about the relationship between Christian alienation and social integration with respect to the Roman social order, made on the level of a de-rhetoricized "real world." Instead, I follow Daniel Boyarin (paraphrasing Jacob Neusner) in asking the question, "Once we know that we cannot know certain things, what else do we know, precisely by knowing what we cannot know?"[14]

One thing we know, I would argue, is that the multiple ends to which Christians deployed the topos belong as part of the story of early Christian history. Therefore, instead of following Meeks in his characterization of the tensions present here as indicative of a "not completely escapable" sociohistorical reality, I would maintain that to narrate these tensions in terms of "deliberate strategies of differentiation" (to return again to Laurence Moore)[15] does greater justice to the complexities of the extant textual data. In this narration (or emplotment) of early Christian history, "alien identity" becomes not a flat historical reality or a site of irresolvable tensions, but rather "an imaginative space created by rhetoric,"[16] one that allowed Christians to maintain their distinctive identity—even as they situated that identity in relation to Roman society in complex ways, to varying degrees both assimilationist and resistant (as we have seen in multiple registers and with a variety of emphases in 1 Peter, Hebrews, *Diognetus*, and *Hermas*). Furthermore, this type of historical narrative opens up space to take seriously not only the different ways that the alien topos could be used for constructing and maintaining identity, but also the competing stances taken by Christians on what could constitute legitimate Christian identity at all (as we saw so starkly in the *Apocryphon of James*). In this way, the alien topos finds its place within a larger narrative of Christian origins not based on the Eusebian meta-narrative of the triumph of orthodoxy, but rather focused on the rival claims and multiple voices that both produced and constituted the early movement.

Yet no narrative is innocent or uninterested—in this case neither the Eusebian version nor the "diversity of Christian origins" story so prevalent in current scholarship (and with which I align myself). This brings me then to a crucial ethical question about the writing of history, well-expressed recently by Karen King as follows: "How, then, should we speak differently? How might we represent the history of Christianity and to what ends? For whom should this history be written? What story of truth and identity ought it to tell?"[17] I find the self-reflexive orientation of these questions helpful not only for thinking about historiography and sociohistorical reconstruction of the first and second centuries, but also for looking beyond antiquity to the ongoing life of the Christian alien topos. Given the dialectic at work between present-day Christian communities and (at least some of) the ancient texts that make use of the topos, it seems appropriate to turn now to the contemporary field of Christian identity formation. To revisit a question posed in the introduction, what are the implications (both theological and political) of the topos's different possibilities? What bearing do its diverse ancient uses have on the theological articulation of Christian identity in terms of the self as other today?

Constructing Christian Difference Beyond the Second Century

But as for you, you are a foreigner in this world, a citizen of Jerusalem, the city above. Our citizenship, the apostle says, is in heaven. You have your own reg-isters, your own calendar; you have nothing to do with the joys of the world; nay, you are called to the very opposite, for "the world shall rejoice but ye shall mourn."[18]

For thoroughly a stranger and sojourner in the whole of life is every such one, who, inhabiting the city, despises the things in the city which are admired by oth-ers, and lives in the city as in a desert, so that the place may not compel him, but his mode of life shows him to be just.[19]

But seeing we are by nature sojourners, let us also be so by choice; that we be not there sojourners and dishonored and cast out. For if we are set upon being citizens here, we shall be so neither here nor there; but if we continue to be so-journers, and live in such wise as sojourners ought to live in, we shall enjoy the freedom of citizens both here and there.[20]

In these selections, we see just a sampling of the vigorous use that the alien topos enjoyed in the writings of patristic authors from the late sec-ond century onward. In fact, the rhetoric proved to have staying power not only through the systematic persecutions of Christianity in the third century, but also the transition to imperial religion in the fourth century and beyond. Here it is worth citing again the summation of Miroslav Volf concerning its influence on the history of Christian identity for-mation across the whole scope of the tradition: "It takes only a brief glance through the history of the church to see [the motif's] potency. By the second century being 'alien' had become central to the self-under-standing of Christians. Later it was essential to monastic and Anabaptist movements alike, to Augustine and Zinzendorf, and, in our own time, to Dietrich Bonhoeffer (*The Cost of Discipleship*) no less than to Jim Wallis (*Sojourners*) or Stanley Hauerwas (*Resident Aliens*)."[21] Indeed, in contem-porary Christian discourse in the United States, this move to construct the self as other, so strongly rooted in the history of the tradition, is alive and well, and continues to be used in the articulation of Christian iden-tity to varying theological, social, and political ends.

As we saw in the introduction, both Hauerwas/Willimon and Volf ap-peal to notions of the Christian self as an alien figure in order to present their respective visions for contemporary Christian identity and practice. In his examination of 1 Peter, Volf does so in a way that seeks to leave rhetorical space for certain kinds of cultural integration and accommo-dation through a distinction between "hard" and "soft" difference. By contrast, Hauerwas and Willimon turn to Philippians 3.20 (opting for the evocative translation of Moffatt: "We are a colony of heaven"[22]) and other New Testament texts to draw a starker rhetorical line, using the topos to argue for Christian identity not in terms of "the sustenance of a service club within a generally Christian culture, but the survival of a *colony* within an *alien society.*"[23] Drawing a similar note of contrast between the church and the surrounding culture, Joyce Hollyday and Jim Wallis articulate the vision of the journal *Sojourners* by appeal to the alien topos of Hebrews 11, in which, according to their reading, "the people of God are seen as pilgrims and strangers in the world because of their loyalty, not to the values of the world, but to God's way of justice and peace."[24]

These examples show that the turn to the alien topos in contemporary (American) Christian discourse tends to find its justification in part by drawing on ancient texts (often—but not always—with a particular emphasis on canonical texts such as Philippians, Hebrews, and 1 Peter). We can find particularly striking instances of this in biblical commentaries that seek to bridge the gap between antiquity and contemporary life. For example, Scot McKnight argues for the following "application" of the alien topos through his exegesis of 1 Peter 2.11–12:

The church, Peter says, is a countercultural alternative to society and culture. . . . But how will this work out today? First, we need to recognize that the forces working today to enculturate the mandates and truth of the gospel and to swallow holiness are *not as overtly physical as they were in Peter's day.* But the threat to the church is not to be minimized. While Peter's churches could spot those opposed to them because they had seen such people beat on Christians physically, we must have discernment to perceive the same kind of pressure today on the church and on Christian living. In particular, we have the forces of modernization, privatization and secularization.[25]

In response to these "forces" of modernity that he constructs as a looming threat, McKnight calls for an articulation of Christian identity which "[emphasizes] that Christians are different and will often be unaccepted by society. . . . The Christian is the one who is countercultural because he or she is out of step with the trends and passions in culture. It is not this way because we are trying to be odd; we are odd because we are trying to be godly."[26] Elsewhere in his analysis of the epistle, McKnight makes this application of the alien and stranger designation even more concrete: "In the Western world I can think of no group to whom 'social exclusion' might apply any better than to God-fearing Christians on university campuses."[27]

Similarly, in a commentary on Hebrews from the same series, George Guthrie argues that "the message [of chapter 11] to the original hearers must not be missed, for their circumstance must be seen as analogous to that of the patriarchs. Perhaps their current experience of persecution has highlighted the alien nature of their earthly existence. . . . Life must be lived in our challenging, terrestrial cities in light of a better, heavenly country that will be experienced in the future."[28] Guthrie goes on to map out possible outcomes of this alien existence living by faith: "faith can be rewarded with a 'delayed' outcome or even a 'negative' outcome. Abel still got murdered. Abraham had to wait for the son of the promise. Faith can also involve being tortured, mocked, beaten, destitute, stoned, put in prison, generally mistreated, and even mutilated."[29] In this way, Guthrie appropriates the text's evocative language of marginality to ask his readers what in this context is meant to function as a challenging paraenetic question: "How would you live differently if you did not believe? Would there be much difference?"[30] At its root, the question that Guthrie poses here is one about the intersection of identity and practice. How ought one to perform a given understanding of identity? Thus in both examples we see that the language of alien status continues to function today, through interpretation of the ancient biblical texts, as a powerful rhetorical resource for certain Christians to think with about the contours of their identity and its implications for practice.

But contemporary interpretations such as these are not unrelated to the ancient context or the analysis we have pursued in this study. In McKnight's commentary in particular, one can see clearly how he constructs a line of historical continuity by translating one kind of singular and monolithic "alien status"—experienced by early Christians and embodied in physical persecution—into another—experienced by present-day Christians and embodied in "the forces of modernization, privatization and secularization." This translation process (and its function to construct continuity) becomes explicit in McKnight's exhortation to his audience regarding the need "to perceive *the same kind of pressure today* on the church and on Christian living."[31] Yet if the singularity of the ancient situation cannot be maintained, then what does this mean for the unbroken historical line between two uniform milieus that McKnight seeks to draw here? Do the complexities of the topos's ancient usage in some way point to the need to nuance, complicate, or otherwise critique aspects of these contemporary deployments?

Alterity, Theological Identity, and Rhetoric

What problems does foreignness solve for us?[32]

The resident alien topos is a rich and vibrant rhetorical resource—and has functioned as such, both historically and today. There is much to be gained from an appeal to what is unmistakably an extremely powerful rhetoric for the articulation of a distinctive and cohesive group identity. For example, with respect to the nineteenth and twentieth century American context (construed more broadly than just the Mormons), Laurence Moore argues that "over the years sectarian dissent has provided an extraordinary number of people with strategies of success when others were lacking. In conscious and unconscious ways, [these people] built a usable social identity for themselves by stressing the degree to which polite society called them the scum of the earth and the filth of creation. In those charges, they found the badge of respectability and, at least sometimes, a path to upward social mobility and greatly enhanced power in the social and political world around them."[33]

Indeed, turning to the language of alien and foreign status to articulate one's identity is a way of making that identity matter—a way of rendering it not only legible as a distinct entity but also potent in its peculiar doubleness. We inherit a discourse in which the category of the foreigner can still activate an ambivalence that is ancient in its roots, a site of "desire and derision" at once enthralling and repellent.[34] As Julia Kristeva maintains, with respect to the contemporary situation of foreigners in France, "Since you remain uncurably different and unacceptable, you are an object of fascination: one notices you, one talks about you, one hates you or admires you, or both at the same time. But you are not an ordinary, negligible presence, you are not a Mr. or Mrs. Nobody. You are a problem, a desire—positive or negative, never neutral."[35] And as I have argued throughout, there is something compelling about this curious intersection of problem and desire in the alien figure, making the topos a powerful rhetorical tool that can be used efficaciously to numerous ends.

This is, in fact, what we have seen in this examination of first- and second-century Christian sources. The language of alienation functions impressively to stake different kinds of ground in a pluralistic cultural landscape. While purporting to describe an objective situation in which a group is excluded or marginalized from the cultural mainstream, the topos can actually open up a rhetorical space for an identity grounded in conventional/centrist practices (à la 1 Peter and Hebrews). It can also be used to challenge a hegemonic discourse of identity, even as it appropriates the very terms and ideals of that discourse (à la *Diognetus*). Or it can serve as a vehicle to polemicize against people, beliefs, and ways of life (à la *Hermas*). The paradoxical genius of a rhetoric of marginality is that it allows all this, while at the same time continually serving to reinscribe group identity in powerfully cohesive terms.

Yet there are also risks that accompany the project of constructing the self as other that I see as potentially quite serious and problematic. For one thing, the tensions that we have seen in Hebrews and other ancient texts between a radical rhetoric of outsider status and a more conventional paraenetic vision are reflected today on the contemporary American stage in discussions like those of McKnight and Guthrie examined above, as well as the theological positionings of Hauerwas and others. As

Alan Wolfe points out in response to Hauerwas and Willimon, "sociologically speaking, *Resident Aliens* fails to capture much of the actual realities of American religious life, including the fact that untold numbers of religious conservatives are quite at home in the culture around them." In Wolfe's analysis, the rhetoric which insists that "believers have no place at the table of modernity" is absurd, even somewhat perverse.[36]

To put this in Bourdieuian terms, positioning oneself in a relationship of alienation to a cultural field is itself a practice within that field (in this case one that still lays claim to a kind of privileged status). There is no place to stand outside the various fields of culture from which a group can make these claims—there is only rhetoric to this effect. As Stuart Hall contends,

Cultural identity is not a fixed essence at all, lying unchanged outside history and culture. It is not some universal and transcendental spirit inside us on which history has made no fundamental mark. It is not once-and-for-all. It is not a fixed origin to which we can make some final and absolute return. . . . It is always constructed through memory, fantasy, narrative, and myth. Cultural identities are the points of identification, the unstable points of identification or suture, which are made, within the discourses of history and culture. Not an essence but a *positioning*. Hence, there is always a politics of identity, a politics of position, which has no absolute guarantee in an unproblematic, transcendental "law of origin."[37]

If this is the case, then Christian "alien identity" cannot be take as a given or as a pristine essence to be recovered and/or preserved—not today any more than in the ancient world. Through the analysis pursued here, the figure of the ancient Christian alien has emerged as a composite, a fissured image formed not from a single position but from a shifting set of multiple positions. So too in contemporary Christian discourse, we need to be willing to ask hard questions about the various politics of theological identity involved in different renditions of the Christian self as other.

Aliens, Sojourners, and Theological Responsibility

So then, you are no longer strangers and resident aliens, but fellow citizens. (Ephesians 2.19)

By making the above argument, I do not mean to imply that the alien topos ought never to be invoked in a contemporary context, or that Christians are not or should not be different. Nor am I contending (and I wish to be clear here) that marginality, persecution, and/or victimization can be reduced to social and discursive constructions. Rather, I hope that this examination of the variable uses of the alien topos in

Christian texts of the first and second centuries points to the need to think with greater nuance, complexity, and self-reflexivity about what we are doing when make the decision (no matter how appropriate that decision may be, given external circumstances) to draw upon the topos to construct religious identity. As Elizabeth Castelli reminds us (with reference to martyrdom—a different but not unrelated discourse of identity), "we have some choices about how we craft the stories that we tell."[38] And with those choices comes the need for both critical self-consciousness and theological responsibility.

Daniel Boyarin has recently argued in a different context that "the valence of [an identity claim] shifts . . . with the political status of the group making the claim."[39] Following Boyarin on this point, my argument here is not that claims to alien status based on religious identity are necessarily problematic, but rather that they are contextual, and as such, contain embedded strategies which should not be exempt from socio-rhetorical analysis and critique. In light of this, we can (and to my mind, ought to) ask ourselves what the difference is between an appeal to alterity as identity on the part of Wolfe's "religious conservatives . . . quite at home in the culture around them," and similar claims on the part of various "subaltern collectives"[40]—as well as what difference that difference makes.

A colorful illustration of just how much difference such contextualization makes can be found in an example drawn from the political sphere (though not without its connections to questions of religious identity). In 2004, *Time Magazine's* coverage of the hotly contested American presidential election offered the following reflection on the scandal provoked by a CBS story based on a false set of memos disparaging President George W. Bush's record in the National Guard: "The network's mess [once the authenticity of the memos was called into question] served members of the Bush campaign beautifully. . . . It fed their story line that they are once again *fighting as outsiders. When you control the White House, both houses of Congress and the Supreme Court, it's a neat trick to act like an underdog.* But to the extent the Republicans could turn the Liberal Media into the Establishment enemy, liken themselves to Thomas Paine and Martin Luther, nail their charges to the door, distribute their pamphlets, rally their faithful, it was in the interest of giving their base a tyrant to battle."[41]

Returning then to the religious sphere, I contend that there is a need for those who would construct communal theological identity in terms of alienation and marginality to be attentive to the multiple uses and possibilities of the alien topos in the contemporary cultural context as well as in the ancient one. Here I have in view not only the multiplicity of the topos's positive possibilities for formulating and reinforcing cohesive group identity. Also needed is a critical self-awareness of the conversations that a robust deployment of the topos may potentially shut down and the potential for abuses that it can open up.

For example, what happens to the space for theological critique of a group's practices, commitments, and beliefs (from outside or inside the group) in the context of an identity narrative of alien status? While logically there is no necessary relationship between the two (and thus nothing necessarily problematic), the latter may in fact function in subtle or unconscious ways to suppress the former. As we have seen, the rhetoric of alien identity can work powerfully to validate the practical ways that people live, relate to one another, and engage the world around them. And so the very structure of the valorized alien trope *may* yield the effect (unintended or perhaps even intended) of rendering a community's practices and attitudes relatively immune from critique—since any critique or questioning (particularly from the outside) only fuels the general plausibility of the narrative that positions the group at the cultural margins. Thus, while by no means an inevitable result, an alien identity stance can offer a rhetorical justification to ignore the need for the critical reassessment of one's own practices and ways of thinking—both individually and institutionally.

Similarly, what are the ways that Christian responsibility for the marginalized other might play out in the face of an identity rhetoric that lays such a strong claim to a position of alterity for itself? How might the Christian alien respond to an ethical injunction such as that of Emmanuel Levinas? "Before the Other, the I is infinitely responsible. The Other is the poor and destitute one, and nothing which concerns this Stranger can leave the I indifferent."[42] Here the other makes an ethical demand on the self from the position of the other's alterity. But in what way am I to respond to that demand, speaking to the other in his or her full integrity as "other," when I myself have occupied the space of the other already (at least rhetorically)?

The Hebrew Bible offers us one option, highlighting the possibility that an identity rooted in alien status may lead to a greater concern for (and solidarity with) others who are marginalized. This is the theological logic that drives a verse like Leviticus 19.33–34: "When a resident alien sojourns with you in your land, do not oppress that one. The resident alien sojourning with you will be to you as a citizen among you. You will love that one as yourself because you were resident aliens in the land of Egypt." We may perhaps see something similar (though the text never makes the link explicit) in Hebrews' juxtaposition of the alien topos with the exhortation of 13.2–3 to care for strangers, prisoners, and those being tortured.

But, on the other hand, this is not always the case. If I may venture a personal anecdote, I vividly remember listening to a youth pastor in suburban Philadelphia in the mid-1990s as she dismissed the importance of engaging the Rwandan genocide either theologically or politically to any substantive degree—*except* to whatever extent the genocide might be culled as homiletic fodder for reflecting on her own community's experience of suburban American Christian alienation. While such an example is admittedly extreme, theologically repulsive, and (hopefully) extremely rare (and would no doubt be disavowed even by many within this pastor's theological community), the fact that such a statement could be viewed as plausible at all points to possibilities that the alien topos may, under certain circumstances, allow (or even encourage)—wherein a rhetorical emphasis on the self as other can strangle the space needed to take seriously the alterity of others who are not ourselves.

So I conclude then by arguing, not for the alien topos's eradication from contemporary theological reflection, but rather for its necessary contextualization—thereby allowing the topos to be held theologically and politically accountable for the work that it performs at the intersections of Christian identity and practice. From a theological point of view (at least for some), this may constitute a certain loss. For from the standpoint of those who live within theological worlds in which much is staked on the "givenness" of their identity as aliens and sojourners, the critical analysis of the alien topos that I offer here may seem profoundly to miss the point. Is Foucault right when he remarks that "there is always something ludicrous in philosophical discourse when it tries, from the outside, to dictate to others, to tell them where their truth is and how to find it, or when it works up a case against them in the language of naive positivity"?[43] While I hope to have offered more here than only a case framed in the language of naive positivity, I recognize that the plea I make for greater self-reflexivity (and through it, ethical and theological responsibility) may entail giving up a certain theological romanticism that is not without its benefits. Hauerwas and Willimon appeal to the "exciting sense of adventure" that an identity rooted in the imagery and rhetorical power of the alien topos evokes—and this exhilarating thrill of one's own divinely sanctioned marginality may prove difficult or even impossible to maintain (at least in its first uncritical rush) in light of what I advocate here. But some losses are worth losing—and indeed are constitutive of new forms of theological identity.

With this in mind, then, I return finally, out of the various texts we have examined, to the *Apocryphon of James*. This is not in the interests of arguing that it be given a normative hearing, or of advocating for its particular soteriology. Rather, I wish to conclude by noting once again the way in which the apocryphon's distinctive stance throws the *constructed* nature of Christian alien identity into sharp relief. That is to say, *Ap.*

Jas. most clearly exposes what the other ancient texts also subtly hint at: the use of the alien topos as part of an ongoing conversation about the nature of Christian identity. I will therefore close with the appropriately acute query that *Ap. Jas.* poses to its readers: what is the way of strangers in relation to one's city? In other words, the relation of strangers to the city is not a given but a *question*, one that admits of multiple answers. And each of these answers entails a set of rhetorical strategies that carries practical implications. At the very least then, the theological, social, and political contexts in which the question is asked and answered need critical and self-conscious exploration.

Abbreviations

Ancient Texts

Abr.	Philo, *De Abrahamo*
Acts Thecla	*Acts of (Paul and) Thecla*
Acts Thom.	*Acts of Thomas*
Agr.	Philo, *De agricultura*
Ant.	Josephus, *Jewish Antiquities*
Ap. Jas.	NHC I,2 *Apocryphon of James*
1 Apoc. Jas.	NHC V,3 *(First) Apocalypse of James*
Apoc. Peter	NHC VII,3 *Apocalypse of Peter*
Apol.	Tertullian, *Apology*
1 Apol.	Justin Martyr, *First Apology*
Ath. pol.	Aristotle, *Constitution of Athens*
2 Bar.	*2 Baruch (Syriac Apocalypse)*
CD	*Damascus Document*
Cher.	Philo, *De cherubim*
1 Chron	1 Chronicles
1 Clem.	*1 Clement*
2 Clem.	*2 Clement*
Conf.	Philo, *De confusione linguarum*
2 Cor	2 Corinthians
Det.	Philo, *Quod deterius potiori insidari soleat*
Deut	Deuteronomy
Diatr.	Epictetus, *Diatribai (Dissertationes)*
Diogn.	*Epistle to Diognetus*
Ebr.	Philo, *De ebrietate*
Eloc.	Demetrius, *Style*
Ep.	Seneca (the Younger), *Epistulae morales*
Eph	Ephesians
Ezek	Ezekiel
Flacc.	Philo, *In Flaccum*

Gen	Genesis
Gig.	Philo, *De gigantibus*
Gos. Thom.	NHC II,2 *Gospel of Thomas*
Heb	Hebrews
Her.	Philo, *Quis rerum divinarum heres sit*
Herm. Mand.	Shepherd of Hermas, *Mandates*
Herm. Sim.	Shepherd of Hermas, *Similitudes*
Herm. Vis.	Shepherd of Hermas, *Visions*
Hist. eccl.	Eusebius, *Ecclesiastical History*
Isa	Isaiah
Jas	James
Lam	Lamentations
Leg. (Athenagoras)	Athenagoras, *Legatio pro Christianis*
Leg. (Cicero)	Cicero, *De legibus*
Leg. (Philo)	Philo, *Legum allegoriae*
Legat.	Philo, *Legatio ad Gaium*
Lev	Leviticus
LXX	Septuagint
Mart. Pol.	*Martyrdom of Polycarp*
Matt	Matthew
Metam.	Ovid, *Metamorphoses*
Mor.	Plutarch, *Moralia*
Mos.	Philo, *De vita Mosis*
Num	Numbers
Od.	Homer, *Odyssey*
Paed.	Clement of Alexandria, *Paedagogus*
1 Pet	1 Peter
Phaed.	Plato, *Phaedo*
Phil	Philippians
Pol. *Phil.*	Polycarp, *To the Philippians*
Ps	Psalms
Rev	Revelation
Rhet.	Aristotle, *Rhetoric*
Rom	Romans
Sib. Or.	*Sibylline Oracles*
Somn.	Philo, *De somniis*
Spec. Laws	Philo, *De specialibus legibus*
[Subl.]	Longinus, *On the Sublime*
Var. hist.	Aelian, *Varia historia*
Virt.	Philo, *De virtutibus*
Wis	Wisdom of Solomon

Scholarly Journals, Series, and Other Secondary Sources

AB	The Anchor Bible
AJT	*Asia Journal of Theology*
ANF	*Ante-Nicene Fathers*
ANRW	*Aufstieg und Niedergang der römischen Welt: Geschichte und Kultur Roms im Spiegel der neueren Forschung*
Anton	*Antonianum*
ATANT	Abhandlungen zur Theologie des Alten und Neuen Testaments
BAGD	Bauer, W., W.F. Arndt, F.W. Gingrich, and F.W. Danker, *Greek-English Lexicon of the New Testament and Other Christian Literature*
BCH	*Bulletin de correspondance hellénique*
BeO	*Bibbia e oriente*
BibS(N)	Biblische Studien (Neukirchen, 1951–)
CahRB	Cahiers de la Revue biblique
CBP	Cahiers de biblia patristica
CBQMS	Catholic Biblical Quarterly Monograph Series
DPL	*Dictionary of Paul and His Letters*
EBib	Études bibliques
ETR	*Études théologiques et religieuses*
ExAud	*Ex auditu*
HNT	Handbuch zum Neuen Testament
HTR	*Harvard Theological Review*
HTS	Harvard Theological Studies
JBL	*Journal of Biblical Literature*
JECS	*Journal of Early Christian Studies*
JTS	*Journal of Theological Studies*
LCL	Loeb Classical Library
LD	Lectio divina
NABPR	National Association of Baptist Professors of Religion Special Studies Series
NedTT	*Nederlands theologisch tijdschrift*
NHC	Nag Hammadi Codices
NHS	Nag Hammadi Studies
NICNT	New International Commentary on the New Testament
NPNF	*Nicene and Post-Nicene Fathers*
NRSV	New Revised Standard Version
NTS	*New Testament Studies*
OCD	*Oxford Classical Dictionary*
PG	Patrologia graeca

PW	*Paulys Realencyclopädie der classischen Altertumswissenschaft* (New edition G. Wissowa)
RCT	*Revista catalana de teología*
RelSRev	*Religious Studies Review*
RevExp	*Review and Expositor*
RHR	*Revue de l'histoire des religions*
RivB	*Rivista biblica italiana*
RSR	*Recherches de science religieuse*
SBLDS	Society of Biblical Literature Dissertation Series
SBLMS	Society of Biblical Literature Monograph Series
SC	Sources chrétiennes
SGU	Studia Graeca Upsaliensia
SPhilo	*Studia philonica*
StNT	Studien zum Neuen Testament
TBT	*The Bible Today*
TDNT	*Theological Dictionary of the New Testament*
TS	*Theological Studies*
TynBul	*Tyndale Bulletin*
USQR	*Union Seminary Quarterly Review*
VC	*Vigiliae christianae*
VP	*Vita e pensiero*
WUNT	Wissenschaftliche Untersuchungen zum Neuen Testament
ZNW	*Zeitschrift für neutestamentliche Wissenschaft und die Kunde der älteren Kirche*

Notes

Introduction

Epigraph: Roland H. Bainton, "The Early Church and War," HTR 39 (1946): 203.

1. *1 Clem.* prescript. Note also the related reference in *1 Clem.* 54.4.
2. See Pol. *Phil.* prescript, *Mart. Pol.* prescript. On the use of sojourning language in the *Martyrdom of Polycarp*, see Frederick W. Weidmann, " 'To Sojourn' or 'To Dwell'? Scripture and Identity in *The Martyrdom of Polycarp*," in *Reading in Christian Communities: Essays on Interpretation in the Early Church*, ed. Charles A. Bobertz and David Brakke (Notre Dame, Ind.: University of Notre Dame Press, 2002), 29–40.
3. *2 Clem.* 5.5; cf. also 5.1.
4. These definitions of Greek terms are commonly accepted but can be found in both H. G. Liddell, R. Scott, H. S. Jones, *A Greek-English Lexicon*, 9th ed. (Oxford: Oxford University Press, 1996); Walter Bauer et al., eds. *A Greek-English Lexicon of the New Testament and Other Early Christian Literature*, based on Walter Bauer's *Griechisch-deutsches Wörterbuch*, 3rd ed. (Chicago: University of Chicago Press, 2000).
5. Augustine, *City of God* 15.1 (*NPNF¹* 2:284–85).
6. Stanley Hauerwas and William H. Willimon, *Resident Aliens: Life in the Christian Colony* (Nashville, Tenn.: Abingdon Press, 1989), 12.
7. Miroslav Volf, "Soft Difference: Theological Reflections on the Relation Between Church and Culture in 1 Peter," *ExAud* 10 (1994): 16–17. Volf himself can also be placed in this stream, albeit in a tempered form. In his reflections on the question of Christian alterity in 1 Peter, he argues for Christian identity in terms of what he calls "soft difference": "For people who live the soft difference, mission fundamentally takes the form of witness and invitation. They seek to win others without pressure or manipulation, sometimes even 'without a word' (1 Peter 3.1)." Here Volf seeks to distance himself from the kind of "hard difference" that he associates with "open or hidden pressures, manipulation, and threats" (with respect to the other from whom one differs); he also wishes to leave room for certain kinds of Christian acculturation and accommodation. But nevertheless, his basic interpretive orientation is to conceptualize Christian identity in terms of its fundamental difference: "To make a difference, one must be different." Volf, "Soft Difference," 24.
8. Here I have in view interpellation in the Althusserian sense of hailing individuals in a way that seeks to constitute them as particular kinds of subjects. See

Louis Althusser, "Ideology and Ideological State Apparatuses (Notes Towards an Investigation)," in *Lenin and Philosophy and Other Essays*, trans. Ben Brewster (New York: Monthly Review Press, 1971), 175. Also Judith Butler, *Excitable Speech: A Politics of the Performative* (New York: Routledge, 1997), 32–34.

9. Hans Jonas, *The Gnostic Religion: The Message of the Alien God and the Beginnings of Christianity* (Boston: Beacon Press, 1958), 49–50.

10. R. Laurence Moore, *Religious Outsiders and the Making of Americans* (Oxford: Oxford University Press, 1986), 27.

11. Moore, *Religious Outsiders*, 29. Moore notes that polygamy was not practiced by a large majority of nineteenth-century Mormons and did not become a significant part of polemical literature against the group until over a decade after its founding. As he argues, "Interestingly, other American religious groups that adopted distinct sexual practices and followed them consistently, the Shakers and the Oneida 'perfectionists,' for example, were far less persecuted than the Mormons. In assembling a historical reality, one need not abandon the reasonable proposition that the practice of plural marriage constituted one difference between Mormons and other Americans. The problem is that this difference took on rather greater significance, and led to far greater conflict, than any objective difference in value system would have warranted." As for other "peculiarities of the Mormon faith," the early Mormon position contained significant theological novelty but "was generally in line with other liberalizing trends that provoked religious controversy [but *not* scandalized outcry] in the nineteenth century. Theologically, in fact, Mormonism was in its beginnings a dull affair." See Moore, *Religious Outsiders*, 28–30.

12. Moore, *Religious Outsiders*, 29.

13. Moore, *Religious Outsiders*, 31, 46, emphasis added.

14. Jonathan Z. Smith, *Relating Religion: Essays in the Study of Religion* (Chicago: University of Chicago Press, 2004), 230.

15. Smith, *Relating Religion*, 245.

16. Jonathan Z. Smith, "What a Difference a Difference Makes," in *"To See Ourselves as Others See Us": Christians, Jews, "Others" in Late Antiquity*, ed. Jacob Neusner and Ernest S. Frerichs (Chico, Calif.: Scholars Press, 1985), 15 (emphasis added).

17. Smith, "What a Difference," 47.

18. See as representative: Paul Cartledge, *The Greeks: A Portrait of Self and Others* (New York: Oxford University Press, 1993); Jonathan Hall, *Ethnic Identity in Greek Antiquity* (Cambridge: Cambridge University Press, 1997); François Hartog, *The Mirror of Herodotus: The Representation of the Other in the Writing of History* (Berkeley: University of California Press, 1988).

19. Passing references (a word or phrase) can be found in the New Testament in Luke 24.18, Acts 7.4–6, 29, 13.17 and Ephesians 2.19, though none of these speak directly to the issue of Christian identity conceived in terms of alien status. More relevant is Philippians 3.20 ("Our citizenship is in heaven"), even if it does not use the figure of the alien/stranger explicitly. Outside the canon (in addition to texts already mentioned), short references appear in Justin Martyr, the *Odes of Solomon*, martyrological literature (e.g., Pontius, *Life and Passion of Cyprian*), various letters cited in Eusebius (Dionysius of Corinth, the letter concerning the martyrs of Lyon and Vienne) and other apocryphal texts. See Eusebius, *Hist. eccl.* 4.23.5–6, 5.1.3. Also cf. *Acts Thecla* 26, *Acts Thom.* 108–13, and from Nag Hammadi, *Gos. Thom.* 42, *1 Apoc. Jas.* 34, *Apoc. Peter* 83.17. Later patristic writers who make use of the topos include Irenaeus, Clement of Alexandria, Origen,

and Augustine, to name only the most prominent. For references, see Johannes Roldanus, "Références patristiques au 'chrétien-étranger' dans les trois premiers siècles," *CBP* 1 (1987): 27–52. Note also that a philological shift takes place in the third and fourth centuries whereby *paroikia* takes on a technical sense of "diocese" in ecclesiastical usage. See Reinhard Feldmeier, "The 'Nation' of Strangers: Social Contempt and Its Theological Interpretation in Ancient Judaism and Early Christianity," in *Ethnicity and the Bible*, ed. M. G. Brett (Leiden: Brill, 1996), 263–64. Also Eusebius, *Hist. eccl.* 3.36.2, 4 as representative.

20. While numerous other texts take up the theme of the Christian as "other" in some way, my concern here is with a *particular conception* of otherness as seen in the language of sojourning, alien status, cities, and citizenship. See John 17.16 as an example of a text that posits Christian "otherness" without turning explicitly to the vocabulary of stranger and alien status.

21. Dating of *Ap. Jas.* will be discussed in Chapter 5.

22. Note that *Ap. Jas.* is not mentioned in Roldanus's otherwise comprehensive and extremely helpful catalogue of references to the Christian as alien and stranger in early Christian literature through the third century. Of course this omission may be unintentional or may signal a different theory of dating the text (given that the extant codices of Nag Hammadi are fourth century). See Roldanus, "Références patristiques."

23. See, for example, Karen L. King, *What Is Gnosticism?* (Cambridge, Mass.: Harvard University Press, 2003); Helmut Koester, *Ancient Christian Gospels: Their History and Development* (Harrisburg, Pa.: Trinity Press International, 1990); Elaine Pagels, *The Gnostic Gospels* (New York: Random House, 1979).

24. Note the foundational debt to the groundbreaking work of Walter Bauer in the early twentieth century, as developed and nuanced by Helmut Koester, James Robinson, and many others. See Walter Bauer, *Orthodoxy and Heresy in Earliest Christianity* (Philadelphia: Fortress Press, 1971); Helmut Koester and James M. Robinson, *Trajectories Through Early Christianity* (Philadelphia: Fortress Press, 1971). For a recent critique that retains an orientation toward the diversity of early Christianity but cautions against the overly facile construction of different Christian "communities" based on indirect evidence from texts, see Frederik Wisse, "Indirect Textual Evidence for the History of Early Christianity and Gnosticism," in *For the Children, Perfect Instruction: Studies in Honor of Hans-Martin Schenke*, ed. Hans-Gebhard Bethge et al. (Leiden: Brill, 2002).

25. Denise Kimber Buell, "Rethinking the Relevance of Race for Early Christian Self-Definition," *HTR* 94, 4 (2001): 473. For a programmatic overview of new directions in reconstructing early Christianity, see Elizabeth Castelli and Hal Taussig, "Drawing Large and Startling Figures: Reimagining Christian Origins by Painting like Picasso," in *Reimagining Christian Origins: A Colloquium Honoring Burton Mack*, ed. Elizabeth Castelli and Hal Taussig (Valley Forge, Pa.: Trinity Press International, 1996).

26. Vincent Wimbush, "'. . . Not of This World . . .': Early Christianities as Rhetorical and Social Formation," in *Reimagining Christian Origins*, ed. Castelli and Taussig, 34 (emphasis original).

27. Notable exceptions to this trend include Feldmeier, "'Nation' of Strangers"; Rowan A. Greer, "Alien Citizens: A Marvellous Paradox," in *Civitas: Religious Interpretations of the City*, ed. Peter S. Hawkins (Atlanta: Scholars Press, 1986), 39–56; Eckhard Plümacher, *Identitätsverlust und Identitätsgewinn: Studien zum Verhältnis von kaiserzeitlicher Stadt und frühem Christentum*, BibS(N) (Neukirchen-Vluyn: Neukirchener Verlag, 1987); Roldanus, "Références patristiques," 27–52.

28. "Identity" in this sense is broadly construed, carrying possible social, political, legal, theological, and/or eschatological connotations depending on the perspective and interests of any particular scholar.

29. John H. Elliott, *A Home for the Homeless: A Sociological Exegesis of 1 Peter, Its Situation and Strategy* (Philadelphia: Fortress Press, 1981), 33.

30. Elliott dates 1 Peter to between 69 and 96 C.E., as well as tentatively proposing an even more specific dating of 73–92 C.E. The latter is based on the sequence of provinces listed in 1 Pet 1:1 that might reflect the reorganization of provincial administration by Vespasian in 72 C.E.. See discussion in John H. Elliott, *1 Peter: A New Translation with Introduction and Commentary*, AB (New York: Doubleday, 2000), 136–38; Elliott, *Home for the Homeless*, 84–87.

31. Elliott, *Home for the Homeless*, 35–36. Elliott makes the further distinction that *paroikos* functions as a technical term with political-legal connotations while *parepidēmos* "refers more generally to the transient visitor who is temporarily residing as a foreigner in a given locality." Elliott, *Home for the Homeless*, 30. Here he draws on a distinction emphasized by Selwyn, who in turn draws on Zahn. See Edward G. Selwyn, *The First Epistle of St. Peter* (London: Macmillan, 1946), 118.

32. Although extremely important in the history of the scholarly conversation around this issue, Elliott's position has not been widely followed. Note however, immediately before the publication of *A Home for the Homeless*, Armand Puig Tàrrech's argument for a similar point: "Quant à leur statut socio-légal, ils sont presque tous des *peregrini* de classe basse, qui cultivent dans des conditions difficiles (souvent en régime de servage féodal) les propriétés appartenant aux classes dominantes, romaines ou locales." Armand Puig Tàrrech, "Le milieu de la Première épître de Pierre," *RCT* 5 (1980): 128. Following the publication of Elliott's work, a handful of scholars have supported his conclusions. See William Dalton, "The Church in 1 Peter," in *Witness of Faith in Life and Worship*, Yearbook—Ecumenical Institute for Theological Research (Jerusalem: The Institute, 1981–1982); Scot McKnight, *1 Peter*, NIV Application Commentary (Grand Rapids, Mich.: Zondervan, 1996), 24–26; John J. Pilch, "'Visiting Strangers' and 'Resident Aliens'," *TBT* 29 (1991). The work of Eckhard Plümacher should perhaps be noted here as well. While Plümacher's study focuses more broadly on the identity crisis reflected in a number of early Christian texts (Hebrews, Ephesians, 1 Peter, *Shepherd of Hermas*), he understands the basic problem of the sub-decurional classes to be exclusion from citizen status—hence the affinity with Elliott. (Plümacher simultaneously argues for an analogous alienation among urban elites due to the increasingly empty role of political leadership in the *polis* under the Roman Empire.) See Plümacher, *Identitätsverlust und Identitätsgewinn*, 10–25, 54–60.

33. Elliott, *Home for the Homeless*, 201.

34. Elliott acknowledges other ancient uses of the term *paroikos*, the main one being the move "to depict the righteous man as a stranger on earth separated from his heavenly home" that he associates primarily with Philo, Hebrews, and "Platonizing Stoicism in general." Elliott, *Home for the Homeless*, 31–32. But he is adamant that 1 Peter contains no such cosmological dualism (or what he calls "pilgrim theology") according to which the addressees are called to think of themselves as pilgrims on earth on the way to their heavenly abode. Elliott, *Home for the Homeless*, 129–32. In support of this position, see Elliott's fascinating catalogue of various translations of 1 Peter 1.1, 1.17, and 2.11. Here he documents a number of attempts to read the text's use of the alien topos in terms of a heaven-earth dualistic cosmology by translating terms like "sojourn" and "resident alien"

in terms of alien status *on earth* when the phrase "on earth" does not appear in the Greek text. Elliott, *Home for the Homeless*, 39–41.

35. See as representative (though epitomizing a spectrum of different opinions about issues of identity, cosmological dualism, sojourning, and diaspora in 1 Peter), Moses Chin, "A Heavenly Home for the Homeless: Aliens and Strangers in 1 Peter," *TynBul* 42 (1991): 96–112; Reinhard Feldmeier, *Die Christen als Fremde: Die Metapher der Fremde in der antiken Welt, im Urchristentum und im 1.Petrusbrief* (Tübingen: Mohr, 1992); Leonhard Goppelt, *A Commentary on 1 Peter*, trans. J. E. Alsup (Grand Rapids, Mich.: Eerdmans, 1993), 61–76; Marie-Louise Lamau, *Des Chrétiens dans le monde: Communautés pétriniennes au 1er siècle*, LD (Paris: Cerf, 1988); Troy W. Martin, *Metaphor and Composition in 1 Peter*, SBLDS (Atlanta, GA: Scholars Press, 1992), 142–43, 88–200; Donald Senior, "The Conduct of Christians in the World (1 Pet 2:11–3:12)," *RevExp* 79 (1982): 427–38. In general, the understanding of metaphor operative in this discussion is a rather narrow one insofar as it conceptualizes the so-called "metaphorical" usage of Petrine alien language in binary terms as the "opposite" of Elliott's legal-"literal" interpretation. While I will retain the use of the terms "metaphor" and "metaphorical" in this sense throughout my analysis (in response to the existing scholarly conversation), it is worth noting that theoretical work on the concept of metaphor has pointed to more robust and variegated understandings of the term. As Thomas McLaughlin argues in an essay on figurative language (of which metaphor is one very important instance), "The systems of meaning and value that make figures possible also produce our way of looking at the world." This point in fact has a certain resonance with my emphasis on the culturally productive aspects of rhetoric as discussed below. See Thomas McLaughlin, "Figurative Language," in *Critical Terms for Literary Study*, ed. Frank Lentricchia and Thomas McLaughlin, 2nd ed. (Chicago: University of Chicago Press, 1995), 87. Also George Lakoff and Mark Johnson, *Metaphors We Live By* (Chicago: University of Chicago Press, 1980).

36. Feldmeier, *Die Christen als Fremde*, 104, my translation from German original. Here Feldmeier is directly in conversation with Elliott's position. The monograph includes an appendix devoted to critiquing Elliott's thesis.

37. Feldmeier, " 'Nation' of Strangers," 258.

38. Feldmeier, " 'Nation' of Strangers," 257, 61. See also Feldmeier's argument for how this social marginalization could be put to missionary advantage in Reinhard Feldmeier, "Die Außenseiter als Avantgarde: Gesellschaftliche Ausgrenzung als missionarische Chance nach dem 1. Petrusbrief," in *Persuasion and Dissuasion in Early Christianity, Ancient Judaism and Hellenism*, ed. Pieter W. van der Horst et al. (Leuven: Peeters, 2003).

39. Though note that in his more recent work, Elliott has backed off from the stringency of his earlier position, admitting that "it is neither necessary nor advisable to require an absolute distinction between literal and figurative usage with respect to these Petrine terms." Instead he argues for a historical process in which a move toward metaphorical usage was based in the experience of *some* Christians as legal resident-aliens and strangers. This modified position allows Elliott to acknowledge the figurative implications of the alien language of 1 Peter for a broader Christian audience in Asia Minor. At the same time, he is able to maintain his emphasis on an original group of actual aliens (and by extension, the sociolegal reality of the *paroikos/oikos* correlation), as well as the text's "predominantly social rather than cosmological perspective." Elliott, *1 Peter*, 481–82. See also the new introduction (esp. xxix–xxx) to the paperback edition of *Home for the Homeless* (Eugene, Ore.: Wipf & Stock, 2005).

40. To summarize a complex conversation (admittedly in overly broad strokes), one can argue that on a sociohistorical level, the Petrine alien topos refers to: (1) The sociolegal status of the Christian community before conversion with no cosmological dualism in view—that is, legal resident aliens, not resident aliens "in the world" (à la Elliott's earlier work). (2) The changed sociolegal status of Christians *after* conversion, for which "the precarious legal status of foreigners . . . provided the closest analogy" (also without recourse to a cosmological dualism). See Paul J. Achtemeier, *1 Peter* (Minneapolis: Fortress Press, 1996), 174–75. (3) A metaphor used to make theological meaning in response to reduced social status—one that allows for a cosmological heaven-earth dualism but does not emphasize it (à la Feldmeier). (4) A metaphor focusing primarily on the sociological implications of the Petrine Christians' nonconformist, alienated status with any possible cosmological implications pushed into the background; see Goppelt, *1 Peter*, 61–76; Senior, "Conduct," 428. (5) A metaphor that *does* emphasize the terminology's potential cosmological and eschatological implications. See Chin, "Heavenly Home," 96–112. (6) An original legal scenario that in time came to have metaphorical and cosmological implications for a broader audience (à la Elliott's later work—see discussion in the previous note).

41. David Balch, "Hellenization/Acculturation in 1 Peter," in *Perspectives on 1 Peter*, ed. Charles H. Talbert, NABPR Special Studies Series (Macon, Ga.: Mercer University Press, 1986), 84–86, 96.

42. Balch, "Hellenization," 87 (citing van Unnik).

43. Balch, "Hellenization," 90, 98–100. As Balch elaborates, "This Christological story was the identity symbol and remained so for Christians, unlike the Roman household *ethos*. I am not emphasizing a mental *idea*. The key identity symbol was a *mythos* not an *ethos*, a sacred story, not a domestic political institution, Christology not codified ethics." See Balch, "Hellenization," 100, emphasis original.

44. On the primacy of *psychē* over *sarx* as a philosophically conventional trope in the ancient world, see further discussion in Chapter 3.

45. Elisabeth Schüssler Fiorenza, *Rhetoric and Ethic: The Politics of Biblical Studies* (Minneapolis: Fortress Press, 1999), 93.

46. Elliott, *Home for the Homeless*, 4–5.

47. For general overviews of the move to sociology in biblical studies and early Christianity in the late 1970s and early 1980s, see Daniel J. Harrington, "Sociological Concepts and the Early Church: A Decade of Research," *TS* 41 (1980); Jonathan Z. Smith, "The Social Description of Early Christianity," *RelSRev* 1 (1975). Important studies that exemplify this scholarly shift include John Gager, *Kingdom and Community: The Social World of Early Christianity* (Englewood Cliffs, N.J.: Prentice-Hall, 1975); Wayne A. Meeks, *The First Urban Christians: The Social World of the Apostle Paul* (New Haven, Conn.: Yale University Press, 1983); Gerd Theissen, *Soziologie der Jesusbewegung: Ein Beitrag zur Entstehungsgeschichte des Urchristentums* (Munich: Kaiser, 1977).

48. Elizabeth Clark, *History, Theory, Text: Historians and the Linguistic Turn* (Cambridge, Mass.: Harvard University Press, 2004), 159. Note that Clark is concerned with a different time period and set of texts within early Christianity, and as such drives a mild interpretive wedge between many earlier materials (such as the texts of the New Testament) and "the long, rhetorically ornate texts of second- to fifth-century Christianity," which she characterizes as "high literary." Clark, *History, Theory, Text*, 7, 166. Yet I would argue (while not necessarily questioning the usefulness of the distinction) that Clark's incisive appraisal of the insights to be

gleaned from theoretical developments in recent critical historiography also has applicability for earlier Christian texts such as those dealt with in this book.

49. Clark, *History, Theory, Text*, 161.

50. A full overview of the diverse intellectual and historiographical trajectories that are often classified as "New Historicism" falls beyond the scope of this inquiry. For a general introduction (with an eye to the relevance of New Historicism for biblical studies), see Gina Hens-Piazza, *The New Historicism* (Minneapolis: Fortress Press, 2002). Also helpful are the essays in H. Aram Vesser, ed., *The New Historicism* (New York: Routledge, 1989). For an accessible example of New Historicism in practice, see Catherine Gallagher and Stephen Greenblatt, *Practicing New Historicism* (Chicago: University of Chicago Press, 2000).

51. For a discussion of this turn in relation to the study of religion (in this case with particular reference to women's and gender studies), see Elizabeth Clark, "Engendering the Study of Religion," in *The Future of the Study of Religion: Proceedings of Congress 2000*, ed. Slavica Jakelic and Lori Pearson (Leiden: Brill, 2004), 217–42. Also in the same volume Amy Hollywood, "Agency and Evidence in Feminist Studies of Religion: A Response to Elizabeth Clark," 243–49.

52. Gabrielle M. Spiegel, *The Past as Text: The Theory and Practice of Medieval Historiography* (Baltimore: Johns Hopkins Press, 1997), 16.

53. Michel Foucault, *The Archaeology of Knowledge and the Discourse on Language*, trans. A. M. Sheridan Smith (New York: Pantheon, 1972), 209 (emphasis added).

54. I draw this phrase from Martin Jay, "Should Intellectual History Take a Linguistic Turn?: Reflections on the Habermas-Gadamer Debate," in *Modern European Intellectual History: Reappraisals and New Perspectives*, ed. Dominick LaCapra and Steven L. Kaplan (Ithaca, N.Y.: Cornell University Press, 1982), 86. However, this is terminology that appears frequently in current discussions of the history of historiography. Cf. Robert F. Berkhofer, *Beyond the Great Story: History as Text and Discourse* (Cambridge, Mass.: Harvard University Press, 1995), 29.

55. Here Elizabeth Clark's metonymic phrase functions as a placeholder for the broader group of social-scientific methodologies and approaches that have been appropriated by scholars of biblical studies and early Christianity. Theorists specifically in view include Mary Douglas, Victor Turner, and Clifford Geertz. See Clark, *History, Theory, Text*, 158.

56. Pierre Bourdieu, *The Field of Cultural Production: Essays on Art and Literature* (Cambridge: Polity Press, 1993), 178–79.

57. Pierre Bourdieu and Loïc J. D. Wacquant, *An Invitation to Reflexive Sociology* (Chicago: University of Chicago Press, 1992), 16–17.

58. Bourdieu and Wacquant, *Reflexive Sociology*, 96.

59. Bourdieu, *Field of Cultural Production*, 181, emphasis original.

60. Bourdieu, *Field of Cultural Production*, 181.

61. Bourdieu and Wacquant, *Reflexive Sociology*, 98, emphasis original. See also Bourdieu and Wacquant, *Reflexive Sociology*, 19.

62. Bourdieu and Wacquant, *Reflexive Sociology*, 98, emphasis original.

63. Bourdieu and Wacquant, *Reflexive Sociology*, 99, emphasis original.

64. Bourdieu and Wacquant, *Reflexive Sociology*, 99.

65. Pierre Bourdieu, *The Logic of Practice*, trans. Richard Nice (Stanford, Calif.: Stanford University Press, 1990), 53.

66. Bourdieu and Wacquant, *Reflexive Sociology*, 126.

67. Pierre Bourdieu, *Outline of a Theory of Practice*, trans. Richard Nice (Cambridge: Cambridge University Press, 1977), 72.

68. Translated in Bourdieu and Wacquant, *Reflexive Sociology*, 22–23, emphasis in translation. For original, see Pierre Bourdieu, *Choses dites* (Paris: Éditions de Minuit, 1987), 96.

69. Bourdieu and Wacquant, *Reflexive Sociology*, 126, emphasis original.

70. Bourdieu and Wacquant, *Reflexive Sociology*, 19.

71. Pierre Bourdieu, *Language and Symbolic Power*, trans. Gino Raymond and Matthew Adamson (Cambridge, Mass.: Harvard University Press, 1991), 38.

72. Bourdieu, *Language and Symbolic Power*, 66, emphasis original.

73. See J. L. Austin, *How To Do Things with Words*, 2nd ed. (Cambridge, Mass.: Harvard University Press, 1975).

74. Bourdieu, *Language and Symbolic Power*, 72 (emphasis original).

75. Bourdieu, *Field of Cultural Production*, 179.

76. Bourdieu, *Field of Cultural Production*, 176.

77. Bourdieu, *Field of Cultural Production*, 183–84.

78. Bourdieu, *Language and Symbolic Power*, 130.

79. Bourdieu, *Language and Symbolic Power*, 133.

80. Bourdieu, *Language and Symbolic Power*, 170.

81. Bourdieu and Wacquant, *Reflexive Sociology*, 119.

82. Bourdieu, *Language and Symbolic Power*, 170.

83. V. N. Voloshinov, *Marxism and the Philosophy of Language*, trans. Ladislav Matejka and I. R. Titunick (Cambridge, Mass.: Harvard University Press, 1986), 105. Bakhtin scholars have debated whether or not certain key texts attributed to Pavel Medvedev and Valentin Voloshinov were in fact authored by Bakhtin himself. While Bakhtinian authorship of these texts was accepted by Clark and Holquist in their important biographical study of the Russian literary theorist, current scholarship on Bakhtin for the most part considers this theory disproved. See Katerina Clark and Michael Holquist, *Mikhail Bakhtin* (Cambridge, Mass.: Harvard University Press, 1984), 146–70; Carol A. Newsom, "Bakhtin," in *Handbook of Postmodern Biblical Interpretation*, ed. A. K. M. Adam (St. Louis: Chalice Press, 2000), 21. Regardless how one settles the authorship question, however, the above quote remains a succinct and apposite expression of a general methodological orientation found in Bakhtin's work.

84. Richard Rorty, "The Pragmatist's Progress," in *Interpretation and Overinterpretation*, ed. Stefano Collini (Cambridge: Cambridge University Press, 1992), 97.

85. Stanley Fish, *Is There a Text in This Class? The Authority of Interpretive Communities* (Cambridge, Mass.: Harvard University Press, 1980), 345.

86. Roland Barthes, "The Death of the Author," in *Image, Music, Text*, trans. Stephen Heath (London: Fontana, 1977), 147–48.

87. Roland Barthes, *S/Z*, trans. Richard Miller (New York: Hill and Wang, 1970), 3.

88. Graham Allen, *Intertextuality* (London: Routledge, 2000), 73.

89. Here I appeal to "cultural code" in a broad sense without employing the technical (and admittedly arbitrary) distinctions in coding evidenced in Barthes's own analysis of Balzac's *Sarrasine* in *S/Z*.

90. Umberto Eco, "Overinterpreting Texts," in *Interpretation and Overinterpretation*, ed. Stefano Collini (Cambridge: Cambridge University Press, 1992), 64.

91. Eco, "Overinterpreting Texts," 65. Here we need not limit the *intentio operis* to a single model reader. Eco notes in the same volume that "when a text is produced not for a single addressee but for a community of readers . . . the author knows that he or she will be interpreted not according to his or her intentions but according to a complex strategy of interactions which also involves readers,

along with their competence in language as a social treasury." Umberto Eco "Between Author and Text," in *Interpretation and Overinterpretation*, 67.

92. Umberto Eco, *The Limits of Interpretation* (Bloomington: Indiana University Press, 1990), 52.

93. Eco, "Overinterpreting Texts," 66.

94. Eco, "Between Author and Text," 88.

95. On the contemporary level, we see an interesting example of this in the way that many scholars read a "pilgrim theology" (drawn from other parts of a larger cultural field) into uses of the alien topos that do not signal it explicitly. (See Elliott's discussion of this phenomenon above, n34.) It is not unreasonable to imagine that similar types of intertextual synthesis took place in actual reading practices with respect to the alien topos in antiquity as well.

Chapter 1. Citizens and Aliens

Epigraph: Lucian, *My Native Land* 8 (Harmon, LCL).

1. Following ancient usage, I group these terms together as part of a single topos. But the terms are in fact not precise synonyms and carry different (if overlapping) valences, thus contributing to the connotative complexity of the topos as a whole.

2. On the applicability of the latter two terms to Greco-Roman antiquity, see below.

3. For a fascinating discussion of the historical relationship between the term "parasite" and notions of otherness, see Jonathan Z. Smith, "What a Difference a Difference Makes," in *"To See Ourselves as Others See Us": Christians, Jews, "Others" in Late Antiquity*, ed. Jacob Neusner and Ernest S. Frerichs (Chico, Calif.: Scholars Press, 1985), 5–14.

4. I take this point and this use of the term "blurriness" from Denise Buell. See especially Denise Kimber Buell, *Why This New Race: Ethnic Reasoning in Early Christianity* (New York: Columbia University Press, 2005), 153. For a somewhat differently oriented take on this same problem, see David Konstan, "*To Hellenikon ethnos*: Ethnicity and the Construction of Ancient Greek Identity," in *Ancient Perceptions of Greek Ethnicity*, ed. Irad Malkin (Washington, D.C.: Center for Hellenic Studies/Harvard University Press, 2001), 30–31.

5. Buell, *New Race*, 32.

6. Daniel Boyarin, *Intertextuality and the Reading of Midrash* (Bloomington: Indiana University Press, 1990), 12. Though Barthes's notion of "cultural codes" (as glossed by Boyarin) is a helpful one, note that Barthes himself is not so interested in *limitations* to meaning (the ways that cultural codes constrain), but puts much greater emphasis on the open-ended and infinite nature of this interplay (thus my recourse to a more explicitly sociological and historical orientation toward language and culture such as Bourdieu's). See Roland Barthes, *S/Z*, trans. Richard Miller (New York: Hill and Wang, 1970); Barthes, "Theory of the Text," in *Untying the Text: A Post-Structuralist Reader*, ed. Robert Young (Boston: Routledge & Kegan Paul, 1981), 31–47.

7. Bourdieu defines this more specifically as "a kind of system of common reference which causes contemporary directors [i.e., cultural producers], even when they do not consciously refer to each other, to be objectively situated in relation to the others, to the extent that they are all interrelated as a function

of the same system of intellectual coordinates and points of reference." Pierre Bourdieu, *The Field of Cultural Production: Essays on Art and Literature* (Cambridge: Polity Press, 1993), 176–77. Here the reference to theatrical production can be taken as illustrative of a more general point.

8. Bourdieu, *Field of Cultural Production*, 176.

9. In 212 c.e., the Emperor Caracalla issued the Antonine Constitution, making citizenship universal for the entire free population throughout the Empire. With this decree, the Roman citizenship quickly ceased to be an issue of much practical and/or legal importance—and other inside/outsider categories such as free versus slave and *honestiores* versus *humiliores* took on an increasing significance. But even after Caracalla's edict, it is unlikely that the category's connotation of definitive insider status shifted very much. While *politically* the "whole world" may have become citizens, the binary opposition of citizen versus foreigner-stranger would have nonetheless remained viable as a sociorhetorical tool for making meaning and demarcating difference. On the historical details, see Michael Crawford, "Citizenship, Roman," *OCD* 334; Adrian N. Sherwin-White, "The Roman Citizenship: A Survey of Its Development into a World Franchise," *ANRW* I.2 (1972): 54–56; Colin Wells, *The Roman Empire*, 2nd ed. (Cambridge, Mass.: Harvard University Press, 1992), 214–15, 66.

10. While the legal rights and status of women in the Roman Empire is a complex question to which there can be no monolithic answer, in general, a woman's status was embedded in the status of the male to whom she was attached. Thus Roman women could be of citizen status without being citizens in the fullest legal sense.

11. See Plato, *Laws* 737–43; Aristotle, *Politics*, esp. 1265–77, 1326–32. On the history of citizenship in the Athenian *polis* and other classical city-states, see John Kenyon Davies, "Citizenship, Greek," *OCD* 333–34; Philip Brook Manville, *The Origins of Citizenship in Ancient Athens* (Princeton, N.J.: Princeton University Press, 1990); Peter Riesenberg, *Citizenship in the Western Tradition: Plato to Rousseau* (Chapel Hill: University of North Carolina Press, 1992).

12. In this way, the political freedoms and limitations of other groups (defined as various shades and degrees of the "un-citizen") were determined with respect to the category of Athenian citizenship. These groups included slaves, freedmen, and metics/*paroikoi* (noncitizen foreigners living in Athens). In the broader Greek context, also worthy of mention is the category of *perioikoi*, a designation for "neighbouring people frequently constituting groups of subjects or half-citizens, normally with local self government; but it could also be applied to outright slaves." Though *perioikoi* could be found in multiple locales in Greece, they are best known in association with Sparta. See Paul Cartledge, "Periokoi," *OCD* 1140–41.

13. Davies, "Citizenship, Greek," 334.

14. Riesenberg, *Citizenship*, 52.

15. Furthermore, while legionaries were in theory supposed to be drawn exclusively from the citizenry, in actual practice, provincials were recruited and granted citizenship. See Crawford, *OCD* 334; D. B. Saddington, "Race Relations in the Early Roman Empire," *ANRW* II, 3 (1975): 128.

16. For a detailed discussion of these various routes to citizenship, see Adrian N. Sherwin-White, *The Roman Citizenship*, 2nd ed. (Oxford: Clarendon Press, 1973).

17. While the origins are obscure, by the fourth century b.c.e., Roman expansion in Italy was proceeding in the context of a group of communities called

the Latin League (of which Rome was the most powerful member). Early on Roman tribal colonies and so-called "Latin communities" lived side by side and intermixed. Indeed in this period, Roman colonists would leave Rome (and their Roman citizenship) to be part of the development of Latin communities. But in 338, a conflict arose between Rome and the Latin League, ending with the total domination of Rome, the end of the league, and the enfranchisement of the Latin communities (but note—*not* full citizenship). The third and second centuries BCE saw Italy emerge as a patchwork of Latin states as well as *socii* (allies). Through the course of the second century, the Romans became increasingly domineering toward the Latin communities and allies, treating them simply as subjects and a source of Italian manpower. Tensions rose and the result was the so-called Social War of 90–88 B.C.E., in which the communities of the Latin name and the allies/*socii* fought against the Romans. The Romans managed to divide their opposition by offering full Roman citizenship/status to the Latin communities, which they immediately accepted. The historical details are unclear, but Rome eventually offered citizenship to the allies as well and Italy became united as a Roman state. See Crawford, *OCD* 334–35; Henrik Mouritsen, *Italian Unification: A Study in Ancient and Modern Historiography* (London: Institute of Classical Studies, School of Advanced Study, University of London, 1998); Riesenberg, *Citizenship*, 71–73; Sherwin-White, *The Roman Citizenship*; Sherwin-White, "Roman Citizenship: A Survey," 23–58.

18. Besides these three, other auxiliary categories added further complexity to the system. For example, rather than advancing up the scale on its own, a community could be assigned to a neighboring *municipium* by *attributio*. It would then be administered and overseen by means of its attachment to another entity within the system. See Saddington, "Race Relations," 127. Another term, *peregrini*, was used to designate the free citizens of foreign states with whom Rome had made treaties. While Rome effectively controlled these areas, their populations made up a different category (foreigners), one not explicitly situated in the system of advancement. But usage of the term *peregrini* was also somewhat fluid and could refer to communities that were in fact eventually transformed into Roman citizens via Latin status or promotion to the level of a *municipium.* See Sherwin-White, *The Roman Citizenship*, 268–69; Sherwin-White, "Roman Citizenship: A Survey," 42.

19. Primarily in the western provinces, this most commonly took the form of transitioning from the lowest grade under the Roman aegis, *civitas* (pl. *civitates*), to the status of a *municipium.* Scholars debate the precise significance of this move. According to D. B. Saddington, the promotion from *civitas* to *municipium* in effect "gave citizenship to existing communities. Generally this was in recognition of the fact that the community concerned had reached an adequate level of Roman culture. The readiness of the Romans to grant this status was a powerful incentive for local communities in the provinces to model their institutions on the Roman pattern." Saddington, "Race Relations," 126. But Sherwin-White summarizes a counter-position, which maintains that the use of the term *municipium* in provincial documents of the early Empire more commonly refers to the granting of Latin status rather than full Roman citizenship. Sherwin-White, "Roman Citizenship: A Survey," 40–41. Above the *municipium* stood the grade of *colonia*, designating a community of Roman citizens who colonized a particular area, setting it up so as to mimic/encapsulate the government and civic space of Rome (though communities could also apply for promotion to this status, the eventual result being a certain number of provincial colonies that were not

originally settled by Roman citizens). At first provincial *coloniae* were not particularly prestigious, but emerged out of a straightforward political and logistical necessity: there was a need to provide discharged legionaries with land upon retirement. But by the time of Trajan (98–117 C.E.), the *coloniae* had become "the summit of civic dignity in the provincial system . . . regarded, with the ever increasing Romanisation of the western provinces, as the highest grade of civic promotion." Sherwin-White, "Roman Citizenship: A Survey," 44–45. Admittedly this generalization operates from a very particular point of view, one oriented toward Roman imperial interests. Furthermore, the meaning and function of administrative designations such as *colonia* were not monolithic across the Empire. Susan Alcock has drawn attention to the reality of "provinces developing in different ways, at different speeds, and subject above all to a specific history of interaction with the ruling power," producing in turn a "heterogeneity of responses to Roman domination." See Susan E. Alcock, *Graecia Capta: The Landscape of Roman Greece* (Cambridge: Cambridge University Press, 1993), 221. Thus in the Greek East, for example, the *colonia* was not necessarily the highest or most desirable civic category, at least from a point of view that emphasized loyalty to the citizenship of one's city. Indeed, local response to Rome's remapping of the Greek civic landscape exhibits (in Alcock's phrase) "signs both of accommodation and of resistance." Alcock, *Graecia Capta*, 230.

20. Sherwin-White, "Roman Citizenship: A Survey," 54.

21. Cicero, *Leg.*, 2.2.5 (Keyes, LCL).

22. Jonathan Hall, *Ethnic Identity in Greek Antiquity* (Cambridge: Cambridge University Press, 1997), 19.

23. Buell, *New Race*, 13.

24. Buell, *New Race*, 13.

25. Benjamin Isaac, *The Invention of Racism in Classical Antiquity* (Princeton, N.J.: Princeton University Press, 2004), 37.

26. Isaac, *Invention of Racism*, 38.

27. Note that Isaac himself argues that race is a construct (citing recent scientific advances in blood typing and DNA analysis) but maintains that some perception of race (i.e., immutable characteristics that define group identity) was nonetheless present in antiquity: "Race, then, does not exist, but it is extremely difficult to combat the acceptance of something that does not exist and yet is widely believed to exist." Isaac, *Invention of Racism*, 30–31.

28. In addition to the monograph already cited, see also Denise Kimber Buell, "Race and Universalism in Early Christianity," *JECS* 10, 4 (2002): 429–68; Denise Kimber Buell, "Rethinking the Relevance of Race for Early Christian Self-Definition," *HTR* 94, 4 (2001): 449–76. In many ways following Buell's lead (but without resort to the terminology of "race"), see Caroline Johnson Hodge, *If Sons, Then Heirs: A Study of Kinship and Ethnicity in the Letters of Paul* (New York: Oxford University Press, 2007).

29. Buell, *New Race*, 21.

30. Buell, *New Race*, 7. See also Irad Malkin, "Introduction," in *Ancient Perceptions of Greek Ethnicity*, ed. Irad Malkin (Washington, D.C.: Center for Hellenic Studies/Harvard University Press, 2001), 1–28; Irad Malkin, *The Returns of Odysseus: Colonization and Ethnicity* (Berkeley: University of California Press, 1998), 55–61; Ann Laura Stoler, *Race and the Education of Desire: Foucault's History of Sexuality and the Colonial Order of Things* (Durham, N.C.: Duke University Press, 1995).

31. Buell, "Race and Universalism," 433.

32. Buell, *New Race*, 14.

33. Buell, *New Race*, 153.

34. For example, in his treatment of Egypt, Herodotus explains that "[Egyptian] customs are the exact opposite of other folks." As he elaborates at great length: "Among them the women run the market and shops, while the men, indoors, weave; and, in this weaving, while other people push the woof upward, the Egyptians push it down. The men carry burdens on their heads; the women carry theirs on their shoulders. The women piss standing upright, but the men do it squatting. The people ease nature's needs in the houses but eat outdoors in the streets . . . . Other people keep the daily life of animals separate from their own, but the Egyptians live theirs close together with their animals. Others live on wheat and barley, but such a diet is the greatest of disgraces to an Egyptian; they make their bread from a coarse grain, which some of them call zeia, or spelt. They knead dough with their feet but mud with their hands, and they lift dung with their hands. Other men leave their genitals as they were at birth, save such as have learned from the Egyptians; but the Egyptians circumcise. Every man has two garments, but each woman only one. The rings of their sails and the sheets are elsewhere fastened outside the boats, but the Egyptians fasten them inside. The Greeks write and calculate moving their hands from left to right, but the Egyptians from right to left. That is what they *do*, but they *say* they are moving to the right and the Greeks to the left." Herodotus, *The History* 2.35–36 (Grene, emphasis original to translation).

35. François Hartog, *The Mirror of Herodotus: The Representation of the Other in the Writing of History* (Berkeley: University of California Press, 1988), 213.

36. According to Hartog, "It is not hard to foresee that the discourse of autochthony was bound to reflect on the representation of nomadism and that the Athenian, that imaginary autochthonous being, had need of an equally imaginary nomad. The Scythian conveniently fitted the bill." Hartog, *Mirror of Herodotus*, 11.

37. Herodotus, *The History* 4.76 (Grene).

38. Herodotus, *The History* 4.76 (Grene).

39. Herodotus, *The History* 4.78 (Grene).

40. Herodotus, *The History* 4.80 (Grene).

41. See Mary Beard, "The Roman and the Foreign: The Cult of the 'Great Mother' In Imperial Rome," in *Shamanism, History and the State*, ed. Nicholas Thomas and Caroline Humphrey (Ann Arbor: University of Michigan Press, 1994), 164–90; Mary Beard et al., *Religions of Rome*, vol. 1 (Cambridge: Cambridge University Press, 1998); Robert Turcan, *The Cults of the Roman Empire*, trans. Antonia Nevill (Oxford: Blackwell, 1996); H. S. Versnel, *Inconsistencies in Greek and Roman Religion I: Ter Unus; Isis, Dionysos, Hermes; Three Studies in Henotheism* (Leiden: Brill, 1990), 96–205.

42. Hartog, *Mirror of Herodotus*, 70.

43. Hartog, *Mirror of Herodotus*, 110.

44. Hartog, *Mirror of Herodotus*, 111.

45. Michel de Certeau, *The Practice of Everyday Life*, trans. Steven Rendall (Berkeley: University of California Press, 1984), 128. On travel literature and encounter with the other in antiquity, see Colin Adams and Ray Laurence, *Travel and Geography in the Roman Empire* (New York: Routledge, 2001); Simon Goldhill, ed., *Being Greek Under Rome: Cultural Identity, the Second Sophistic, and the Development of Empire* (Cambridge: Cambridge University Press, 2001); François Hartog, *Memories of Odysseus: Frontier Tales from Ancient Greece*, trans. Janet Lloyd (Edinburgh: Edinburgh University Press, 2001); Laura Nasrallah, "Mapping the World: Jus-

tin, Tatian, Lucian, and the Second Sophistic," *HTR* 98 (2005): 283–314; James Romm, *The Edges of the Earth in Ancient Thought: Geography, Exploration, and Fiction* (Princeton, N.J.: Princeton University Press, 1992).

46. Aristotle, *Politics* 1265a (Rackham, LCL).

47. Isaac, *Invention of Racism*, 503. Of course as Isaac points out, the polarity tends to shift in the Roman period from East and West to North and South, a more suitable axis on which to propagate the notion "that Italy and Rome are sited ideally in the middle, which makes them a suitable nucleus for universal rule." See Isaac, *Invention of Racism*, 85, see also the detailed discussion at 82–101.

48. Juvenal 3.60–65 (LCL, Ramsay).

49. Juvenal, 6.511–626 (LCL, Ramsay).

50. David Noy, *Foreigners at Rome: Citizens and Strangers* (London: Duckworth, 2000), 37–48. On the political, cultural, and religious complexities of the city of Rome's diversity, see Catharine Edwards and Gregory Woolf, eds., *Rome the Cosmopolis* (Cambridge: Cambridge University Press, 2003); Jürgen Zangenberg and Michael Labahn, eds., *Christians as a Religious Minority in a Multicultural City* (London: T&T Clark, 2004).

51. Tacitus, *Germania* 15 (Hutton/Warmington, LCL).

52. Tacitus, *Germania* 4 (Hutton/Warmington, LCL); cf. also 35. For the designation of Germans as "barbarians," see *Germania* 18.

53. On the classical polarization between Greek and barbarian, see Edith Hall, *Inventing the Barbarian: Greek Self-Definition Through Tragedy* (Oxford: Clarendon Press, 1989), 1–2.

54. Hartog, *Memories*, 163.

55. On the Greek side, Arnaldo Momigliano explores the ways in which Greek historians of Rome like Polybius (c.200–118 B.C.E.) and Posidonius (c.135–151) colluded in this process, so as to become (as he argues) "agents, not only historians, of the Roman expansion. . . . By singling out the Romans as the nation with which the Greeks had the greatest natural affinity, they pushed Celts and Carthaginians into a different category. This was the category of barbarians, and Greek scholars were traditionally famous for exploring barbarian lands and making them intelligible to the civilized." Arnaldo Momigliano, *Alien Wisdom: The Limits of Hellenization* (Cambridge: Cambridge University Press, 1975), 48–49. For a recent (and more complicated) reappraisal of this dynamic, see David Konstan, ed., *Greeks on Greekness: Viewing the Greek Past Under the Roman Empire* (Cambridge: Cambridge Philological Society/Cambridge University Press, 2006).

56. Saddington, "Race Relations," 117–18.

57. See Suetonius' reference to certain Gauls as *semibarbari* in *Lives of the Caesars* 1.76.3.

58. Hartog, *Memories*, 163.

59. See Juvenal 3.60–125 (LCL, Ramsay).

60. For multiple examples of this particular ambivalence, see J. P. V. D. Balsdon, *Romans and Aliens* (London: Duckworth, 1979), 30–58. Also Mary Beard and Michael H. Crawford, *Rome in the Late Republic: Problems and Interpretations* (London: Duckworth, 1985), 12–24.

61. Momigliano, *Alien Wisdom*, 14.

62. Homi K. Bhabha, *The Location of Culture* (London: Routledge, 1994), 67 (emphasis original).

63. Tim Whitmarsh, *Greek Literature and the Roman Empire: The Politics of Imitation* (Oxford: Oxford University Press, 2001), 14–15.

64. Whitmarsh, *Greek Literature*, 18.

65. Certeau, *Practice*, 127.

66. Jan Felix Gaertner, "The Discourse of Displacement in Greco-Roman Antiquity," in *Writing Exile: The Discourse of Displacement in Greco-Roman Antiquity and Beyond*, ed. Jan Felix Gaertner (Leiden: Brill, 2007), 2–3.

67. Gaertner, "Discourse of Displacement," 9–10.

68. Hartog, *Memories*, 19.

69. Whitmarsh, *Greek Literature*, 138. Relevant Greek sources for this view in addition to Plato and Aristotle are cataloged in Ernst Doblhofer, *Exil und Emigration: Zum Erlebnis der Heimatferne in der römischen Literatur* (Darmstadt: Wissenschaftliche Buchgesellschaft, 1987), 21–40.

70. On this interplay in Roman literature, see Gaertner, "Discourse of Displacement," 4, 13–18. Also Heinz-Günther Nesselrath, "Later Greek Voices on the Predicament of Exile," in *Writing Exile: The Discourse of Displacement in Greco-Roman Antiquity and Beyond*, ed. Jan Felix Gaertner (Leiden: Brill, 2007), 87–108.

71. Cicero, *Letters to Atticus* 3.15 (Winstedt, LCL). On exile as complaint in Cicero, see Jo-Marie Claassen, *Displaced Persons: The Literature of Exile from Cicero to Boethius* (London: Duckworth, 1999), 83–85. For related themes, see also Ovid, *The Poems of Exile: Tristia and the Black Sea Letters*, trans. Peter Green (Berkeley: University of California Press, 2005).

72. Favorinus, *On Exile* 6.1–2, translation from Appendix I of Whitmarsh, *Greek Literature*, 302–24 (second bracketed phrase in original). On the traditional elements of this catalog and their presence in earlier Greek literature, see Nesselrath, "Later Greek Voices," 87–108.

73. Ps 137:1–6, NRSV.

74. Erich S. Gruen, *Diaspora: Jews Amidst Greeks and Romans* (Cambridge, MA: Harvard University Press, 2002), 5.

75. Gaertner, "Discourse of Displacement," 10.

76. Thucydides, *History of the Peloponnesian War* 5.26 (Warner).

77. Diogenes Laertius, *Lives of Eminent Philosophers* 6.49 (Hicks, LCL).

78. See Gaertner's critique of Claassen for attributing too much originality to Roman writers like Cicero and Ovid, thereby missing the importance of the earlier Greek tradition to their reflections on exile. Gaertner, "Discourse of Displacement," 14–16.

79. Cicero, *Tusculan Disputations* 5.107–8 (King, LCL).

80. Seneca, *Consolation to Helvia* 5.6–6.1 (Basore, LCL).

81. Seneca, *Consolation to Helvia* 8.5 (Basore, LCL).

82. Whitmarsh, *Greek Literature*, 135.

83. On Greek writers' construction of themselves as exiles in relation to Roman power, see Tim Whitmarsh, " 'Greece Is the World': Exile and Identity in the Second Sophistic," in *Being Greek Under Rome: Cultural Identity, the Second Sophistic and the Development of Empire*, ed. Simon Goldhill (Cambridge: Cambridge University Press, 2001), 269–305; Whitmarsh, *Greek Literature*, 133–80. Whitmarsh argues with reference to the Second Sophistic that writers on exile "strategically reorient the language of cultural self-definition which was current in [an] earlier period, reconfiguring (sometimes explicitly) the relationship between self and polis in terms more appropriate to the enormous world-empire of the Roman principate. . . . The language of exile thus also implies a polemical engagement with Roman power, and the vaunted transcendence of humiliation and suffering imposed by exile advertises the philosopher's superiority to imperial dominion."

Whitmarsh, "Greece Is the World," 271, 275. Whitmarsh's argument examines the following treatises: Musionius Rufus, *That Exile is Not an Evil*; Dio Chrysostom, *On Exile (13th Oration)*; Favorinus, *On Exile*.

84. The historicity of some of these claims has been questioned. On the problem of Favorinus's exile, see Claassen, *Displaced Persons*, 271n121; Whitmarsh, *Greek Literature*, 168–9. On the possibility of a "fiction of exile" in Ovid, see Claassen, *Displaced Persons*, 34, 295n88.

85. I take the term from Whitmarsh, *Greek Literature*, 139.

86. Judith Butler, *Excitable Speech: A Politics of the Performative* (New York: Routledge, 1997), 14.

87. Butler, *Excitable Speech*, 1.

88. Empedocles was a philosopher who lived c.484–424 BCE. See Diogenes Laertius 8.51–77.

89. Plutarch, *Mor.* 607 (de Lacy and Einarson, LCL).

90. Whitmarsh, *Greek Literature*, 138.

91. For the latter, see Deut 10.18, 14.29, 16.11,14 as representative.

92. For discussion and debate on the nature of this legal status in ancient Israel, see Bernhard A. Asen, "The Stranger (ger) in Old Testament Tradition," in *Christianity and the Stranger: Historical Essays* (Atlanta: Scholars Press, 1995), 16–35; Christoph Bultmann, *Der Fremde im antiken Juda: eine Untersuchung zum sozialen Typenbegriff "ger" und seinem Bedeutungswandel in der alttestamentlichen Gesetzgebung* (Göttingen: Vandenhoeck & Ruprecht, 1992); Matty Cohen, "Le 'ger' biblique et son statut socio-religieux," *RHR* 207 (1990): 131–58; Saul Olyan, *Rites and Rank: Hierarchy in Biblical Representations of Cult* (Princeton, N.J.: Princeton University Press, 2000), 63–102; F. A. Spina, "Israelites as gerim, 'Sojourners' in Social and Historical Context," in *The Word of the Lord Shall Go Forth: Essays in Honor of David Noel Freedman*, ed. Carol L. Meyers and M. O'Connor (Minona Lake, Ind.: Eisenbrauns, 1983), 321–35.

93. José E. Ramírez Kidd, *Alterity and Identity in Israel: The "ger" in the Old Testament* (Berlin: Gruyter, 1999).

94. Translations from the Hebrew are my own.

95. Kidd, *Alterity and Identity*, 83, 88–89.

96. Kidd, *Alterity and Identity*, 83, emphasis original; transliteration added. In Kidd's reconstruction, Deut 10.19 represents a generalizing tendency of the more basic principle that is applied only to Egyptians in Deut 23.8. See Kidd, *Alterity and Identity*, 89.

97. Kidd, *Alterity and Identity*, 99. Cf. also Psalm 119.19: "I am a resident-alien (*ger*) on the earth."

98. Kidd, *Alterity and Identity*, 132, transliteration added. Feldmeier also makes a similar point: "Israel does not fall apart as a result of these negative experiences [exile and diaspora] but *is able to interpret this experience of alienation theologically and thus to integrate it in its self-understanding and its relationship to God*. This comes to expression for example in the self-designation as 'strangers and sojourners' which is applied figuratively to the Israelites in the land." Reinhard Feldmeier, "The 'Nation' of Strangers: Social Contempt and Its Theological Interpretation in Ancient Judaism and Early Christianity," in *Ethnicity and the Bible*, ed. M. G. Brett (Leiden: Brill, 1996), 245, emphasis original.

99. More specifically, *prosēlytos* is used 78 times, *paroikos* eleven times, *g(e)iōras* twice, and *xenos* once. For textual references see Kidd, *Alterity and Identity*, 119. See also further detailed discussion in Luis Mercado, "The Language of Sojourning in the Abraham Midrash in Hebrews 11:8–19: Its Old Testament Basis,

Exegetical Traditions and Function in the Epistle to the Hebrews" (Th.D. dissertation, Harvard University, 1966).

100. See discussion in Kidd, *Alterity and Identity*, 119–23.

101. Another relevant parallel (albeit not one explicitly in dialogue with Hellenistic philosophical motifs) has been noted by Feldmeier in the Qumranic literature. Citing primarily the Damascus Document, he explains that "the Essenes deliberately and provocatively describe themselves as those banished to the wilderness, as those who have converted from Israel and dwell in a strange land." Feldmeier, "'Nation' of Strangers," 249. See especially CD 6:4–5: "The Well is the Law, and those who dug it were converts of Israel who went out of the land of Judah to sojourn in the land of Damascus." Translation from Geza Vermes, ed., *The Dead Sea Scrolls in English*, 4th ed. (Sheffield: Sheffield Academic Press, 1995).

102. Philo, *Conf.* 77–79, 81 (Colson, LCL), translation slightly modified.

103. LXX: "They said to Pharaoh, 'We have come to sojourn in the land. For there is no pasture for the livestock of your servants, for the famine has grown strong in the land of Canaan. Now then, let your servants settle in the land of Goshen" (*eipan de tō pharaō Paroikein en tē gē hēkamen; ou gar estin nomē tois ktēnesin tōn paidōn sou, enischysen gar ho limos en gē Chanaan; nun oun kataoikēsomen hoi paides sou en gē Gesem*). While an allusion is perhaps probable, given this loose correspondence, the decision of the Loeb editor to mark the text as a quotation seems overly optimistic.

104. Philo, *Agr.* 65 (Colson and Whitaker, LCL), translation slightly modified. Cf. *Her.* 82–85, 267. Note also the discussion in *De cherubim* where Philo's emphasis is not so much on the *valorized* status of the sojourner state as the way in which every person is a resident-alien and foreigner in comparison to God, the only true citizen (*hoti monos kyriōs ho theos politēs esti, paroikon de kai epēlyton to genēton hapan, Cher.* 121).

105. Buell, *New Race*, 153. On the problems involved in defining "religion" in Greco-Roman antiquity and in situating early Christianity as a religion, see Buell, *New Race*, 59–62. Also Beard et al., *Religions of Rome*, x–xi; Dale B. Martin, *Inventing Superstition: From the Hippocratics to the Christians* (Cambridge, Mass.: Harvard University Press, 2004), 17, 125–39.

Chapter 2. Going to Jesus "Outside the Camp": Alien Identity in Hebrews

Jonathan Z. Smith, "What a Difference a Difference Makes," in *"To See Ourselves As Others See Us": Christians, Jews, "Others" in Late Antiquity*, ed. Jacob Neusner and Ernest S. Frerichs (Chico, Calif.: Scholars Press, 1985), 10.

1. Pierre Bourdieu, *Language and Symbolic Power*, trans. Gino Raymond and Matthew Adamson (Cambridge, Mass.: Harvard University Press, 1991), 242.

2. Harold W. Attridge, *The Epistle to the Hebrews* (Philadelphia: Fortress Press, 1989), 1.

3. In antiquity, the Eastern church tended to associate Hebrews with Paul or a Pauline disciple, while in the West the text was not widely accepted as Pauline until the fifth century when backed by the authority of Augustine and Jerome. Since the Reformation, scholars have largely recognized that Hebrews cannot have been written by Paul, noting the vast differences in style, content, and theological orientation between it and the Pauline corpus. Other proposals for an

author have included Apollos, Barnabas, Priscilla, and Silas, to name a few. Many locales have also been suggested for situating the text's addressees. Palestine and Rome are the two most common, with many current scholars favoring Rome. See discussion of these and other introductory questions in Attridge, *Hebrews*, 1–13; Craig R. Koester, *Hebrews: A New Translation with Introduction and Commentary*, AB (New York: Doubleday, 2001), 41–63. For a general analysis of the structure of the text, see Albert Vanhoye, *La structure littéraire de l'Épître aux Hébreux*, 2nd ed. (Paris: Desclée de Brouwer, 1976).

4. The issues involved in dating Hebrews tend to center around the question of whether the text should be situated pre- or post-70 C.E. (the destruction of the Jerusalem temple). While numerous commentators have pointed both to the text's use of the present tense in its discussion of cultic activity and to its failure to make any reference to the temple's devastation as evidence of a pre-70 dating, it should be noted that the primary concern of Hebrews is not with the temple cult but with its precursor, the Pentateuchal tabernacle. Arguments for a post-70 date include the text's well-developed Christology and parallels with later New Testament literature such as Luke-Acts, the Pastoral Epistles, and 1 Peter. However, it is impossible to settle this question conclusively. The reference in 2.3 to an earlier generation of Christian believers implies that Hebrews does not belong to the initial years of the movement, allowing us to place it at 60 C.E. or later. The mention of Timothy in 13.23 (assuming this is in fact Timothy the companion of Paul) points to a date no later than the end of the first century. However, the *terminus ad quem* is often set even more specifically at 96 C.E., based on *1 Clement*'s supposed dependence on Hebrews. While Attridge notes that both the dependence and this dating of *1 Clement* have been challenged, he settles on 60 to 100 C.E. as "the most probable range of dates within which Hebrews was composed." See full discussion in Attridge, *Hebrews*, 6–9. Also Koester, *Hebrews*, 50–54.

5. See Lawrence Wills, "The Form of the Sermon in Hellenistic Judaism and Early Christianity," *HTR* 77 (1984): 277–99. Also C. Clifton Black, "The Rhetorical Form of the Hellenistic Jewish and Early Christian Sermon: A Response to Lawrence Wills," *HTR* 81 (1988): 1–18.

6. For a thorough discussion of Hebrews' deliberative and epideictic features, see David A. deSilva, *Perseverance in Gratitude: A Socio-Rhetorical Commentary on the Epistle "to the Hebrews"* (Grand Rapids, Mich.: Eerdmans, 2000), 46–58.

7. Ernst Käsemann, *The Wandering People of God: An Investigation of the Letter to the Hebrews*, trans. Roy A. Harrisville and Irving L. Sandberg (Minneapolis: Augsburg, 1984), 44. The rest of Käsemann's thesis, which situates the theology of Hebrews as a reworking of the "Gnostic myth of the redeemed Redeemer," has been widely discredited. As Attridge argues, "Käsemann's analysis of the [wandering] motif as Gnostic is too specific. . . . The soteriology implicit in the imagery here is commonplace in the Hellenistic world and is not the property of a single religious phenomenon such as Gnosticism." Attridge, *Hebrews*, 328 n. 7. Thus in Craig Koester's estimation, "Renewed emphasis on the pilgrimage motif, rather than his history-of-religions hypothesis, is Käsemann's abiding contribution." See Käsemann, *Wandering*, 174–82; Koester, *Hebrews*, 60–61. Note also Johnsson's later study, which builds on Käsemann's work, narrowing the scope of "wandering" to a more focused (but closely related) "pilgrimage" motif. Here Johnsson works with a phenomenological model of pilgrimage, juxtaposing it against the text's cultic language in order to characterize "the Christians of Hebrews . . . as a cultic community on the move." William G. Johnsson, "The Pilgrimage Motif in the Book of Hebrews," *JBL* 97, 2 (1978): 250.

8. P. J. Arowele, "The Pilgrim People of God—An African's Reflections on the Motif of Sojourn in the Epistle to the Hebrews," *AJT* 4 (1990): 441.

9. For a comprehensive study of the use of this term in the Septuagint as well as Greco-Roman and Hellenistic Jewish sources, see Luis Mercado, "The Language of Sojourning in the Abraham Midrash in Hebrews 11:8–19: Its Old Testament Basis, Exegetical Traditions and Function in the Epistle to the Hebrews" (Th.D. dissertation, Harvard University, 1966).

10. Here I follow post-structuralist critiques of a general source/origin orientation toward textual analysis. Foucault expresses this trend well when he problematizes "the notion of influence, which provides a support—of too magical a kind to be very amenable to analysis—for the facts of transmission and communication; which refers to an apparently causal process (but with neither rigorous delimitation nor theoretical definition) the phenomena of resemblance or repetition." Michel Foucault, *The Archaeology of Knowledge and the Discourse on Language*, trans. A. M. Sheridan Smith (New York: Pantheon, 1972), 21.

11. *Abr.* 62. Note the difference from Philo's use of the Abraham figure cited in Chapter 1.

12. I do not wish to overplay this point, given that *katoikeō* is the same verb used in Heb 11.9 to refer to Abraham, Isaac, and Jacob dwelling in tents in the land of promise. However, when each passage is looked at in context (especially the reference to a transient dwelling place such as tents in the case of Hebrews), the contrast seems clear.

13. Reinhard Feldmeier, "The 'Nation' of Strangers: Social Contempt and Its Theological Interpretation in Ancient Judaism and Early Christianity," in *Ethnicity and the Bible*, ed. M. G. Brett (Leiden: Brill, 1996), 247–48, emphasis original.

14. According to Aune, this use of *pistei* ("by faith") to structure the catalogue of *exempla* is "one of the most extensive uses of anaphora in ancient literature." David E. Aune, *The Westminster Dictionary of New Testament and Early Christian Literature and Rhetoric* (Louisville, Ky.: Westminster John Knox Press, 2003), 34.

15. Note also that this move continues to shape the patriarchal sojourning narrative to Hebrews' particular ends. Compare how this contrasts, for example, to the assertion of Gen 37.1 that Jacob settled in the land in which his father sojourned (*Katōkei de Iakōb en tē gē hou parōkēsen ho patēr autou*).

16. DeSilva, *Perseverance*, 380.

17. Here I am not positing a "Hebrews Christianity" or a singular "Hebrews community." Rather, I am using the term "community" to highlight the social and collective implications of the text's rhetorical strategy. Thus I am interested not so much in any *particular* historical community as in the function of Hebrews' rhetoric for communal identity formation, a usage that allows for the fluidity of multiple audiences and reading contexts.

18. Pamela M. Eisenbaum, *The Jewish Heroes of Christian History: Hebrews 11 in Literary Context*, SBLDS, ed. Pheme Perkins (Atlanta: Scholars Press, 1997), 87.

19. The well-known debate over the textual problems of Heb 11.11 falls beyond the scope of this inquiry.

20. Eisenbaum, *Jewish Heroes*, 161.

21. Scholars debate the precise referent of the phrase *houtoi pantes*. On the one hand, Attridge is most likely correct in his contention that it refers principally to the three patriarchs rather than all the heroes mentioned thus far (he notes that the *houtoi pantes* logically could not include Enoch who did not see death, *tou mē idein thanaton*, 11.5). See Attridge, *Hebrews*, 329. (Though note that Eisenbaum offers a counterargument that the phrase refers to all the heroes mentioned up

to this point. See Eisenbaum, *Jewish Heroes*, 160–61.) At the very least, however, we ought to consider the possibility of some sort of link between the *houtoi pantes* and the line of Abraham's descendants referenced in 11.12. The overall structure of Hebrews 11 (with its emphasis on individuals acting in faith) and the fact that the innumerable descendants are only described as an objective result of Abraham's faith (not subjects of their own action) make it unlikely that the descendants of 11.12 are meant to be the direct referent of *houtoi pantes* in 11.13. But at the same time the immediate proximity of verses 12 and 13 leaves space for readers to make a loose interpretive connection between the two. Therefore, the *houtoi pantes* may function as a rhetorical encouragement for an audience (appropriating a place in this lineage as "Abraham's descendants") to see themselves and their own community in the reinforcement of identity that is to follow.

22. Attridge, *Hebrews*, 329.

23. See the extended citations from Plutarch and Philo in Chapter 1, which appropriately illustrate this tendency.

24. For a general discussion of the unusual term *parepidēmos*, see W. Grundmann, "*Parepidēmos*," *TDNT* 2: 64–65. John Elliott contends (with reference to 1 Peter) that *parepidēmos* "refers more generally to the transient visitor who is temporarily residing as a foreigner in a given locality," in contrast to the technical-legal usage of *paroikos*. John H. Elliott, *A Home for the Homeless: A Sociological Exegesis of 1 Peter, Its Situation and Strategy* (Philadelphia: Fortress Press, 1981), 30. Attridge offers a contrasting position, focusing on the relationship between Hebrews 11.13 and the scriptural use of the expression *paroikos kai parepidēmos* (Gen 23.4, Ps 39(38).13). On his reading of 11.13, *parepidēmos* is the technical designation for "resident alien" and *xenoi* is a more evocative substitution for *paroikoi* in the scriptural phrase (cf. also the use of *xenoi kai paroikoi* in Eph 2.19).

25. Here I see a functional similarity between the rhetorical work done by this narrative of scriptural lineage and the rhetorical operation of rites of institution and investiture as analyzed by Bourdieu. See Bourdieu, *Language and Symbolic Power*, 119.

26. This question has provoked much scholarly discussion. According to Seeberg, the *homologia* ought to be understood as a fixed and standardized verbal confession of the community. Alfred Seeberg, *Der Brief an die Hebräer* (Leipzig: Quelle & Meyer, 1912), 32. Käsemann responds to this argument with slightly more caution, but does argue that "the *homologia* of Hebrews not only denotes the primitive Christian liturgy of the community, *but that in addition the Christology of Hebrews represents a detailed exposition and interpretation of the community's liturgical homologia.*" Käsemann, *Wandering*, 171, emphasis original, transliteration added. Attridge suggests a profession of faith that "took place within liturgical contexts with some formula or formulas. . . . Given the prominence of the title 'son' in Hebrews, it is likely that the community's confession of Jesus as Son of God was involved." Attridge, *Hebrews*, 108. See also Koester, *Hebrews*, 126–27.

27. In drawing this connection between this use of the verb *homologeō* and the text's earlier references to "the confession," I would not want to push Attridge's theory (see previous note) so far as to posit a liturgical formula within Hebrews' community that involved the identification of the community as strangers and sojourners (though neither is there reason to rule out this possibility).

28. Koester, *Hebrews*, 293.

29. Note the contrasting nuance between 11.15 and the more typically Middle Platonic trajectory—one which emphasizes the return of the sojourning soul to the heavenly homeland from which it set out.

30. With the exception of 13.2—see discussion below.

31. Eisenbaum, *Jewish Heroes*, 184.

32. Here "reward" functions analogously to the various "entrance" metaphors already used—i.e., one gains it through solidarity with the text's constructed margins.

33. This appeal to a *polis* resonates with the notion of a "true citizenship" already implicit in 11.16.

34. The contention of some scholars that chapter 13 is a secondary addition is unconvincing, especially given key aspects of literary unity with the rest of the text, such as will be examined below. For a brief overview, see Attridge, *Hebrews*, 384–85.

35. Attridge, *Hebrews*, 397.

36. Helmut Koester, "'Outside the Camp': Hebrews 13:9–14," *HTR* 55 (1962): 300, emphasis original.

37. Cf. *Ebr.* 100, *Gig.* 54, *Leg.* 2, 54–55, *Det.* 160.

38. James Moffatt, *A Critical and Exegetical Commentary on the Epistle to the Hebrews* (New York: Scribner's, 1924), 235, transliteration added. See also as representative, Herbert Braun, *An die Hebräer*, HNT (Tübingen: J.C.B. Mohr (Paul Siebeck), 1984), 467; Gerd Theissen, *Untersuchungen zum Hebräerbrief*, StNT (Gütersloh: Mohn, 1969), 104.

39. F. F. Bruce, *The Epistle to the Hebrews*, NICNT (Grand Rapids, Mich.: Eerdmans, 1964), 403. Other representative examples include Floyd V. Filson, *"Yesterday": A Study of Hebrews in the Light of Chapter 13* (Naperville, Ill.: Alec. Allenson, 1967), 60–65; Philip E. Hughes, *A Commentary on the Epistle to the Hebrews* (Grand Rapids, Mich.: Eerdmans, 1977), 580.

40. Koester, "Outside," 303.

41. See the full discussion in Attridge, *Hebrews*, 394–96.

42. In this case, it is not just my methodological orientation that necessitates the move to readers and multiple interpretive possibilities. Rather, the possibility of various interpretations seems to be an actual part of the text's strategy, characterized by Attridge in terms of its "deliberate ambiguity." See Attridge, *Hebrews*, 396.

43. Roland Barthes, "Theory of the Text," in *Untying the Text: A Post-Structuralist Reader*, ed. Robert Young (Boston: Routledge & Kegan Paul, 1981), 42.

44. Robin Lane Fox, *Pagans and Christians* (San Francisco: HarperCollins, 1986), 89.

45. Here Beard et al. offer the example of Augustus "banning Egyptian rites within the *pomerium*—so 'restoring' (or maybe 'inventing') a principle that the worship of foreign gods should not occur within the sacred boundary of Rome"; Mary Beard et al., *Religions of Rome*, vol. 1 (Cambridge: Cambridge University Press, 1998), 180. Note also that the Roman *coloniae* in the first and second centuries C.E. modeled their own religious institutions on those of the capital, including the establishment of a sacred boundary. Thus the connotative significance of the *pomerium* would have extended far beyond the city of Rome itself. See Beard et al., *Religions of Rome*, 328–29.

46. Mary Beard, "The Roman and the Foreign: The Cult of the 'Great Mother' in Imperial Rome," in *Shamanism, History and the State*, ed. Nicholas Thomas and Caroline Humphrey (Ann Arbor: University of Michigan Press, 1994), 181.

47. For the former option, see the approach in Cyril Bailey, *Phases in the Religion of Ancient Rome* (Westport, Conn.: Greenwood Press, 1972), 183. The latter position is well expressed by Maarten Vermaseren: "The Romans had brought their

ancestral Goddess ["ancestral" in light of Rome's traditional connection to Troy] to the new country and provided her with proper accommodation, only then to discover how widely and profoundly their own attitude differed from the Asian mentality. They were shocked by the Eastern rites, with their loud ululations and wild dances, with their entrancing rhythms, which by pipe and tambourine whipped up the people into ecstasies of bloody self-flagellation and self-injury." Maarten J. Vermaseren, *Cybele and Attis: The Myth and the Cult*, trans. A. M. H. Lemmers (London: Thames and Hudson, 1977), 96. Cf. also Franz Cumont, *The Oriental Religions in Roman Paganism* (New York: Dover Publications, 1956), 51–53; John Ferguson, *The Religions of the Roman Empire* (Ithaca, N.Y.: Cornell University Press, 1970), 27; H. H. Scullard, *Festivals and Ceremonies of the Roman Republic* (Ithaca, N.Y.: Cornell University Press, 1981), 21.

48. Beard, "Roman and the Foreign," 166.

49. Nor does the relevance of this Magna Mater example rely on following current scholarly trends to locate Hebrews in the city of Rome. Though I am sympathetic to this position, locating the text any more specifically than the Roman Empire in the late first century C.E. is immaterial to the point I seek to make here.

50. Suggestions for the referent of this *thysiastērion* have included the eucharist, the cross/Christ's death and the heavenly sanctuary of Heb 8–9. See discussion in Koester, *Hebrews*, 568–69.

51. Beard et al., *Religions of Rome*, 166.

52. Koester, "Outside," 302.

53. Cf. Gen 18.1–8, Homer *Od.* 17.485–87, Ovid *Metam.* 8.626ff.

54. See for example, Koester, *Hebrews*, 565.

55. See the approach in Attridge, *Hebrews*, 386–88.

56. Denise Kimber Buell, *Why This New Race: Ethnic Reasoning in Early Christianity* (New York: Columbia University Press, 2005), 61.

57. For example, the Qumran community, Philo's Therapeutae (as described in *De Vita Contemplativa*), or more radical forms of Cynicism.

58. Wayne A. Meeks, *The Origins of Christian Morality: The First Two Centuries* (New Haven, Conn.: Yale University Press, 1993), 37.

59. See discussion in the Introduction and R. Laurence Moore, *Religious Outsiders and the Making of Americans* (Oxford: Oxford University Press, 1986), 46.

60. Ceslas Spicq, *L'Épître aux Hébreux*, 2 vols., EBib (Paris: Gabalda, 1952), 1.243.

61. According to Reinhard Feldmeier, "ancient society saw [the early Christians] as *a foreign body*, whose very existence jeopardised its foundations, whose spread disturbed peace and order, and hence in every respect, *had destructive effects*." Feldmeier, "'Nation' of Strangers," 255–56, emphasis original. In a similar vein, Attridge argues, "The image of the sojourning strangers, Abraham, Sarah, Isaac, Jacob, and Joseph (11:8–22), buoyed by their hopes for a true heavenly homeland, is neither a description of the technical legal situation of the addressees, nor is it purely metaphorical, describing the state of the soul lost in the world of matter . . . . It is, rather, an appropriate image for a community that has suffered the social ostracism and obloquy described in chapter 10." Harold W. Attridge, "Paraenesis in a Homily: The Possible Location of, and Socialization in, the 'Epistle to the Hebrews'," *Semeia* 50 (1990): 219.

62. Thus P. J. Arowele argues, "The concept of the pilgrim church was an important ecclesiological development, arising . . . from the need to re-define the church's self-understanding in the world in the circumstances of the delayed par-

ousia. With it, the church was no longer simply the community of those anxiously expecting the end of the world but a body which must live through a long period of striving and witnessing on earth." Arowele, "Pilgrim People," 449.

63. Foucault, *Archaeology*, 47.

64. Thanks to Virginia Burrus for helping me with this formulation.

65. Bourdieu, *Language and Symbolic Power*, 105.

66. Judith Perkins, *The Suffering Self: Pain and Narrative Representation in the Early Christian Era* (London: Routledge, 1995), 9.

67. Bourdieu, *Language and Symbolic Power*, 119–20. Here Bourdieu's interest is in ritual acts of institution. Following the general contours of his philosophy of language, however, I argue that the reiteration of a narrative can function in a similar way—particularly when a community comes to view a text as sacred or otherwise authoritative.

Chapter 3. Outsiders by Virtue of Outdoing: The Epistle to Diognetus

1. John Elliott, for example, drives an interpretive wedge between the two canonical texts, 1 Peter and Hebrews, arguing that 1 Peter uses the alien topos in a "literal-legal" sense while Hebrews roots its usage in Platonic cosmology. He then reads the late first- and second-century evidence in light of this split. In this way, Elliott is able to assign the epistolary prescript evidence of *1 Clement* to the trajectory of 1 Peter, while placing *2 Clement* 5 and *Diognetus* 5–6 in the conceptual stream of Hebrews. See John H. Elliott, *1 Peter: A New Translation with Introduction and Commentary*, AB (New York: Doubleday, 2000), 482–83. Other scholars take a more generalized view: by not reading the alien motifs of 1 Peter and Hebrews in tension with one another, they are able to take the second-century evidence as simply part of the broader *Wirkungsgeschichte* of the New Testament texts. See, for example, Johannes Roldanus, "Références patristiques au 'chrétien-étranger' dans les trois premiers siècles," *CBP* 1 (1987): 27–52. Note, however, that while Roldanus frames his discussion in terms of how "cette conscience . . . s'inspirait de quelques textes néotestamentaires qui attestent notamment la condition d'étranger du croyant" (27), his analysis of pre-Irenaean second-century texts is also cognizant of the lack of direct biblical citations in these texts. Roldanus solves this problematic tension in his mildly source-critical approach by resorting to terms such as "echo," "allusion," and "key-word" (*mots-clés*) in order to understand and situate second-century evidence such as that found in *2 Clement*, *Diognetus*, and *Hermas* (see 29–30, 33–34).

2. *Diognetus* is difficult to date with certainty, but is generally placed in the later second century (sometimes early third), based on internal affinities with the genre of second-century Christian apologetic. See Robert M. Grant, *Greek Apologists of the Second Century* (Philadelphia: Westminster Press, 1988), 178–79; Clayton N. Jeffords, *Reading the Apostolic Fathers* (Peabody, Mass.: Hendrickson, 1996), 162. For the purposes of this analysis, I follow the general scholarly trend to treat *Diognetus* as a mid/late second-century apologetic text. The project at hand does not require any greater specificity, and in any event attempts to situate the text more precisely in terms of chronology or authorship have proven speculative and unconvincing. See, for example, P. Andriessen, "The Authorship of the Epistula ad Diognetum," *VC* 1 (1947): 129–36; L.W. Barnard, "The Epistle Ad Diognetum: Two Units from One Author?" *ZNW* 56 (1964): 136–37; R. H. Connolly, "The Date and Authorship of the Epistle to Diognetus," *JTS* 36 (1935): 347–53; Grant, *Apologists*, 178.

3. The *editio princeps* was published in 1592 by Henri Estienne (Stephanus), derived from an earlier transcription. See discussion in Bart D. Ehrman, ed., *The Apostolic Fathers*, 2 vols., LCL (Cambridge, Mass.: Harvard University Press, 2003), 2.128–29. Modern editions of the Greek text include E. H. Blakeney, *The Epistle to Diognetus* (London: Society for Promoting Christian Knowledge, 1943); Ehrman, ed., *Apostolic Fathers*, 2.121–59; Kirsopp Lake, *The Apostolic Fathers*, 2 vols., LCL (Cambridge, Mass.: Harvard University Press, 1913), 2.347–79; Henri-Irénée Marrou, *À Diognète*, SC (Paris: Cerf, 1951); Henry G. Meecham, *The Epistle to Diognetus: The Greek Text with Introduction, Translation and Notes* (Manchester: Manchester University Press, 1949); J. J. Thierry, *The Epistle to Diognetus*, Textus minores (Leiden: Brill, 1964); Klaus Wengst, *Didache (Apostellehre), Barnabasbrief, Zweiter Klemensbrief, Schrift an Diognet*, Schriften des Urchristentums (Darmstadt: Wissenschaftliche Buchgesellschaft, 1984). For a brief overview of introductory issues and secondary literature in English, see Jeffords, *Apostolic Fathers*, 159–69. For a much more extensive catalogue of scholarly literature in multiple languages (as well as a more complete list of Greek editions), see Enrico Norelli, *A Diogneto: Introduzione, traduzione, e note*, Letture cristiane del primo millennio (Milan: Figlie di S. Paolo, 1991), 65–71. I am greatly indebted to Taylor Petrey in this analysis for his help with the translation of several important secondary texts on *Diognetus* written in Italian.

4. See discussion in Adolf von Harnack, *Geschichte der altchristlichen Literatur bis Eusebius*, 2 vols., 2nd ed. (Leipzig: Hinrichs, 1958), 1.515; Wengst, *Didache*, 287–90. For various scholarly positions on the authorship question in the later fragment, see Barnard, "Two Units," 130–37; R. H. Connolly, "Ad Diognetum xi–xii," *JTS* 37 (1936): 2–15; R. G. Tanner, "The Epistle to Diognetus and Contemporary Greek Thought," in *Studia Patristica*, vol. 15 (Berlin: Akademie-Verlag, 1984), 497–98.

5. Ehrman, ed., *Apostolic Fathers*, 2.122.

6. Helmut Koester, *Introduction to the New Testament*, 2 vols., 2nd ed. (New York: Walter de Gruyter, 1982), 342. As David Aune elaborates, "The *logos protreptikos* . . . is an oral or literary genre used by philosophers for outsiders. It is rooted in both the rhetorical and philosophical protreptic traditions and must be distinguished from both. The central function of *logoi protreptikoi*, within a philosophical context, was to encourage *conversion*. Conversion is possible only when a belief system is considered ultimately true and excludes alternative or competitive traditions. Yet the term 'conversion' is not fully appropriate, since there were several levels of acceptance involved in adopting the philosophical way of life, and these involved both cognitive and behavioral commitment: (1) the love of wisdom (*philosophia*) generally, (2) the selection of a particular philosophical school superior to the others, and (3) the discipline to persevere in advanced study in that school. However, *logoi protreptikoi* also characteristically included a strong element of dissuasion (*apotropein*) or censure (*elenchein*) aimed at freeing the person from erroneous beliefs and practices." David E. Aune, "Romans as a *Logos Protreptikos*," in *The Romans Debate: Revised and Expanded Edition*, ed. Karl P. Donfried (Peabody, Mass.: Hendrickson, 1991), 280, emphasis original. See also the discussion of protreptic literature in David E. Aune, *The Westminster Dictionary of New Testament and Early Christian Literature and Rhetoric* (Louisville, Ky.: Westminster John Knox Press, 2003), 383–86. On Christianity as a "philosophy" in the second century, see Aune, "Romans," 285–87; Pierre Hadot, *Philosophy as a Way of Life: Spiritual Exercises from Socrates to Foucault*, trans. Michael Chase (Oxford: Blackwell, 1995), 126–44. Key ancient works related to the *logos protreptikos*

146 Notes to Pages 64–69

include Plato's *Euthydemus*, Aristotle's *Protrepticus* (fragmentary), Cicero's *Hortensius* (fragmentary), and Iamblichus' *Protrepticus*.

7. Aune, *Dictionary*, 52. Elsewhere Aune notes an interesting parallel function for protreptic literature in the later Neoplatonic tradition (late third/early fourth cent.): "Because of the largely technical nature of the *Synagoge* within which [Iamblichus's] *Protrepticus* was buried, it does not seem to have been directed to outsiders, but rather to confirm insiders of the choice of Neoplatonism which they had already made." Aune, "Romans," 284.

8. Grant, *Apologists*, 9.

9. Here the manuscript reads *esthesi* ("clothing"). However, as Meecham argues, "the threefold correspondence with v. 2 (cities, speech, life) favours the term 'customs.'" Meecham, *Diognetus*, 108. Indeed the majority of editors follow this emendation. Norelli takes the minority view, arguing for *esthos*/"clothing," a poetic variant of the more familiar term *esthēs* used in 5.4. See Norelli, *A Diogneto*, 140.

10. Cf. Heb 11.16, *Herm. Sim.* 1.1ff. The notion of a heavenly citizenship is still operative in *Diognetus* (cf. 5.9, 6.8). It is just not the immediate or primary emphasis at the opening of chapter 5.

11. Here Marrou has argued that the "new race" language in 1.1 is actually a designation that the text rejects and actively seeks to refute in chapters 5–6: "l'idée [Christians as a *triton genos*] pouvait être susceptible de recevoir une utilisation apologétique, mais notre auteur, visant plus loin et plus profondément, la refuse; il n'accepte pas de voir les Chrétiens isolés en quelque sorte par leur spécificité même, parqués en un ghetto; leur religion est universelle." Marrou, *A Diognète*, 132. While Marrou's point that the text is not isolating or ghettoizing Christians is a sound one, his negative reading of *kainon touto genos* misses the important tension that helps to drive the use of the alien topos in chapter 5. Cf. also Giuseppe Lazzati, "I cristiani 'anima del mondo' secondo un documento del II secolo," *VP* 55 (1972): 66.

12. Norelli, *A Diogneto*, 90.

13. Denise Kimber Buell, "Rethinking the Relevance of Race for Early Christian Self-Definition," *HTR* 94, 4 (2001): 464.

14. On the rhetorical functions of the Greek/barbarian distinction in antiquity, see the discussion in Chapter 1. Norelli also notes the variant interpretation of J. C. Th. von Otto (writing in the late nineteenth century) who argues that the barbarians in view here are actually Jews (see Norelli, *A Diogneto*, 91). This reading has little to support it; most likely Otto is overly influenced by the Jew-Greek polarity in 5.17 and elsewhere.

15. Denise Kimber Buell, *Why This New Race: Ethnic Reasoning in Early Christianity* (New York: Columbia University Press, 2005), 31.

16. Buell, *New Race*, 31.

17. Reinhard Feldmeier, "The 'Nation' of Strangers: Social Contempt and its Theological Interpretation in Ancient Judaism and Early Christianity," in *Ethnicity and the Bible*, ed. M. G. Brett (Leiden: Brill, 1996), 265.

18. On a similar note, Norelli argues that the use of the verb *hypomenō* here probably indicates something like "internal detachment" (*un distacco interiore*). See Norelli, *A Diogneto*, 91.

19. As such, *Diognetus* makes a rhetorical move thoroughly at home in the world of second-century Christian apologetics. Cf. Justin Martyr, *1 Apol.* 17, Athenagoras, *Leg.* 32–33.

20. Norelli points out the contrast between this attitude and any sort of ascetic

stance, even a moderate position such as Justin Martyr's in *1 Apol.* 29.1: "We do not marry except for raising children" (*ouk egamoumen ei mē epi paidōn anatrophē*). See Norelli, *A Diogneto*, 92. For the text of Justin, see Edgar J. Goodspeed, ed., *Die ältesten Apologeten: Texte mit kurzen Einleitungen* (Göttingen: Vandenhoeck & Ruprecht, 1984), 45.

21. J.R. Sallares, "Infanticide," *OCD* 757. For a survey of the relevant ancient sources, secondary literature, and methodological issues involved in studying ancient abandonment of infants, see John Boswell, *The Kindness of Strangers: The Abandonment of Children in Western Europe from Late Antiquity to the Renaissance* (New York: Pantheon, 1988), 53–179. Also William Harris, "Child-Exposure in the Roman Empire," *JRS* 84 (1994): 1–22.

22. Boswell, *Kindness*, 91.

23. Epictetus, *Diatr.* 1.23.7–10 (Oldfather, LCL).

24. Aelian, *Var. hist.* 2.7 (Wilson, LCL).

25. Philo, *Spec. Laws* 3.115–16 (Colson, LCL). Cf. also *Virt.* 131–33, *Mos.* 1.10–11. For an analysis of this issue in Philo, see Adele Reinhartz, "Philo on Infanticide," *SPhilo* 4 (1992): 42–58.

26. P. W. van der Horst, ed., *The Sentences of Pseudo-Phocylides* (Leiden: Brill, 1978), v. 185, translation mine.

27. Boswell, *Kindness*, 88.

28. Note also that early Christian views on the topic are themselves not monolithic. Athenagoras (mid second cent.) explicitly equates exposure with child-murder (*kai mē ektithenai men to gennēthen, hōs tōn ektithentōn teknoktonountōn*). See Athenagoras, *Leg.* 35.2. (Goodspeed, ed., *Die ältesten Apologeten*, 356.) However, Boswell notes a slightly more ambiguous attitude to the practice in some other early Christian writers. For example, Justin Martyr (d. c.165) is concerned about child-murder (*1 Apol.* 29.1), but argues that nearly all those who are exposed (*ektithenai*) go on to prostitution (*hoti tous pantas schedon horōmen epi porneia proagontas*). He then expresses concern that one might unknowingly end up having incestuous intercourse with one's own child or sibling. See Justin, *1 Apol.* 27.1. (Goodspeed, ed., *Die ältesten Apologeten*, 44.) Clement of Alexandria (c.150–c.215) makes this point even more clearly: "So fathers, not being mindful of the children they have exposed, have sex in ignorance with a son who is a prostitute or wanton daughters" (*paidi porneusanti kai machlōsais thygatrasin agnoēsantes pollakis mignyntai pateres, ou memnēmenoi tōn ektethentōn paidiōn*). See Clement of Alexandria, *Paed.* 3.3; Otto Stählin, ed., *Clemens Alexandrinus*, vol. 1 (Berlin: Akademie-Verlag, 1972), 249. Note also the presence of both concerns (i.e., murder and incest) together in the same discussion in Tertullian (c.160–c.225), *Apol.* 9. Henricus Hoppe, ed., *Tertulliani Apologeticum*, CSEL (Vindobonae: Hoelder-Pichler-Tempsky, 1939), 23–27. This connection made by certain Christian writers between exposure and the possibility of incest seems to signal a fuzzier attitude towards the act of exposure itself. As Boswell points out, "prohibitions of other activities such as promiscuity and recourse to prostitutes are predicated on the consequences of Christian parents having exposed children." Boswell, *Kindness*, 177.

29. The term *koitēn* in 5.7 is a correction (followed by most editors of the text) from the manuscript's *koinēn*. Reading *koinēn* instead results in the phrase *trapezan koinēn . . . all' ou koinēn trapezan*, a play on the multiple meanings of the word. Thus Meecham proposes "a common board, but no polluted one." See discussions in Meecham, *Diognetus*, 110–11; Norelli, *A Diogneto*, 140–41.

30. Meecham, *Diognetus*, 111, transliteration added.

31. On hospitality in the ancient world and early Christianity, see G. Stählin,

"The Custom of Hospitality," TDNT 5:17–25; Abraham J. Malherbe, *Social Aspects of Early Christianity*, 2nd ed. (Philadelphia: Fortress Press, 1983), 92–112.

32. Norelli, *A Diogneto*, 92.

33. For a full discussion of this ideal across ancient philosophical schools, see Pierre Hadot, *What is Ancient Philosophy?* trans. Michael Chase (Cambridge, Mass.: Harvard University Press, 2002), 220–31.

34. As Pierre Hadot explains, "For the Stoics, the person who is 'awake' is always perfectly conscious not only of what he *does* but of what he *is*. In other words, he is aware of his place in the universe and of his relationship to God. His self-consciousness is, first and foremost, a moral consciousness. A person endowed with such consciousness seeks to purify and rectify his intentions at every instant. He is constantly on the lookout for signs within himself of any motive for action other than the will to do good. Such self-consciousness is not, however, merely a moral conscience; it is also cosmic consciousness. The 'attentive' person lives constantly in the presence of God and is constantly remembering God, joyfully consenting to the will of universal reason, and he sees all things with the eyes of God himself. Such is the philosophical attitude *par excellence*. It is also the attitude of the Christian philosopher." Hadot, *Way of Life*, 130, emphasis original. On the assimilation between Christianity and ancient philosophical ideals in general, see 26–44.

35. See discussion in the Introduction as well as Umberto Eco, "Overinterpreting Texts," in *Interpretation and Overinterpretation*, ed. Stefano Collini (Cambridge: Cambridge University Press, 1992), 64–65.

36. Commentators predictably connect the phrase *all' en ouranō politeuontai* to Phil 3.20 (*hēmōn gar to politeuma en ouranois hyparchei*). See as representative, Rudolf Brändle, *Die Ethik der 'Schrift an Diognet': Eine Wiederaufnahme paulinischer und johanneischer Theologie am Ausgang des zweiten Jahrhunderts*, ATANT (Zürich: Theologischer Verlag Zürich, 1975), 82; Meecham, *Diognetus*, 111; Norelli, *A Diogneto*, 92. However, given my larger argument that the alien topos functioned as a cultural resource in early Christianity available for deployment in *various* ways, drawing this explicit connection with Philippians on the level of direct textual dependence does not seem necessary.

37. Norelli, *A Diogneto*, 92 (see further discussion, 92–93n14).

38. Thanks to Jennifer Knust for pushing me on this point.

39. Elizabeth Castelli, *Martyrdom and Memory: Early Christian Culture Making* (New York: Columbia University Press, 2004), 57.

40. Judith Perkins, *The Suffering Self: Pain and Narrative Representation in the Early Christian Era* (London: Routledge, 1995), 115.

41. For a brief overview and ancient parallels, see C. G. Kruse, "Afflictions, Trials, Hardships," *DPL* 18–20 and S. J. Hafemann, "Suffering," *DPL* 920–21.

42. These discussions deal not only with the supposed points of contact between *Diognetus* and the *peristasis* catalogues but also with important differences in function and orientation. See Marrou, *À Diognète*, 128; Meecham, *Diognetus*, 112; Norelli, *A Diogneto*, 93.

43. Norelli, *A Diogneto*, 93. On homoioteleuton, see W. B. Stanford, *The Sound of Greek: Studies in the Greek Theory and Practice of Euphony*, Sather Classical Lectures (Berkeley: University of California Press, 1967), 84–85. But, as Stanford points out, "the frequent similarities of the case-endings made rhymes in end-syllables of words less noticeable to [Greek-speakers] than to us" (84). Thus the rhymed endings that Norelli calls attention to in 5.11–17 may not in fact be an intentional rhetorical device. For an unmistakable example of the rhetorically motivated use of homoioteleuton, however, see *Diognetus* 12.8b-9.

44. On asyndeton in general, see J. D. Denniston, *Greek Prose Style* (Oxford: Clarendon Press, 1960), 99–123; Eberhard W. Güting and David L. Mealand, *Asyndeton in Paul: A Text-Critical and Statistical Enquiry into Pauline Style*, Studies in the Bible and Early Christianity (Lewiston, N.Y.: Edwin Mellon, 1998), 1–8. Note also that a number of asyndetic comparisons are also found in *Diognetus* 6.2–10.

45. See the discussion in Aune, *Dictionary*, 137–39. On the use of the *kai-adversativus*, see Jerker Blomqvist, *Das sogenannte KAI adversativum: Zur Semantik einer griechischen Partikel*, SGU (Stockholm: Almqvist & Wiksell, 1979).

46. Heinrich Lausberg, *Handbook of Literary Rhetoric: A Foundation for Literary Study*, trans. Matthew T. Bliss et al. (Leiden: Brill, 1998), §79. According to the treatise *On The Sublime* (first century C.E.?), "[asyndetic] phrases being disconnected, and yet none the less rapid, give the idea of an agitation which both checks the utterance and at the same time drives it on." Longinus, [*Subl.*] 19 (trans. Fyfe in Aristotle, *Poetics*, LCL). Similarly the treatise *On Style* (date unknown—most likely late Hellenistic, early Roman): "The disjointed style is perhaps better for immediacy, and that same style is also called the actor's style since the asyndeton stimulates dramatic delivery." Demetrius, *Eloc.* 193 (trans. Innes in Aristotle, *Poetics*, LCL).

47. See Aune, *Dictionary*, 138.

48. See for example, Philo, *Legat.* 200, Josephus, *Ant.* 4.183, Acts 10.28.

49. Aune, *Dictionary*, 138.

50. *Synkrisis* and *comparatio* function as technical terms for comparison in ancient rhetoric. According to Lausberg, *synkrisis* is "the comparison of the praise . . . of two persons or things. The comparison may be made between equal or unequal objects." Lausberg, *Literary Rhetoric*, §1130. Aristotle offers theoretical reflection on the amplifying power of *synkrisis* in epideictic rhetoric: "If he [the object of praise] does not furnish you with enough material in himself, you must compare him with others. . . . And you must compare him with illustrious personages, for it affords ground for amplification and is noble, if he can be proved better than men of worth. Amplification is with good reason ranked as one of the forms of praise, since it consists in superiority, and superiority is one of the things that are noble. That is why, if you cannot compare him with illustrious personages, you must compare him with ordinary persons, since superiority is thought to indicate virtue. Speaking generally, of the topics common to all rhetorical arguments, amplification is most suitable for epideictic speakers, whose subject is actions which are not disputed, so that all that remains to be done is to attribute beauty and importance to them." Aristotle, *Rhet.* 1.9.38–40 (Freese, LCL).

51. Marrou argues that the vision of the soul/body relationship advanced here stands in distinct contrast to the Platonic tradition which advocates "le caractère irréductible de leur opposition." He therefore contends that *Diognetus* 6 should be understood entirely in terms of Stoicism. See Marrou, *À Diognète*, 138–39. However, Robert Joly objects to Marrou's position, noting that the term *speirō* (*espartai*, 6.2) "ne figure pas au lexique des *Stoïcorum Veterum Fragmenta*. Pour traduire la présence de l'âme au corps, les fragments que nous possédons emploient *diēkon* (*diēkō*—pervade, fill) ou *kekramai* (*kerannymi*—mix, mingle)." Robert Joly, *Christianisme et Philosophie: Études sur Justin et les Apologistes grecs du deuxième siècle* (Bruxelles: Editions de l'Université de Bruxelles, 1973), 204, transliteration added. Furthermore, Joly protests the shifting senses of *kosmos* necessitated by Marrou's reading (an implied Roman world in *Diognetus* 5—i.e., the term *kosmos* is not actually used—and the universe in *Diognetus* 6), and thus looks to numerous sources (Plutarch, Plato's *Phaedo*, Pindar, Aeschylus) to argue that the anal-

ogy should be read in terms of "le mysticisme païen, orphico-pythagoricien."
Joly, *Christianisme et Philosophie*, 208. Tanner accepts Joly's critiques of Marrou but
makes a renewed case for Stoicism, arguing that the entire treatise is an "internal
Stoic debate" in which the term *kosmos* functions amphibolously, and the term
espartai "was intended to introduce an incidental implication of the Stoic sense of
logos spermatikos as well as its main Orphic-Pythagorean significance." Tanner, "Diognetus," 503, transliteration added. Similarly, Tibiletti argues for a Stoic background, but one that comes mediated through Jewish wisdom literature. He cites
in particular the use of *synechō* in Wis 1.7. See Carlo Tibiletti, "Azione cosmica dei
cristiani in 'A Diogneto' 6, 7," 4 (1983): 35–37.
    52. A. A. Long, "Stoic Psychology," in *The Cambridge History of Hellenistic Phi-
losophy*, ed. Keimpe Algra et al. (Cambridge: Cambridge University Press, 1999),
561. Note in addition the affinities to the "world soul" of Plato's *Timaeus* (34b).
The notion of the soul interspersed throughout the human organism can also
be found in Epicurus (*hē psychē sōma esti leptomeres par' holon to athroisma parespar-
menon, Ep. Hdt.* 63). See Cyril Bailey, ed., *Epicurus: The Extant Remains* (Oxford:
Clarendon Press, 1926), 39. However, here the idea actually functions quite differently from what we see in *Diognetus* 6, due to the Epicurean emphasis on the
mutual dependence of the soul and the body: "One of Epicurus' most cherished
doctrines is that the *psuche* dies with the rest of the body, and much attention is
paid to establishing this claim." See Stephen Everson, "Epicurean Psychology," in
The Cambridge History of Hellenistic Philosophy, ed. Keimpe Algra et al. (Cambridge:
Cambridge University Press, 1999), 545.
    53. Indeed, as Long points out, Stoic anthropological theory has "an ethical af-
finity to Platonic dualism," making the sort of "on the ground" synthesis argued
for here quite plausible. See Long, "Stoic Psychology," 562.
    54. See especially, *Phaed.* 62b, "that we human beings are in a kind of prison"
(*hōs en tini phroura esmen hoi anthrōpoi*); cf. also *Phaed.* 82e. Note also the related
discussion in Chapter One on the soul as sojourner on earth in Philo (esp. *Conf.*
77–78, 81) and Plutarch *Mor.* 607.
    55. On the use of *sōma* and *sarx* as equivalent terms, see Meecham, *Diognetus*,
114.
    56. Here Rudolf Brändle has argued for the direct influence of Johannine
theology (cf. John 15.19, 17.11, 14, 16). See Brändle, *Die Ethik*, 85–86. Regardless of the genealogical origin of these phrases however (*en tō kosmō, ouk eisin ek
tou kosmou* etc.), as Norelli notes (correctly to my mind), they seem to function
quite differently in the context of *Diognetus* 5–6; given the analogue of the soul/
body relation, no "radical ontological opposition" between the Christian and the
world is in view. See Norelli, *A Diogneto*, 97.
    57. The manuscript reads *menontes* ("they remain") instead of *men ontes*. Edi-
tors have followed Estienne's emendation for sense and because of the correla-
tive *de.* See discussion in Meecham, *Diognetus*, 114.
    58. Norelli, *A Diogneto*, 97. On the invisibility of Christian *theosebeia*, see BAGD
s.v. theosebeia which argues that the reference is to a lack of visible cultic practice.
(If this is the case, we can note how the text cleverly turns a potential critique
of Christians into a further positive correlation with the soul as opposed to the
body.) Judith Lieu offers the intriguing suggestion that this emphasis on the
invisibility of Christian practice may reflect an apologetic polemic against the vis-
ibility of Jewish practices of social separation. See Judith M. Lieu, *Neither Jew nor
Greek? Constructing Early Christianity* (London: T&T Clark, 2002), 183.
    59. Again Norelli notes a mild imbalance in the parallelism: "l'anima è im-

mortale per natura, secondo la tradizione greca, invece i cristiani attendono l'incorruttibilità dopo la morte." Norelli, *A Diogneto*, 99.

60. Lieu, *Neither Jew Nor Greek?* 182–83.

61. See discussion in H. Koester, "*synechō, synochē*," *TDNT* 7:877–88.

62. Norelli, *A Diogneto*, 99.

63. For a critique of the theory that this verse represents a prohibition against suicide, see Giuseppe Lazzati, "*Ad Diognetum* VI 10: Proibizione del suicidio?," in *Studia Patristica*, ed. F. L. Cross, vol. 4 (Berlin: Akademie-Verlag, 1961), 291–97.

64. Koester, *Introduction*, 2.354.

65. Pierre Bourdieu, *In Other Words: Essays Towards a Reflexive Sociology*, trans. Matthew Adamson (Stanford, Calif.: Stanford University Press, 1990), 137.

Chapter 4. Foreign Countries and Alien Assets in the Shepherd of Hermas

1. For a thorough overview of scholarly debates about genre, as well as discussion of the text's manuscript history, major theological themes, and other introductory issues, see Carolyn Osiek, *Shepherd of Hermas* (Minneapolis: Fortress Press, 1999), 1–38. On the genre issue, see also Carolyn Osiek, "The Genre and Function of *The Shepherd of Hermas*," *Semeia* 36 (1986): 113–21. Various critical editions of the text have been published from 1672 on; the two in use today are Robert Joly, *Hermas le Pasteur*, 2nd ed., SC (Paris: Cerf, 1986); Molly Whittaker, ed., *Der Hirt des Hermas*, Die Apostolischen Väter (Berlin: Akademie-Verlag, 1956). For easy reference, the Greek text can be found in the Loeb Classical Library editions of *The Apostolic Fathers*, with English translation by Kirsopp Lake (1913) or Bart Ehrman (2003).

2. According to Carolyn Osiek, "There are three pegs upon which all theories of [the text's] date hang: the Hermas of Rom 16:14, the reference to Clement in *Vis.* 2.4.3, and the *Muratorian Canon*." Osiek, *Hermas*, 18. The Hermas mentioned in Romans could not have lived any later than the end of the first century, but there is no reason to conclude that this Hermas is necessarily the author of the *Shepherd of Hermas* (Origen seems to be the earliest to make this connection). Similarly, the reference to Clement cannot be definitively tied to Clement of Rome. As for the *Muratorian Canon*, it maintains that "Hermas wrote the Shepherd quite lately in our time in the city of Rome, when on the throne of the church of the city of Rome the bishop Pius, his brother, was seated" (*Muratorian Canon* 73–77). Osiek notes in her earlier work on *Hermas* (following Dibelius) that while the *Muratorian Canon* "is anachronistic in its placement of *Hermas* and the monarchical episcopate together, . . . anachronism regarding the rise of the Roman episcopate is typical of later writers, beginning in the second century, so that this factor alone does not disprove the reliability of the text." See Carolyn Osiek, *Rich and Poor in the Shepherd of Hermas: An Exegetical-Social Investigation*, CBQMS (Washington, D.C.: Catholic Biblical Association of America, 1983), 11–12. Thus if we treat the *Muratorian Canon* evidence as trustworthy and follow Eusebius' dating for Pius as bishop of Rome (see *Hist. eccl.* 4.11.6), this would place the text in the middle of the second century. On the other hand, it is possible (and indeed likely) that the text was composed over a considerable period of time—even when one posits a single author. (While many scholars of the late nineteenth and early twentieth centuries held to multiple authorship of *Hermas*, most scholars today argue for a single author writing over an extended time period.) Thus Osiek's conclusion seems sound: "The best assignment of date is an

expanded duration of time beginning from the very last years of the first century, but stretching through most of the first half of the second." Osiek, *Hermas*, 20.

3. The case for the composite nature of *Hermas* is by no means incontrovertible. While the manuscript tradition shows unmistakable signs of fragmentation, Osiek points out that this could be the later result of the text being considered too long and unwieldy. As she points out, patristic quotations from all three sections "seem to be persuasive evidence that at the end of the second century the text was circulating as a unity in both Egypt and North Africa and that divisions occurred later." See further discussion in Osiek, *Hermas*, 3–4. Also Philippe Henne, *L'unité du Pasteur d'Hermas*, CahRB (Paris: Gabalda, 1992).

4. Heb 11.13, *Diogn.* 5.4–5.

5. Dale B. Martin, *Slavery as Salvation: The Metaphor of Slavery in Pauline Christianity* (New Haven, Conn.: Yale University Press, 1990), 49.

6. Cf. Acts 16.17, 1 Pet 2.16 (also Titus 1.1, Jas 1.1), *2 Clem.* 20.1. In the text itself, cf. *Herm. Mand.* 5.2.1, 6.2.4, 8.10.

7. Jonathan Z. Smith, "What a Difference a Difference Makes," in *"To See Ourselves as Others See Us": Christians, Jews, "Others" in Late Antiquity*, ed. Jacob Neusner and Ernest S. Frerichs (Chico, Calif.: Scholars Press, 1985), 15. As Smith aptly puts it, "a 'theory of the other' requires those complex political and linguistic projects necessary to enable us to think, to situate, and to speak of 'others' in relation to the way in which we think, situate and speak about ourselves." Smith, "What a Difference," 48.

8. Thus *epi* (*tēs*) *xenēs* can mean simply "abroad." Cf. the emphasis on the foreignness of a particular *place* in question, rather than the foreign *status* of the person/people in question (with respect to that place) in the following: Epictetus *Diatr.* 1.27.5, Plutarch *Mor.* 576c, Philo, *Legat.* 15, Josephus, *Ant.* 18.344.

9. Joly sees a heaven/earth distinction here, but cites Zahn as allowing that "this city" represents Rome and its empire. See Joly, *Hermas*, 210–11. Snyder follows Zahn, arguing that the opposition represents church and state, while Osiek critiques these categories as "anachronistically institutionalized." See Osiek, *Hermas*, 158; Graydon F. Snyder, *The Shepherd of Hermas*, The Apostolic Fathers, ed. Robert M. Grant (London: Nelson, 1968), 95.

10. Cf. for example, Ezek 48.15–35, Heb 11.10–16, 12.22–24, 13.14, Rev 21, *4 Ezra* 10.26–7, *2 Bar.* 4.1–7, Philo, *Somn.* 2.250–51.

11. Osiek, *Hermas*, 158 (emphasis added).

12. Note especially Hebrews 13.14, *Diognetus* 6.8.

13. *Ant.* in critical editions; see Migne PG 89.1413–1855.

14. See Joly, *Hermas*, 210.

15. Osiek, *Hermas*, 157.

16. See, for example, *Herm. Vis.* 2.2.5, *Herm. Vis.* 5.7, *Herm. Mand.* 4.3.1–7.

17. See the similar evaluation of the well-known "impossibility of repentance" passage (6.4–12) in Craig R. Koester, *Hebrews: A New Translation with Introduction and Commentary*, AB (New York: Doubleday, 2001), 321.

18. According to Osiek, "*Dipsychia* ('double-soulness' or 'doublemindedness') and its related verb and adjective occur 55 times in *Hermas*: *dipsychia* ('double-mindedness') 16 times, *dipsychein* ('to be doubleminded') 20 times, and *dipsychos* ('doubleminded') 19 times—as contrasted to a total of 10 times in all other early Christian literature up to this time." Osiek, *Hermas*, 30, transliteration added. For parallels and further discussion, see Oscar J. F. Seitz, "Antecedents and Signification of the Term *Dipsuchos*," *JBL* 66 (1947): 211–19; Oscar J. F. Seitz, "Relationship of the Shepherd of Hermas to the Epistle of James," *JBL* 63 (1944): 131–40.

19. Pierre Bourdieu, *Language and Symbolic Power*, trans. Gino Raymond and Matthew Adamson (Cambridge, Mass.: Harvard University Press, 1991), 133.

20. The change between plural and singular address/verb forms throughout the similitude is most likely insignificant. As Osiek summarizes, "The chapter begins in the plural (v. 1) and switches to the rhetorical singular in vv. 3–6, then back to the paraenetic plural until the end." Osiek, *Rich and Poor*, 54n30. Thus while the parable storyline sometimes carries the sense of the singular, the paraenetic thrust of the plural is dominant overall.

21. Osiek's study, *Rich and Poor in the Shepherd of Hermas*, provides a thorough examination of this topic, cataloguing references to wealth and the wealthy, business and worldly affairs, the poor and needy, and widows and orphans. See the discussion of relevant texts in Osiek, *Rich and Poor*, 39–57, especially 41–45. As she remarks, "The rich are at times severely criticized, but they are never condemned without hope. Their traditional obligation to give to the needy is reinforced . . . there can be no doubt that the paraenesis of *Hermas* about wealth and poverty is intended for the rich, who are presented as insiders called to repentance" (57). Similarly, James Jeffers argues: "Hermas condemns the conspicuous consumption by wealthy Roman Christians who are members of the *populus urbanus* . . . . [The relevant examples] suggest that Hermas knew of 'rich' persons only in terms of successful freeborns and freedmen below the aristocracy." James S. Jeffers, *Conflict at Rome: Social Order and Hierarchy in Early Christiantiy* (Minneapolis: Fortress Press, 1991), 116. Both scholars conclude that the congregation/audience in view is made up largely of wealthy freedmen. While this argument is historically plausible, it must remain conjectural. However, the attention that Osiek and Jeffers draw to the text's preponderant rhetorical concern with economic matters (rather than simply the issue of repentance) remains extremely helpful.

22. Jeffers, *Conflict*, 139.

23. Osiek, *Rich and Poor*, 53. Similarly, both Brox and Dibelius aver that the question of emperor, devil, or other precise referent cannot be strictly settled. See Norbert Brox, *Der Hirt des Hermas*, Kommentar zu den Apostolischen Vätern (Göttingen: Vandenhoeck & Ruprecht, 1991), 286; Martin Dibelius, *Der Hirt des Hermas* (Tübingen: J.C.B. Mohr (Paul Siebeck), 1923), 551.

24. Osiek, *Hermas*, 159.

25. Note also that in an imperial context, further specification might be dangerous. See James C. Scott, *Domination and the Arts of Resistance: Hidden Transcripts* (New Haven, Conn.: Yale University Press, 1990).

26. Martin Leutzsch, *Die Wahrnehmung sozialer Wirklichkeit im "Hirten des Hermas"* (Göttingen: Vandenhoeck & Ruprecht, 1989), 201.

27. O. Murray, "Kingship," *OCD* 807.

28. Dio Chrysostom, *Kingship* 3.44 (translation mine).

29. Dio Chrysostom, *Borysthenic Discourse (Or. 36)* 20 (translation mine).

30. See David E. Aune, *The Westminster Dictionary of New Testament and Early Christian Literature and Rhetoric* (Louisville, Ky.: Westminster John Knox Press, 2003), 129; Stanley K. Stowers, *The Diatribe and Paul's Letter to the Romans* (Chico, Calif.: Scholars Press, 1981).

31. Osiek notes the unexpected mildness of the term (which can also mean "unprofitable" or "disadvantageous") but argues that "its occurrence elsewhere in Hermas [*Man.* 4.3.6; 5.1.4, 2.2; 6.2.6] indicates a more serious meaning." Osiek, *Hermas*, 159.

32. Note that the terminology of denial is necessitated by the narrative logic of the parable—i.e., the mutual exclusivity between the laws of the two *poleis* (1.3–

5). Thus the sense of denying the Christian confession (which eventually takes on a technical function in later martyrologies) does not seem to be in view.

33. Osiek reads this term as an adaptation of a Stoic virtue, "independence based on minimal needs." Osiek, *Hermas*, 139. See also Osiek, *Rich and Poor*, 53–55. As Martin Hengel notes, the amount of ascetic rigor implied in the term *autarkeia* (versus allowance of a kind of "bourgeois" moderation) can vary according to context. See Martin Hengel, *Earliest Christianity*, trans. John Bowden (London: SCM Press, 1986), 202–7. Also G. Kittel, "*autarkeia, autarkēs*," TDNT 1:466–67.

34. The two Latin versions and the Ethiopic both attest *anybristōs agalliōmenos*. Codex Athous attests *anybristōs kai agalliōmenōs* ("without hindrance and gladly").

35. Cf. the more detailed exhortation found in *Herm. Mand.* 8.10: "So hear these things which follow: to render service to widows, to take care of orphans and those in need, to rescue the servants of God from distress, to be hospitable (for doing good is found in hospitality), to resist nobody, to be peaceable, to be more impoverished than all people, to reverence the elderly, to practice justice, to protect fellowship, to submit to insult, to be forbearing, to bear no grudge, to encourage those who are weary in spirit, not to reject those who have been led to sin in the faith, but to convert them and encourage them, to admonish those who sin, not to oppress debtors and poor people and whatever is similar to these things." See also discussion in Carolyn Osiek, "The Ransom of Captives: Evolution of a Tradition," *HTR* 74 (1981): 371–72.

36. Cf. Jas 1.27.

37. Thanks to Jennifer Knust for this provocative suggestion.

38. Note the further reflection on this theme and the mutual interdependence of the poor and the rich in *Herm. Sim.* 2.5–10.

39. Note the contrast to how the description of the eschatological city functions in a text such as Rev 21.

40. Osiek's characterization of v. 11 as "a new and extraneous exhortation against covetousness and theft" is perhaps a bit overdrawn, given the explicit return to the language of foreign/alien status, which has served throughout as a key rhetorical motif to hold the entire similitude together.

41. Reinhard Feldmeier, "The 'Nation' of Strangers: Social Contempt and its Theological Interpretation in Ancient Judaism and Early Christianity," in *Ethnicity and the Bible*, ed. M. G. Brett (Leiden: Brill, 1996), 265. See also Reinhard Feldmeier, *Die Christen als Fremde: Die Metapher der Fremde in der antiken Welt, im Urchristentum und im 1.Petrusbrief* (Tübingen: J.C.B. Mohr, 1992), 213–14.

42. Seneca, *Epistle* 17.5–7 (translation mine).

43. Note that later in this same letter, Seneca makes it clear that his principal concern is the state of the soul, regardless of whether one is poor or rich in practice (see 17.12).

44. Brad Inwood and Pierluigi Donini, "Stoic Ethics," in *The Cambridge History of Hellenistic Philosophy*, ed. Keimpe Algra, Jonathan Barnes, Jaap Mansfeld, and Malcolm Schofield (Cambridge: Cambridge University Press, 1999), 722.

45. Inwood and Donini, "Stoic Ethics," 734.

46. James A. Francis, *Subversive Virtue: Asceticism and Authority in the Second-Century Pagan World* (University Park: Pennsylvania State University Press, 1995), 182.

47. Pierre Bourdieu, *In Other Words: Essays Towards a Reflexive Sociology*, trans. Matthew Adamson (Stanford, Calif.: Stanford University Press, 1990), 61.

48. Of course in actual practice, second-century audiences surely engaged *Her-*

mas intertextually, producing its meaning in dialogue with other uses of the alien topos with which they were familiar (such as those seen in 1 Peter, Hebrews, *Diognetus*, etc.) The probable result—a reading that *does* foreground an insider identity equated with valorized outsider status—is just as likely to have occurred in the second century as it is today (as evidenced by contemporary scholarly readings that collapse different uses of the topos in these texts into a single-voiced motif that is uniform in purpose and meaning). Nevertheless, the point still holds true that valorized outsider status is not *Hermas*'s primary focus here.

49. Bourdieu, *In Other Words*, 61.

50. Michel de Certeau, *The Practice of Everyday Life*, trans. Steven Rendall (Berkeley: University of California Press, 1984), 105–6.

51. Bourdieu, *In Other Words*, 75.

Chapter 5. Strangers and Soteriology in the Apocryphon of James

Epigraph: Mikhail M. Bakhtin, "Discourse in the Novel," in *The Dialogic Imagination*, ed. Michael Holquist, trans. Caryl Emerson and Michael Holquist (Austin: University of Texas Press, 1981), 276.

1. For the *editio princeps*, see Michel Malinine et al., eds., *Epistula Iacobi Apocrypha: Codex Jung F. I^r-F. VIII^v (p. 1–16)* (Zürich: Rascher Verlag, 1968). The primary edition used for this study can be found in Francis E. Williams, "The Apocryphon of James," in *Nag Hammadi Codex I (The Jung Codex): Introductions, Texts, Translations, Notes*, ed. Harold W. Attridge, 2 vols., NHS (Leiden: Brill, 1985), 1.13–53, 2.7–37. I have also consulted Dankwart Kirchner, *Epistula Jacobi Apocrypha: Die zweite Schrift aus Nag-Hammadi-Codex I* (Berlin: Akademie-Verlag, 1989).

2. As Helmut Koester notes, "Because of the association of James with Peter . . . it is tempting to identify James with the brother of Jesus. However, no such identification occurs in the document. Rather, James appears, like Peter, as one of the twelve disciples." Helmut Koester, *Ancient Christian Gospels: Their History and Development* (Harrisburg, Pa.: Trinity Press International, 1990), 188 n. 2. van Unnik offers the suggestion that the James in question is in fact James the son of Zebedee rather than the brother of Jesus. W. C. van Unnik, "The Origin of the Recently Discovered 'Apocryphon Jacobi'," *VC* 10 (1956): 153–54.

3. Cameron bases this argument on a comparative study of early Christian technical usage of the term "remembering" (*pmeeue*) with reference to the words of Jesus (*Ap. Jas.* 2.10). See Ron Cameron, *Sayings Traditions in the Apocryphon of James*, HTS (Philadelphia: Fortress Press, 1984), 122–23.

4. Pheme Perkins, "Johannine Traditions in *Ap. Jas.* (NHC I,2)," *JBL* 101 (1982): 403.

5. According to Ron Cameron's form-critical study, the literary form of *Ap. Jas.* can be outlined as follows: 1) 1.1–8: prescript; 2) 1.8–2.7: proem; 3) 2.7–39: account of the post-resurrection appearance of Jesus; 4) 2.39–15.5: the body of Jesus' discourse and dialogue with James and Peter; 5) 15.5–16.11: account of the ascension; 6) 16.12–30: postscript. Thus the text is in fact a case of mixed genres. A large section of dialogue and discourse is embedded within a narrative, which is in turn framed by a letter. See Cameron, *Sayings Traditions*, 3. Also Donald Rouleau, *L'Épître Apocryphe de Jacques*, Bibliothèque Copte de Nag Hammadi, ed. Jacques Ménard et al. (Québec: Presses de l'Université Laval, 1987), 10–11. Still, in spite of the epistolary framework, we can classify the bulk of the text as a

post-resurrection dialogue between Jesus and two of his disciples. See J. van der Vliet, "Spirit and Prophecy in the Epistula Iacobi Apocrypha (NHC I,2)," *VC* 44 (1990): 25. More specifically, Cameron has suggested that the letter frame of *Ap. Jas.* functions rhetorically to "appeal to individual disciples as special recipients of the revelation and authoritative witnesses of the traditions," while the appeal to writing in Hebrew "is intended to locate this text in the earliest stages of the tradition," similar to Papias's statement about the Gospel of Matthew. See Cameron, *Sayings Traditions*, 121–2. Also Eusebius, *Hist. eccl.* 3.39.16.

6. Pheme Perkins, *The Gnostic Dialogue: The Early Church and the Crisis of Gnosticism* (New York: Paulist Press, 1980), 25. See also Kurt Rudolph, "Der gnostische Dialog als literarische Genus," in *Probleme der koptischen Literatur*, ed. Peter Nagel (Halle-Wittenberg: Wissenschaftliche Beiträge der Martin-Luther-Universität, 1968), 85–107.

7. Perkins, *Gnostic Dialogue*, 145. Perkins is not alone in this classification. Note the tendency on the part of many other scholars to identify the text as "Gnostic." See as representative, Dankwart Kirchner, "The Apocryphon of James," in *New Testament Apocrypha*, ed. Wilhelm Schneemelcher, trans. R. McL. Wilson, 2 vols., 2nd ed. (Louisville, KY: Westminster / John Knox Press, 1991), 1.290–91; John Painter, *Just James: The Brother of Jesus in History and Tradition*, 2nd ed. (Columbia: University of South Carolina Press, 2004), 164, 68; Henri-Charles Puech and Gilles Quispel, "Les Écrits gnostiques du Codex Jung," *VC* 8 (1954): 20–22; G. Röwekamp, "James (the younger), Literature about," in *Dictionary of Early Christian Literature*, ed. Siegmar Döpp and Wilhelm Geerlings, trans. Matthew O'Connell (New York: Crossroad Publishing Company, 2000), 317; Gerd Theissen and Annette Merz, *The Historical Jesus: A Comprehensive Guide*, trans. John Bowden (Minneapolis: Fortress Press, 1998), 42. For a counter-position, see W. C. van Unnik, *Newly Discovered Gnostic Writings: A Preliminary Survey of the Nag-Hammadi Find* (Naperville, Ill.: Alec R. Allenson, 1960), 87–88. Cf. also the form-critical approach taken in Cameron, *Sayings Traditions*, 1–3; Koester, *Ancient Christian Gospels*, 187–200.

8. See Karen L. King, *What Is Gnosticism?* (Cambridge, Mass.: Harvard University Press, 2003); Michael Williams, *Rethinking "Gnosticism": An Argument for Dismantling a Dubious Category* (Princeton, N.C.: Princeton University Press, 1996).

9. Van der Vliet, "Spirit and Prophecy," 26. Charles Hedrick makes a similar point even more strongly, characterizing this passage as "an outright denial of Jesus' own authority to admit sinners into the Kingdom of God." Charles W. Hedrick, "Kingdom Sayings and Parables of Jesus in *The Apocryphon of James*: Tradition and Redaction," *NTS* 29 (1983): 21.

10. Francis Williams suggests that "man" simply reflects a translation variant of "Son of Man" on the part of the Coptic translator. But he also allows for the possibility that a theological distinction is being made here, using the term to demonstrate that the text "equated the term 'Son of Man' specifically with the humanity of Christ." See Williams, "Apocryphon of James," 2.11. While it certainly seems plausible that this use of *prōme* could be read in the context of early Christological debates as a statement about the humanity of Christ, in my opinion, the strategy of the text does not seem to be signaling this link explicitly. In any event, the important point is that both *pšēre ⁿmprōme* in 3.14/3.17 and *prōme* in 3.20 here refer to Jesus.

11. Apparently equivalent here to the "kingdom of the heavens." See Williams, "Apocryphon of James," 1.23.

12. Given the explicit context of 4.19 (*šō[pe] če eretⁿmmēh abal ḥ̇m ppneuma*), fullness should most likely be associated with the Spirit.

13. See 3.40–4.1, 4.24–30, 5.35–6.1, 6.21–27, 6.32–33, 13.26–36.

14. Similarly, Jesus' statement in 13.23–25 ("For you, I have placed myself under the curse, in order that you may be saved"/ *ahiteeit nēt^en ha psahoue jekase ^entōt^en eretnaoujeei*) needs to be read in light of the overarching soteriological agenda of the text in its entirety. Here I would take issue with the scholarly position that reads 13.23–25 as an affirmation of the crucifixion as atonement. (See for example, Douglas M. Parrott, "Gnostic and Orthodox Disciples in the Second and Third Centuries," in *Nag Hammadi, Gnosticism & Early Christianity*, ed. Charles W. Hedrick and Robert Hodgson, Jr. (Peabody, Mass.: Hendrickson, 1986), 212.) While the language used here certainly resonates with the discussion of "the curse" in Galatians 3.13 ("Christ set us free from the curse of the law, by becoming a curse on our behalf"), this does not necessarily indicate that the kind of atonement theology seen in Galatians is present in the soteriology of *Ap. Jas.* Rather, in the context of *Ap. Jas.*, Jesus' placement of himself under the curse functions within a schema of salvation that does not necessarily privilege Jesus' suffering as somehow uniquely important or salvific but instead deems "suffering and death, not as good in and of themselves, but as necessary consequences of teaching the gospel." King, *Gnosticism*, 210. See further discussion below.

15. King, *Gnosticism*, 209. See also Earl Richard, *Jesus: One and Many: The Christological Concept of New Testament Authors* (Wilmington, Del.: Michael Glazier, 1988), 527.

16. Note that van der Vliet takes the *jōk abol* of 4.13 in its second-century technical sense as a reference to martyrdom. See van der Vliet, "Spirit and Prophecy," 26.

17. David Brakke, "Parables and Plain Speech in the Fourth Gospel and the Apocryphon of James," *JECS* 7, no. 2 (1999): 215.

18. King, *Gnosticism*, 210–11.

19. Brakke, "Parables and Plain Speech," 215.

20. Brakke, "Parables and Plain Speech," 206.

21. For *allogenēs*, see Num 3.10; *allotrios*, John 10.5; *geiōras*, Isa 14.1; *xenos*, Lam 5.2; *prosēlutos*, Ezek 22.7.

22. Here I somewhat freely translate *ahro*, a particle of reproach that "expresses astonishment or puzzled regret"; see Bentley Layton, *A Coptic Grammar* (Wiesbaden: Harrassowitz Verlag, 2000), §243.

23. Given the context, the alternative translation "without prayers" seems unlikely. I am therefore reading *aj^en* as a Subachmimic variant for *ej^en*—thus "on account of prayers" or more colloquially, "by prayers."

24. In addition to the examples cited here, see also the epigraph of Chapter 1 attributed to Lucian of Samosata.

25. Dio Chrysostom, *Sixty-Sixth Discourse* 15.

26. Marcus Aurelius, *Meditations* 4.29 (translation mine).

27. Though another level of complexity is added to the dialogical picture when we turn our attention from the *intentio operis* of *Ap. Jas.* to the question of the text's early readers. That is to say—regardless of the apocryphon's deliberate attempts to activate specific intertexts (which I am arguing is not the case here)—the rhetorical effectiveness of the appeal to the alien-stranger category in *Ap. Jas.* would be powerfully heightened for a second-century audience were they in fact to read its ironic polemic in light of the *Hermas* passage or other similar deployments of the alien topos.

28. Frederik Wisse, "Indirect Textual Evidence for the History of Early Christianity and Gnosticism," in *For the Children, Perfect Instruction: Studies in Honor*

of Hans-Martin Schenke, ed. Hans-Gebhard Bethge et al. (Leiden: Brill, 2002), 227, 229.

29. Bakhtin, "Discourse," 276.

Conclusion

1. Rowan A. Greer, "Alien Citizens: A Marvelous Paradox," in *Civitas: Religious Interpretations of the City*, ed. Peter S. Hawkins (Atlanta: Scholars Press, 1986), 39.

2. Greer, "Alien Citizens," 41.

3. Greer, "Alien Citizens," 56.

4. Bonnie Honig, *Democracy and the Foreigner* (Princeton, N.J.: Princeton University Press, 2001), 2.

5. Elizabeth Castelli and Hal Taussig, "Drawing Large and Startling Figures: Reimagining Christian Origins by Painting like Picasso," in *Reimagining Christian Origins: A Colloquium Honoring Burton Mack*, ed. Elizabeth Castelli and Hal Taussig (Valley Forge, Pa.: Trinity Press International, 1996), 16.

6. Karen L. King, *What Is Gnosticism?* (Cambridge, Mass.: Harvard University Press, 2003), 235.

7. Martin Hengel, *Earliest Christianity*, trans. John Bowden (London: SCM Press, 1986), 189.

8. See as representative Elizabeth Castelli, *Martyrdom and Memory: Early Christian Culture Making* (New York: Columbia University Press, 2004), 37; Henry Chadwick, *The Early Church*, 2nd ed. (London: Penguin, 1993), 31; Justo L. González, *The Story of Christianity*, 2 vols. (New York: HarperCollins, 1984), 1.48–49.

9. Wayne A. Meeks, *The First Urban Christians: The Social World of the Apostle Paul* (New Haven, Conn.: Yale University Press, 1983), 105.

10. Hayden White, *Tropics of Discourse: Essays in Cultural Criticism* (Baltimore: John Hopkins University Press, 1978), 82, emphasis original.

11. White, *Tropics of Discourse*, 84, emphasis original. To flesh out this concept, White graphically illustrates how a set of events (*a, b, c, d, e, . . . , n*) can be plotted in a variety of ways (not just *A, b, c, d, e, . . . , n* but also *a, B, c, d, e, . . . , n* or *a, b, c, D, e, . . . , n*) such that "the capitalized letters indicate the privileged status given to certain events or sets of events in the series by which they are endowed with explanatory force." White, *Tropics of Discourse*, 92. In contradistinction to what he terms the "chronicle" (a recording of events in order without the form of an explanatory narrative), he articulates various modes of narrative emplotment found in the Western literary tradition (romance, tragedy, comedy, farce/satire). These in turn are part of a larger theory of historiography that is exceedingly complex in its many variables, including a series of tropes (metaphor, metonymy, synecdoche, irony) by which, according to White, historians prefigure the historical field upon which they construct and emplot their accounts, as well as four modes of argument and four modes of "ideological implication" not outlined here. See Hayden White, *Metahistory* (Baltimore: John Hopkins University Press, 1973). Recognition of White's various modes of emplotment highlights again his more foundational insight that "A narrative account is always a figurative account, an allegory. To leave this figurative element out of consideration in the analysis of a narrative is to miss not only its aspect as allegory but also the performance in language by which a chronicle is transformed into a narrative." See Hayden White, *The Content of the Form: Narrative Discourse and Historical Representation* (Baltimore: John Hopkins University Press, 1987), 43, 48. For my purposes,

however, it is not necessary to apply this theoretical apparatus in all its many complexities to a reconstruction of early Christianity. White's basic methodological insight proves illuminating all the same: "the *shape* of the *relationships* which will appear to be inherent in the objects inhabiting the field will in reality have been imposed on the field by the investigator in the very *act of identifying and describing* the objects that he finds there. The implication is that historians *constitute* their subjects as possible objects of narrative representation by the very language they use to *describe* them." White, *Tropics of Discourse*, 95, emphasis original.

12. Meeks, *First Urban Christians*, 157. Here Meeks draws the language of "old" and "new" modes of socialization from Victor Turner's ritual theory. He uses Turner's framework to understand first the transition that occurred in the ritual of early Christian baptism, but also the ongoing tensions of conflicting modes of socialization on the other side of the baptismal experience. Meeks grounds this ongoing dimension theoretically in Turner's extension of the concept of *liminality* to include not just the "liminal" phase of an initiation ritual but also an ongoing "'anti-structural' component in more complex social situations, including the condition of marginal groups within complex societies." See further discussion in Meeks, *First Urban Christians*, 88–89, 156–57. Also Victor Turner, *The Ritual Process: Structure and Anti-Structure* (Chicago: Aldine, 1969), 94–130.

13. Elizabeth Clark, *History, Theory, Text: Historians and the Linguistic Turn* (Cambridge, Mass.: Harvard University Press, 2004), 160–61.

14. Daniel Boyarin, *Borderlines: The Partition of Judaeo-Christianity* (Philadelphia: University of Pennsylvania Press, 2004), 71.

15. R. Laurence Moore, *Religious Outsiders and the Making of Americans* (Oxford: Oxford University Press, 1986), 33.

16. Moore, *Religious Outsiders*, 43.

17. King, *Gnosticism*, 235.

18. Tertullian, *The Crown* 13 (*ANF* 3.101)

19. Clement of Alexandria, *Miscellanies* 7.12 (*ANF* 2.545).

20. John Chrysostom, *Homilies on Second Corinthians* 16 (*NPNF*[1] 12.359).

21. Miroslav Volf, "Soft Difference: Theological Reflections on the Relation Between Church and Culture in 1 Peter," *ExAud* 10 (1994): 16–17.

22. Stanley Hauerwas and William H. Willimon, *Resident Aliens: Life in the Christian Colony* (Nashville, Tenn.: Abingdon Press, 1989), 11.

23. Hauerwas and Willimon, *Resident Aliens*, 115, emphasis original. See also Volf, "Soft Difference," 15–30.

24. Joyce Hollyday and Jim Wallis, eds., *Cloud of Witnesses* (Maryknoll, N.Y.: Orbis Books, 1991), xiv.

25. Scot McKnight, *1 Peter*, NIV Application Commentary (Grand Rapids, Mich.: Zondervan, 1996), 136–7, emphasis original.

26. McKnight, *1 Peter*, 140.

27. McKnight, *1 Peter*, 62.

28. George H. Guthrie, *Hebrews*, NIV Application Commentary (Grand Rapids, Mich.: Zondervan, 1998), 379.

29. Guthrie, *Hebrews*, 389.

30. Guthrie, *Hebrews*, 390.

31. Emphasis added.

32. Honig, *Democracy and the Foreigner*, 4.

33. Moore, *Religious Outsiders*, 46.

34. See the related discussion in Chapter 1. I take the quoted phrase from Homi K. Bhabha, *The Location of Culture* (London: Routledge, 1994), 67.

35. Julia Kristeva, *Strangers to Ourselves*, trans. Leon S. Roudiez (New York: Columbia University Press, 1991), 39.

36. Alan Wolfe, *The Transformation of American Religion: How We Actually Live Our Faith* (New York: Free Press, 2003), 250–51.

37. Stuart Hall, "Cultural Identity and Diaspora," in *Theorizing Diaspora: A Reader*, ed. Jana Evens Braziel and Anita Mannur (Malden, Mass.: Blackwell, 2003), 237, emphasis original.

38. Castelli, *Martyrdom and Memory*, 202.

39. Daniel Boyarin, *A Radical Jew: Paul and the Politics of Identity* (Berkeley: University of California Press, 1994), 241–42.

40. I take this phrase from Boyarin, *Radical Jew*, 242.

41. Nancy Gibbs, "Blue Truth, Red Truth," *Time Magazine*, 27 September 2004, 27 (emphasis added).

42. Emmanuel Levinas, "Transcendence and Height," in *Emmanuel Levinas: Basic Philosophical Writings*, ed. Adriaan T. Peperzak, Simon Critchley, and Robert Bernasconi (Bloomington: Indiana University Press, 1996), 18.

43. Michel Foucault, *The Use of Pleasure: Volume 2 of the History of Sexuality*, trans. Robert Hurley (New York: Random House, 1985), 9.

Bibliography

Achtemeier, Paul J. *1 Peter.* Hermeneia. Minneapolis: Fortress Press, 1996.

———. "Review of J. Elliott, *A Home for the Homeless: A Sociological Exegesis of 1 Peter, Its Situation and Strategy.*" *JBL* 103 (1984): 130–33.

Adams, Colin, and Ray Laurence. *Travel and Geography in the Roman Empire.* New York: Routledge, 2001.

Adinolfi, Marco. "Stato civile dei Cristiani 'forestieri e pellegrini' (1 Pt 2:11)." *Anton* 42 (1967): 420–34.

Aelian. *Historical Miscellany.* Trans. N. G. Wilson. LCL. Cambridge, Mass.: Harvard University Press, 1997.

Alcock, Susan E. *Graecia Capta: The Landscape of Roman Greece.* Cambridge: Cambridge University Press, 1993.

Allen, Graham. *Intertextuality.* London: Routledge, 2000.

Althusser, Louis. "Ideology and Ideological State Apparatuses (Notes Towards an Investigation)." Pp. 127–86 in Althusser, *Lenin and Philosophy and Other Essays.* Trans. Ben Brewster. New York: Monthly Review Press, 1971.

Anderson, Graham. "Greek Religion in the Roman Empire: Diversities, Convergences, Uncertainties." Pp. 143–63 in *Religious Diversity in the Greco-Roman World,* ed. Dan Cohn-Sherbok and John M. Court. Sheffield: Sheffield Academic Press, 2001.

Andriessen, P. "The Authorship of the Epistula ad Diognetum." *VC* 1 (1947): 129–36.

The Ante-Nicene Fathers. 10 vols. Ed. Alexander Roberts and James Donaldson, 1885–1887. Repr. Peabody, Mass.: Hendrickson, 1994.

Aristotle. *Aristotle.* Trans. Harold P. Cooke et al. 23 vols. LCL. Cambridge, Mass.: Harvard University Press, 1926–1962.

Arowele, P. J. "The Pilgrim People of God: An African's Reflections on the Motif of Sojourn in the Epistle to the Hebrews." *AJT* 4 (1990): 438–55.

Asen, Bernhard A. "The Stranger (*ger*) in Old Testament Tradition." Pp. 16–35 in *Christianity and the Stranger: Historical Essays,* ed. Francis W. Nichols. Atlanta: Scholars Press, 1995.

Attridge, Harold W. *The Epistle to the Hebrews.* Hermeneia. Philadelphia: Fortress Press, 1989.

———. "Paraenesis in a Homily: The Possible Location of, and Socialization in, the 'Epistle to the Hebrews'." *Semeia* 50 (1990): 211–26.

Auffarth, Christoph. "Protecting Strangers: Establishing a Fundamental Value in the Religion of the Ancient Near East and Ancient Greece." *Numen* 39 (1992): 193–214.

Aune, David E. "Romans as a *Logos Protreptikos.*" Pp. 278–96 in *The Romans Debate: Revised and Expanded Edition,* ed. Karl P. Donfried. Peabody, Mass.: Hendrickson, 1991.

————. *The Westminster Dictionary of New Testament and Early Christian Literature and Rhetoric.* Louisville, Ky.: Westminster John Knox Press, 2003.

Aurelius, Marcus. *Meditations.* Trans. Charles Reginald Haines. LCL. Cambridge, Mass.: Harvard University Press, 1930.

Austin, J. L. *How To Do Things with Words.* 2nd ed. Cambridge, Mass: Harvard University Press, 1975.

Bailey, Cyril. *Phases in the Religion of Ancient Rome.* Westport, Conn.: Greenwood Press, 1972.

————, ed. *Epicurus: The Extant Remains.* Oxford: Clarendon Press, 1926.

Bainton, Roland H. "The Early Church and War." *HTR* 39 (1946): 189–212.

Bakhtin, Mikhail M. "Discourse in the Novel." Pp. 259–422 in Bakhtin, *The Dialogic Imagination,* ed. Michael Holquist, trans. Caryl Emerson and Michael Holquist. Austin: University of Texas Press, 1981.

————. *Problems of Dostoevsky's Poetics.* Trans. Caryl Emerson. Minneapolis: University of Minnesota Press, 1984.

Balch, David. "Early Christian Criticism of Patriarchal Authority: 1 Peter 2:11–3:12." *USQR* 39 (1984): 161–73.

————. "Hellenization/Acculturation in 1 Peter." Pp. 79–101 in *Perspectives on 1 Peter,* ed. Charles H. Talbert. NABPR 9. Macon, Ga.: Mercer University Press, 1986.

————. *Let Wives Be Submissive: The Domestic Code in 1 Peter.* SBLMS 26. Chico, Calif.: Scholars Press, 1981.

Balsdon, J. P. V. D. *Romans and Aliens.* London: Duckworth, 1979.

Barclay, John M. G. *Jews in the Mediterranean Diaspora: From Alexander to Trajan (323 BCE–117 CE).* Edinburgh: T&T Clark, 1996.

Barnard, L.W. "The Epistle Ad Diognetum: Two Units from One Author?" *ZNW* 56 (1964): 130–37.

————. "The Shepherd of Hermas in Recent Study." *Heythrop Journal* 9 (1968): 29–36.

Barthes, Roland. "The Death of the Author." Pp. 142–48 in Barthes, *Image, Music, Text,* trans. Stephen Heath. London: Fontana, 1977.

————. *S/Z.* Trans. Richard Miller. New York: Hill and Wang, 1970.

————. "Theory of the Text." Pp. 31–47 in *Untying the Text: A Post-Structuralist Reader,* ed. Robert Young. Boston: Routledge & Kegan Paul, 1981.

Bauer, Johannes B. "An Diognet VI." *VC* 17 (1963): 207–10.

Bauer, Walter. *Orthodoxy and Heresy in Earliest Christianity.* Philadelphia: Fortress Press, 1971. German original: *Rechtgläubigkeit und Ketzerei im ältesten Christentum.* Beiträge zur historischen Theologie 10. Tübingen: Mohr/Siebeck, 1934.

Bauer, Walter, W. F. Arndt, F. W. Gingrich, and F. W. Danker, eds. *A Greek-English Lexicon of the New Testament and Other Early Christian Literature.* 3rd ed. Chicago: University of Chicago Press, 2000.

Beard, Mary. "The Roman and the Foreign: The Cult of the 'Great Mother' in Imperial Rome." Pp. 164–90 in *Shamanism, History, and the State,* ed. Nicholas Thomas and Caroline Humphrey. Ann Arbor: University of Michigan Press, 1994.

Beard, Mary, and Michael H. Crawford. *Rome in the Late Republic: Problems and Interpretations.* London: Duckworth, 1985.

Beard, Mary, John North, and Simon Price. *Religions of Rome.* Vol. 1. Cambridge: Cambridge University Press, 1998.

Belleguic, Thierry, and Clive Thomson. "Dialogical Criticism." Pp. 31–34 in *Encyclopedia of Contemporary Literary Theory,* ed. Irena R. Makaryk. Toronto: University of Toronto Press, 1993.

Benner, Ronald, ed. *Theorizing Citizenship*. Albany: State University of New York Press, 1995.

Berkhofer, Robert F. *Beyond the Great Story: History as Text and Discourse*. Cambridge, Mass.: Harvard University Press, 1995.

Bhabha, Homi K. *The Location of Culture*. London: Routledge, 1994.

Bigg, Charles A. *A Critical and Exegetical Commentary on the Epistles of St. Peter and St. Jude*. International Critical Commentary. Edinburgh: T&T Clark, 1902.

Black, C. Clifton. "The Rhetorical Form of the Hellenistic Jewish and Early Christian Sermon: A Response to Lawrence Wills." *HTR* 81 (1988): 1–18.

Blakeney, E. H. *The Epistle to Diognetus*. London: Society for Promoting Christian Knowledge, 1943.

Blomart, Alain. "Die evocatio und der Transfer fremder Götter von der Peripherie nach Rom." Pp. 99–111 in *Römische Reichsreligion und Provinzialreligion*, ed. Hubert Cancik and Jörg Rüpke. Tübingen: Mohr Siebeck, 1997.

Blomqvist, Jerker. *Das sogenannte KAI adversativum: Zur Semantik einer griechischen Partikel*. Studia Graeca Upsaliensia 13. Stockholm: Almqvist & Wiksell, 1979.

Boesak, Allan, and Wolfram Kistner. "Proclamation and Protest: The Lost Sons/ Outside the Gate." Pp. 74–82 in *Resistance and Hope: South African Essays in Honour of Beyers Naudé*, ed. Charles Villa-Vicencio and John W. de Gruchy. Grand Rapids, Mich.: Eerdmans, 1985.

Boswell, John. *The Kindness of Strangers: The Abandonment of Children in Western Europe from Late Antiquity to the Renaissance*. New York: Pantheon, 1988.

Bourdieu, Pierre. *Choses dites*. Paris: Éditions de Minuit, 1987.

———. *The Field of Cultural Production: Essays on Art and Literature*. Cambridge: Polity Press, 1993.

———. "Genesis and Structure of the Religious Field." In *Comparative Social Research: A Research Annual*, ed. Craig Calhoun. Vol. 13. Greenwich, Conn.: Jai Press, 1991.

———. *In Other Words: Essays Towards a Reflexive Sociology*. Trans. Matthew Adamson. Stanford, Calif.: Stanford University Press, 1990.

———. *Language and Symbolic Power*. Trans. Gino Raymond and Matthew Adamson. Cambridge, Mass.: Harvard University Press, 1991. French original: *Ce que parler veut dire: l'économie des échanges linguistiques*. Paris: Fayard, 1982.

———. *The Logic of Practice*. Trans. Richard Nice. Stanford, Calif.: Stanford University Press, 1990. French original: *Le sens pratique*. Paris: Éditions de Minuit, 1980.

———. *Outline of a Theory of Practice*. Trans. Richard Nice. Cambridge: Cambridge University Press, 1977. French original: *Esquisse d'une théorie de la pratique, précédé de trois études d'ethnologie kabyle*. Geneva: Droz, 1972.

Bourdieu, Pierre, and Loïc J. D. Wacquant. *An Invitation to Reflexive Sociology*. Chicago: University of Chicago Press, 1992.

Bovon, Anne. "La représentation des guerriers perses et la notion de barbare dans la 1re moitié du Ve siècle." *BCH* 87 (1963): 580–602.

Bovon, François. "Foi chrétienne et religion populaire dans la première Épître de Pierre." *Études théologiques et religieuses* 53 (1978): 25–41.

Boyarin, Daniel. *Borderlines: The Partition of Judaeo-Christianity*. Divinations. Philadelphia: University of Pennsylvania Press, 2004.

———. *Intertextuality and the Reading of Midrash*. Bloomington: Indiana University Press, 1990.

———. *A Radical Jew: Paul and the Politics of Identity*. Berkeley: University of California Press, 1994.

Brakke, David. "Parables and Plain Speech in the Fourth Gospel and the Apocryphon of James." *JECS* 7, 2 (1999): 187–218.

Brändle, Rudolf. *Die Ethik der "Schrift an Diognet": Eine Wiederaufnahme paulinischer und johanneischer Theologie am Ausgang des zweiten Jahrhunderts.* ATANT 64. Zürich: Theologischer Verlag Zürich, 1975.

Braun, Herbert. *An die Hebräer.* HNT 14. Tübingen: J.C.B. Mohr (Paul Siebeck), 1984.

Brown, Raymond. "Pilgrimage in Faith: The Christian Life in Hebrews." *Southwestern Journal of Theology* 28 (1985): 28–35.

Brox, Norbert. *Der Hirt des Hermas.* Kommentar zu den Apostolischen Vätern 7. Göttingen: Vandenhoeck & Ruprecht, 1991.

Bruce, F. F. *The Epistle to the Hebrews.* NICNT. Grand Rapids, Mich.: Eerdmans, 1964.

Buell, Denise Kimber. "Race and Universalism in Early Christianity." *JECS* 10, 4 (2002): 429–68.

———. "Rethinking the Relevance of Race for Early Christian Self-Definition." *HTR* 94, 4 (2001): 449–76.

———. *Why This New Race: Ethnic Reasoning in Early Christianity.* New York: Columbia University Press, 2005.

Bultmann, Christoph. *Der Fremde im antiken Juda: eine Untersuchung zum sozialen Typenbegriff "ger" und seinem Bedeutungswandel in der alttestamentlichen Gesetzgebung.* Göttingen: Vandenhoeck & Ruprecht, 1992.

Butler, Judith. *Excitable Speech: A Politics of the Performative.* New York: Routledge, 1997.

Cameron, Ron. *Sayings Traditions in the Apocryphon of James.* HTS 34. Philadelphia: Fortress Press, 1984.

Cardellini, Innocenzo. "Straniere ed 'emigrati-residenti' in una sintesi di teologia storico-biblica." *Rivista Biblica* 40 (1992): 129–81.

Carr, Edward H. *What Is History?* New York: Vintage, 1961.

Cartledge, Paul. *The Greeks: A Portrait of Self and Others.* New York: Oxford University Press, 1993.

Cartledge, Paul, Peter Garnsey, and Erich S. Gruen, eds. *Hellenistic Constructs: Essays in Culture, History, and Historiography.* Berkeley: University of California Press, 1997.

Castelli, Elizabeth. *Martyrdom and Memory: Early Christian Culture Making.* New York: Columbia University Press, 2004.

Castelli, Elizabeth, and Hal Taussig. "Drawing Large and Startling Figures: Reimagining Christian Origins by Painting like Picasso." Pp. 3–20 in *Reimagining Christian Origins: A Colloquium Honoring Burton Mack,* ed. Elizabeth Castelli and Hal Taussig. Valley Forge, Pa.: Trinity Press International, 1996.

Certeau, Michel de. *The Practice of Everyday Life.* Trans. Steven Rendall. Berkeley: University of California Press, 1984.

Chadwick, Henry. *The Early Church.* 2nd ed. London: Penguin, 1993.

Charlesworth, James H., ed. *The Old Testament Pseudepigrapha.* 2 vols. New York: Doubleday, 1983.

Chevallier, M.A. "Condition et vocation des chrétiens en diaspora: Remarques exégétiques sur la 1re épître de Pierre." *Recherches de science religieuse* 48 (1974): 387–400.

Chin, Moses. "A Heavenly Home for the Homeless: Aliens and Strangers in 1 Peter." *Tyndale Bulletin* 42 (1991): 96–112.

Cicero. *Cicero.* Trans. William Falconer et al. 29 vols. LCL. Cambridge, Mass.: Harvard University Press, 1923–1999.

Claassen, Jo-Marie. *Displaced Persons: The Literature of Exile from Cicero to Boethius.* London: Duckworth, 1999.

Clark, Elizabeth. "Engendering the Study of Religion." Pp. 217–42 in *The Future of the Study of Religion: Proceedings of Congress 2000,* ed. Slaviva Jakelic and Lori Pearson. Leiden: Brill, 2004.

———. *History, Theory, Text: Historians and the Linguistic Turn.* Cambridge, Mass.: Harvard University Press, 2004.

Clark, Katerina, and Michael Holquist. *Mikhail Bakhtin.* Cambridge, Mass.: Harvard University Press, 1984.

Cohen, Matty. "Le 'ger' biblique et son statut socio-religieux." *RHR* 207 (1990): 131–58.

Cohen, Shaye J. D. *The Beginnings of Jewishness: Boundaries, Varieties, Uncertainties.* Berkeley: University of California Press, 1999.

Collins, Adela Yarboro. "Insiders and Outsiders in the Book of Revelation and Its Social Context." Pp. 186–218 in *"To See Ourselves as Others See Us": Christians, Jews, "Others" in Late Antiquity,* ed. Jacob Neusner and Ernest S. Frerichs. Chico, Calif.: Scholars Press, 1985.

Collins, John J. *Between Athens and Jerusalem: Jewish Identity in the Hellenistic Diaspora.* New York: Crossroad, 1983.

Connolly, R. H. "Ad Diognetum xi-xii." *JTS* 37 (1936): 2–15.

———. "The Date and Authorship of the Epistle to Diognetus." *JTS* 36 (1935): 347–53.

Cumont, Franz. *The Oriental Religions in Roman Paganism.* New York: Dover, 1956. French original: *Les religions orientales dans le paganisme romain.* Paris: Libraire Orientalist Paul Guethner, 1907.

Dalton, William. "The Church in 1 Peter." Pp. 79–91 in *Witness of Faith in Life and Worship,* Yearbook–Ecumenical Institute for Theological Research. Jerusalem: The Institute, 1981–82.

Dehandschutter, B. "L'Epistula Jacobi apocrypha de Nag Hammadi (CG I,2) comme apocryphe néotestamentaire." *ANRW* II. 25, 6 (1988): 4536–39.

Denniston, J. D. *Greek Prose Style.* Oxford: Clarendon Press, 1960.

deSilva, David A. *Perseverance in Gratitude: A Socio-Rhetorical Commentary on the Epistle "to the Hebrews".* Grand Rapids, Mich.: Eerdmans, 2000.

Dibelius, Martin. *Der Hirt des Hermas.* Tübingen: J.C.B. Mohr (Paul Siebeck), 1923.

Dio Chrysostom. Trans. J. W. Cohoon and H. Lamar Crosby. 5 vols. LCL. Cambridge, Mass.: Harvard University Press, 1932–1952.

Diogenes Laertius. Trans. R. D. Hicks. 2 vols. LCL. Cambridge, Mass.: Harvard University Press, 1925–1927.

Dio's Roman History. Trans. Earnest Cary. 9 vols. LCL. Cambridge, Mass.: Harvard University Press, 1961–1969.

Doblhofer, Ernst. *Exil und Emigration: Zum Erlebnis der Heimatferne in der römischen Literatur.* Darmstadt: Wissenschaftliche Buchgesellschaft, 1987.

Eco, Umberto. "Between Author and Text." Pp. 67–88 in *Interpretation and Overinterpretation,* ed. Stefano Collini. Cambridge: Cambridge University Press, 1992.

———. *The Limits of Interpretation.* Bloomington: Indiana University Press, 1990.

———. "Overinterpreting Texts." Pp. 45–66 in *Interpretation and Overinterpretation,* ed. Stefano Collini. Cambridge: Cambridge University Press, 1992.

Edwards, Catharine, and Gregory Woolf, eds. *Rome the Cosmopolis.* Cambridge: Cambridge University Press, 2003.

Ehrman, Bart D., ed. *The Apostolic Fathers.* 2 vols. LCL. Cambridge, Mass.: Harvard University Press, 2003.

Eisenbaum, Pamela M. *The Jewish Heroes of Christian History: Hebrews 11 in Literary Context.* SBLDS 156. Ed. Pheme Perkins. Atlanta: Scholars Press, 1997.

Elliott, John H. "1 Peter, Its Situation and Strategy: A Discussion with David Balch." Pp. 61–78 in *Perspectives on 1 Peter,* ed. Charles H. Talbert. NABPR 9. Macon, Ga.: Mercer University Press, 1986.

———. *1 Peter: A New Translation with Introduction and Commentary.* AB 37b. New York: Doubleday, 2000.

———. *A Home for the Homeless: A Sociological Exegesis of 1 Peter, Its Situation and Strategy.* Philadelphia: Fortress Press, 1981.

Epictetus. *The Discourses as Reported by Arrian.* Trans. W. A. Oldfather. LCL. Cambridge, Mass.: Harvard University Press, 1925.

Eusebius. *Ecclesiastical History.* Trans. Kirsopp Lake and J. E. L. Oulton. 2 vols. LCL. Cambridge, Mass.: Harvard University Press, 1926–32.

Everson, Stephen. "Epicurean psychology." Pp. 542–59 in *The Cambridge History of Hellenistic Philosophy,* ed. Keimpe Algra, Jonathan Barnes, Jaap Mansfeld, and Malcolm Schofield. Cambridge: Cambridge University Press, 1999.

Feldman, Louis H. "The Concept of Exile in Josephus." Pp. 145–72 in *Exile: Old Testament, Jewish and Christian Conceptions,* ed. James M. Scott. Supplement to *Journal for the Study of Judaism* 56. Leiden: Brill, 1997.

Feldmeier, Reinhard. "Die Außenseiter als Avantgarde: Gesellschaftliche Ausgrenzung als missionarische Chance nach dem 1. Petrusbrief." Pp. 161–78 in *Persuasion and Dissuasion in Early Christianity, Ancient Judaism and Hellenism,* ed. Pieter W. van der Horst, Maarten J. J. Menken, Joop F. M. Smit, and Gert van Oyen. Leuven: Peeters, 2003.

———. *Die Christen als Fremde: Die Metapher der Fremde in der antiken Welt, im Urchristentum und im 1.Petrusbrief.* Tübingen: J.C.B. Mohr, 1992.

———. "The 'Nation' of Strangers: Social Contempt and Its Theological Interpretation in Ancient Judaism and Early Christianity." Pp. 241–70 in *Ethnicity and the Bible,* ed. M. G. Brett. Leiden: Brill, 1996.

Ferguson, John. *The Religions of the Roman Empire.* Ithaca, N.Y.: Cornell University Press, 1970.

Filson, Floyd V. *"Yesterday'": A Study of Hebrews in the Light of Chapter 13.* Naperville, Ill.: Alec R. Allenson, 1967.

Fish, Stanley. *Is There a Text in This Class? The Authority of Interpretive Communities.* Cambridge, Mass.: Harvard University Press, 1980.

Foucault, Michel. *The Archaeology of Knowledge and the Discourse on Language.* Trans. A. M. Sheridan Smith. New York: Pantheon, 1972. French original: *L'Archéologie du Savoir.* Paris: Éditions Gallimard, 1969.

———. *The Use of Pleasure: Volume 2 of the History of Sexuality.* Trans. Robert Hurley. New York: Random House, 1985. French original: *L'Usage des plaisirs.* Paris: Éditions Gallimard, 1984.

Fox, Robin Lane. *Pagans and Christians.* San Francisco: HarperCollins, 1986.

Francis, James A. *Subversive Virtue: Asceticism and Authority in the Second-Century Pagan World.* University Park: Pennsylvania State University Press, 1995.

Frend, W. H. C. *Martyrdom and Persecution in the Early Church.* Oxford: Blackwell, 1965.

Gaertner, Jan Felix. "The Discourse of Displacement in Greco-Roman Antiquity." Pp. 1–20 in *Writing Exile: The Discourse of Displacement in Greco-Roman Antiquity and Beyond,* ed. Jan Felix Gaertner. Leiden: Brill, 2007.

Gager, John. *Kingdom and Community: The Social World of Early Christianity.* Englewood Cliffs, N.J.: Prentice-Hall, 1975.

Gallagher, Catherine, and Stephen Greenblatt. *Practicing New Historicism.* Chicago: University of Chicago Press, 2000.

Gammie, John G. "Paraenetic Literature: Toward the Morphology of a Secondary Genre." *Semeia* 50 (1990): 41–77.

Giet, Stanislas. *Hermas et les pasteurs: les trois auteurs du Pasteur d'Hermas.* Paris: Presses Universitaires de France, 1963.

Goldhill, Simon, ed. *Being Greek Under Rome: Cultural Identity, the Second Sophistic, and the Development of Empire.* Cambridge: Cambridge University Press, 2001.

González, Justo L. *The Story of Christianity.* 2 vols. New York: HarperCollins, 1984.

Goodblatt, David. *Elements of Ancient Jewish Nationalism.* New York: Cambridge University Press, 2006.

Goodspeed, Edgar J., ed. *Die ältesten Apologeten: Texte mit kurzen Einleitungen.* Göttingen: Vandenhoeck & Ruprecht, 1984.

Goppelt, Leonhard. *A Commentary on 1 Peter.* Trans. J. E. Alsup. Grand Rapids, Mich.: Eerdmans, 1993.

———. *Theology of the New Testament.* Trans. J. E. Alsup. Vol. 2. Grand Rapids, Mass.: Eerdmans, 1982.

Grant, Robert M. *Greek Apologists of the Second Century.* Philadelphia: Westminster Press, 1988.

Grässer, Erich. *An Die Hebräer.* 3 vols. Zürich: Neukirchener, 1990.

Gray, Patrick. "Abortion, Infanticide and the Social Rhetoric of the *Apocalypse of Peter.*" *JECS* 9 (2001): 313–37.

Greer, Rowan A. "Alien Citizens: A Marvelous Paradox." Pp. 39–56 in *Civitas: Religious Interpretations of the City,* ed. Peter S. Hawkins. Atlanta: Scholars Press, 1986.

Gruen, Erich S. *Diaspora: Jews Amidst Greeks and Romans.* Cambridge, Mass.: Harvard University Press, 2002.

———. *Heritage and Hellenism: The Reinvention of Jewish Tradition.* Berkeley: University of California Press, 1998.

———. *Studies in Greek Culture and Roman Policy.* Leiden: Brill, 1990.

Guterman, Simon. *Religious Toleration and Persecution in Ancient Rome.* London: Aiglon, 1951.

Guthrie, George H. *Hebrews.* NIV Application Commentary. Grand Rapids, Mich.: Zondervan, 1998.

Güting, Eberhard W., and David L. Mealand. *Asyndeton in Paul: A Text-Critical and Statistical Enquiry into Pauline Style.* Studies in the Bible and Early Christianity 39. Lewiston, N.Y.: Edwin Mellon, 1998.

Haarhoff, T. J. *The Stranger at the Gate: Aspects of Exclusiveness and Co-operation in Ancient Greece and Rome, with Some Reference to Modern Times.* Oxford: Blackwell, 1948.

Hadot, Pierre. *Philosophy as a Way of Life: Spiritual Exercises from Socrates to Foucault.* Trans. Michael Chase. Oxford: Blackwell, 1995.

———. *What Is Ancient Philosophy?* Trans. Michael Chase. Cambridge, Mass.: Harvard University Press, 2002.

Hall, Edith. *Inventing the Barbarian: Greek Self-Definition Through Tragedy.* Oxford: Clarendon Press, 1989.

Hall, Jonathan. *Ethnic Identity in Greek Antiquity.* Cambridge: Cambridge University Press, 1997.

———. *Hellenicity: Between Ethnicity and Culture.* Chicago: University of Chicago Press, 2002.

Hall, Stuart. "Cultural Identity and Diaspora." Pp. 233–46 in *Theorizing Diaspora: A Reader*, ed. Jana Evens Braziel and Anita Mannur. Malden, Mass.: Blackwell, 2003.

Harnack, Adolf von. *Geschichte der altchristlichen Literatur bis Eusebius.* 2 vols. 2nd ed. Leipzig: Hinrichs, 1958.

Harrington, Daniel J. "Sociological Concepts and the Early Church: A Decade of Research." *TS* 41 (1980): 181–90.

Harris, William. "Child-Exposure in the Roman Empire." *JRS* 84 (1994): 1–22.

Hartog, François. *Memories of Odysseus: Frontier Tales from Ancient Greece.* Trans. Janet Lloyd. Edinburgh: Edinburgh University Press, 2001.

———. *The Mirror of Herodotus: The Representation of the Other in the Writing of History.* Berkeley: University of California Press, 1988.

Hauerwas, Stanley, and William H. Willimon. *Resident Aliens: Life in the Christian Colony.* Nashville, Tenn.: Abingdon Press, 1989.

Hawthorne, Gerald F., Ralph P. Martin, and Daniel G. Reid, eds. *Dictionary of Paul and His Letters.* Downers Grove, Ill.: InterVarsity Press, 1993.

Hedrick, Charles W. "Kingdom Sayings and Parables of Jesus in *The Apocryphon of James*: Tradition and Redaction." *NTS* 29 (1983): 1–24.

Heintz, Michael. "*Mimetes Theou* in the *Epistle to Diognetus*." *JECS* 12 (2004): 107–19.

Helderman, Jan. "Anapausis in the Epistula Jacobi Apocrypha." Pp. 34–43 in *Nag Hammadi and Gnosis*, ed. R. McL. Wilson. Leiden: Brill, 1978.

Helmbold, Andrew K. *The Nag Hammadi Gnostic Texts and the Bible.* Grand Rapids, Mich.: Baker, 1967.

Hengel, Martin. *Earliest Christianity.* Trans. John Bowden. London: SCM Press, 1986.

Henne, Philippe. *L'unité du Pasteur d'Hermas.* CahRB 31. Paris: Gabalda, 1992.

Hens-Piazza, Gina. *The New Historicism.* Minneapolis: Fortress Press, 2002.

Herodotus. *The History.* Trans. David Grene. Chicago: University of Chicago Press, 1987.

Hollyday, Joyce, and Jim Wallis, eds. *Cloud of Witnesses.* Maryknoll, N.Y.: Orbis Books, 1991.

Hollywood, Amy. "Agency and Evidence in Feminist Studies of Religion: A Response to Elizabeth Clark." Pp. 243–49 in *The Future of the Study of Religion: Proceedings of Congress 2000*, ed. Slaviva Jakelic and Lori Pearson. Leiden: Brill, 2004.

Homer. *The Odyssey.* Trans. A. T. Murray, ed. George E. Dimock. 2nd ed. LCL. Cambridge, Mass.: Harvard University Press, 1995.

Honig, Bonnie. *Democracy and the Foreigner.* Princeton, N.J.: Princeton University Press, 2001.

Hoppe, Henricus, ed. *Tertulliani Apologeticum.* Corpus scriptorum ecclesiasticorum latinorum 69. Vienna: Hoelder-Pichler-Tempsky, 1939.

Hornblower, Simon, and Anthony Spawforth, eds. *The Oxford Classical Dictionary.* 3rd ed. Oxford: Oxford University Press, 2003.

Hughes, Philip E. *A Commentary on the Epistle to the Hebrews.* Grand Rapids, Mich.: Eerdmans, 1977.

Inwood, Brad, and Pierluigi Donini. "Stoic Ethics." Pp. 675–738 in *The Cambridge History of Hellenistic Philosophy*, ed. Keimpe Algra, Jonathan Barnes, Jaap Mansfeld, and Malcolm Schofield. Cambridge: Cambridge University Press, 1999.

Isaac, Benjamin. *The Invention of Racism in Classical Antiquity.* Princeton, N.J.: Princeton University Press, 2004.

Janssens, Yvonne. "Traits de la Passion dans l'*Epistula Iacobi Apocrypha.*" *Muséon* 88 (1975): 97–101.

Jay, Martin. "Should Intellectual History Take a Linguistic Turn? Reflections on the Habermas-Gadamer Debate." Pp. 86–110 in *Modern European Intellectual History: Reappraisals and New Perspectives,* ed. Dominick LaCapra and Steven L. Kaplan. Ithaca, N.Y.: Cornell University Press, 1982.

Jeffers, James S. *Conflict at Rome: Social Order and Hierarchy in Early Christiantiy.* Minneapolis: Fortress Press, 1991.

————. "Jewish and Christian Families in First-Century Rome." Pp. 128–50 in *Judaism and Christianity in First-Century Rome,* ed. Karl P. Donfried and Peter Richardson. Grand Rapids, Mich.: Eerdmans, 1998.

Jeffords, Clayton N. *Reading the Apostolic Fathers.* Peabody, Mass.: Hendrickson, 1996.

Johnson Hodge, Caroline. *If Sons, Then Heirs: A Study of Kinship and Ethnicity in the Letters of Paul.* New York: Oxford University Press, 2007.

Johnsson, William G. "The Pilgrimage Motif in the Book of Hebrews." *JBL* 97, 2 (1978): 239–51.

Joly, Robert. *Christianisme et Philosophie: Études sur Justin et les Apologistes grecs du deuxième siècle.* Bruxelles: Editions de l'Université de Bruxelles, 1973.

————. *Hermas le Pasteur.* 2nd ed. SC 53. Paris: Éditions du Cerf, 1986.

————. "Le milieu complexe du 'Pasteur d'Hermas'." *ANRW* II.27 (1993): 524–51.

Jonas, Hans. *The Gnostic Religion: The Message of the Alien God and the Beginnings of Christianity.* Boston: Beacon Press, 1958.

Jonge, M. de. "Vreemdelingen en bijwoners: Enige opmerkingen naar aanleding van 1 Pt. 2, 11 en verwante teksten." *Nederlands theologisch tijdschrift* 11 (1956–57): 18–36.

Josephus. *Josephus.* Trans. H. St. J. Thackeray et al. 10 vols. LCL. Cambridge, Mass.: Harvard University Press, 1926–65.

Juvenal and Persius. Trans. G. G. Ramsay. LCL. Cambridge, Mass.: Harvard University Press, 1940.

Kagan, Donald. *Pericles of Athens and the Birth of Democracy: The Triumph of Vision in Leadership.* New York: Touchstone, 1991.

Käsemann, Ernst. *The Wandering People of God: An Investigation of the Letter to the Hebrews.* Trans. Roy A. Harrisville and Irving L. Sandberg. Minneapolis: Augsburg, 1984. German original: *Das wandernde Gottesvolk: Eine Untersuchung zum Hebräerbrief.* 2nd ed. Göttingen: Vandenhoeck & Ruprecht, 1957.

Kidd, José E. Ramírez. *Alterity and Identity in Israel: The "ger" in the Old Testament.* Berlin: Walter de Gruyter, 1999.

King, Karen L. *Revelation of the Unknowable God.* Santa Rosa, Calif.: Polebridge Press, 1995.

————. *What Is Gnosticism?* Cambridge, Mass.: Harvard University Press, 2003.

Kirchner, Dankwart. "The Apocryphon of James." Pp. 285–99 in *New Testament Apocrypha,* ed. Wilhelm Schneemelcher, trans. R. McL. Wilson. 2 vols. 2nd ed. Louisville, Ky.: Westminster/John Knox Press, 1991.

————. *Epistula Jacobi Apocrypha: Die zweite Schrift aus Nag-Hammadi-Codex I.* Berlin: Akademie-Verlag, 1989.

Kittel, Gerhard, and Gerhardt Friedrich, eds. *Theological Dictionary of the New Testament.* 10 vols. Grand Rapids, Mich.: Eerdmans, 1964–76.

Koester, Craig R. *Hebrews: A New Translation with Introduction and Commentary.* AB 36. New York: Doubleday, 2001.

Koester, Helmut. *Ancient Christian Gospels: Their History and Development.* Harrisburg, Pa.: Trinity Press International, 1990.

———. *Introduction to the New Testament.* 2 vols. 2nd ed. New York: Walter de Gruyter, 1982.

———. "'Outside the Camp': Hebrews 13:9–14." *HTR* 55 (1962): 299–315.

Koester, Helmut, and James M. Robinson. *Trajectories Through Early Christianity.* Philadelphia: Fortress Press, 1971.

Konstan, David. "*To Hellenikon ethnos*: Ethnicity and the Construction of Ancient Greek Identity." Pp. 29–50 in *Ancient Perceptions of Greek Ethnicity*, ed. Irad Malkin. Washington, D.C.: Center for Hellenic Studies/Harvard University Press, 2001.

———, ed. *Greeks on Greekness: Viewing the Greek Past Under the Roman Empire.* Cambridge: Cambridge Philological Society/Cambridge University Press, 2006.

Kristeva, Julia. *Strangers to Ourselves.* Trans. Leon S. Roudiez. New York: Columbia University Press, 1991. French original: *Etrangers à nous-mêmes.* Paris: Librairie Artheme Fayard, 1988.

Kuhn, Thomas S. *The Structure of Scientific Revolutions.* 3rd ed. Chicago: University of Chicago Press, 1996.

Lake, Kirsopp. *The Apostolic Fathers.* 2 vols. LCL. Cambridge, Mass.: Harvard University Press, 1913.

———. "The Shepherd of Hermas and Christian Life in Rome in the Second Century." *HTR* 4 (1911): 25–46.

Lakoff, George, and Mark Johnson. *Metaphors We Live By.* Chicago: University of Chicago Press, 1980.

Lamau, Marie-Louise. *Des chrétiens dans le monde: Communautés pétriniennes au 1er siècle.* LD 134. Paris: Cerf, 1988.

Laurence, Ray, and Joanne Berry, eds. *Cultural Identity in the Roman Empire.* London: Routledge, 1998.

Lausberg, Heinrich. *Handbook of Literary Rhetoric: A Foundation for Literary Study.* Trans. Matthew T. Bliss, Annemiek Jansen, and David E. Orton. Leiden: Brill, 1998.

Layton, Bentley. *A Coptic Grammar.* Wiesbaden: Harrassowitz, 2000.

Lazzati, Giuseppe. "*Ad Diognetum* VI 10: Proibizione del suicidio?" Pp. 291–97 in *Studia Patristica*, ed. F. L. Cross. Vol. 4. Berlin: Akademie-Verlag, 1961.

———. "I cristiani 'anima del mondo' secondo un documento del II secolo." *Vita e pensiero* 55 (1972): 757–61.

Leutzsch, Martin. *Die Wahrnehmung sozialer Wirklichkeit im 'Hirten des Hermas'.* Göttingen: Vandenhoeck & Ruprecht, 1989.

Levinas, Emmanuel. "Transcendence and Height." Pp. 11–31 in *Emmanuel Levinas: Basic Philosophical Writings*, ed. Adriaan T. Peperzak, Simon Critchley, and Robert Bernasconi. Bloomington: Indiana University Press, 1996.

Lieu, Judith M. *Neither Jew Nor Greek? Constructing Early Christianity.* London: T&T Clark, 2002.

Lindemann, Andreas. "Paulinische Theologie im Brief am Diognet." Pp. 337–50 in *Kerygma und Logos: Beiträge zu den geistesgeschichtlichen Beziehungen zwischen Antike und Christentum*, ed. Adolf Martin Ritter. Göttingen: Vandenhoeck & Ruprecht, 1979.

Lona, Horacio E. "Zur Structur von Diog 5–6." *VC* 54 (2000): 32–43.

Long, A. A. "Stoic Psychology." Pp. 560–84 in *The Cambridge History of Hellenistic*

Philosophy, ed. Keimpe Algra, Jonathan Barnes, Jaap Mansfeld, and Malcolm Schofield. Cambridge: Cambridge University Press, 1999.

Lucian. Trans. A. M. Harmon, K. Kilburn and M. D. MacLeod. 8 vols. LCL. Cambridge, Mass.: Harvard University Press, 1913–67.

Lysias. Trans. W. R. M. Lamb. LCL. Cambridge, Mass.: Harvard University Press, 1930.

Malherbe, Abraham J. *Moral Exhortation: A Greco-Roman Sourcebook.* Philadelphia: Westminster Press, 1986.

———. *Social Aspects of Early Christianity.* 2nd ed. Philadelphia: Fortress Press, 1983.

Malinine, Michel, Henri-Charles Puech, Gilles Quispel, Walter Till, and Rodolphe Kasser, eds. *Epistula Iacobi Apocrypha: Codex Jung F. I*ʳ-*F. VIII*ᵛ *(p. 1–16).* Zürich: Rascher Verlag, 1968.

Malkin, Irad. "Introduction." Pp. 1–28 in *Ancient Perceptions of Greek Ethnicity*, ed. Irad Malkin. Washington, D.C.: Center for Hellenic Studies/Harvard University Press, 2001.

———. *The Returns of Odysseus: Colonization and Ethnicity.* Berkeley: University of California Press, 1998.

Manville, Philip Brook. *The Origins of Citizenship in Ancient Athens.* Princeton, N.J.: Princeton University Press, 1990.

Marrou, Henri-Irénée. *À Diognète.* SC 33. Paris: Cerf, 1951.

Martin, Dale B. *Inventing Superstition: From the Hippocratics to the Christians.* Cambridge, Mass.: Harvard University Press, 2004.

———. *Slavery as Salvation: The Metaphor of Slavery in Pauline Christianity.* New Haven, Conn.: Yale University Press, 1990.

Martin, Troy W. *Metaphor and Composition in 1 Peter.* SBLDS 131. Atlanta: Scholars Press, 1992.

McKnight, Scot. *1 Peter.* NIV Application Commentary. Grand Rapids, Mich.: Zondervan, 1996.

McLaughlin, Thomas. "Figurative Language." Pp. 80–90 in *Critical Terms for Literary Study*, ed. Frank Lentricchia and Thomas McLaughlin. 2nd ed. Chicago: University of Chicago Press, 1995.

Meecham, Henry G. *The Epistle to Diognetus: The Greek Text with Introduction, Translation and Notes.* Manchester: Manchester University Press, 1949.

Meeks, Wayne A. *The First Urban Christians: The Social World of the Apostle Paul.* New Haven, Conn.: Yale University Press, 1983.

———. *The Origins of Christian Morality: The First Two Centuries.* New Haven, Conn.: Yale University Press, 1993.

Mélèze-Modrzejewski, Joseph. "How To Be a Greek and Yet a Jew in Hellenistic Alexandria." Pp. 65–92 in *Diasporas in Antiquity*, ed. Shaye J. D. Cohen and Ernest S. Frerichs. Atlanta: Scholars Press, 1993.

Ménard, J. E. "Au coeur de la cité: le chrétien philosophe selon l'*À Diognète* 5–6." *Revue des sciences religieuses* 63 (1989): 183–94.

Mercado, Luis. "The Language of Sojourning in the Abraham Midrash in Hebrews 11:8–19: Its Old Testament Basis, Exegetical Traditions and Function in the Epistle to the Hebrews." Th.D. dissertation, Harvard University, 1966.

Metzner, Rainer. *Die Rezeption des Matthäusevangeliums im 1. Petrusbrief: Studien zum traditionsgeschictlichen und theologischen Einfluß des 1. Evangeliums auf den 1. Petrusbrief.* Wissenschaftliche Untersuchungen zum Neuen Testament 2.74. Tübingen: J.C.B. Mohr (Paul Siebeck), 1995.

Moffatt, James. *A Critical and Exegetical Commentary on the Epistle to the Hebrews*. New York: Scribner's, 1924.

Momigliano, Arnaldo. *Alien Wisdom: The Limits of Hellenization*. Cambridge: Cambridge University Press, 1975.

Moore, R. Laurence. *Religious Outsiders and the Making of Americans*. Oxford: Oxford University Press, 1986.

Mouritsen, Henrik. *Italian Unification: A Study in Ancient and Modern Historiography*. London: Institute of Classical Studies, School of Advanced Study, University of London, 1998.

Nasrallah, Laura. "Mapping the World: Justin, Tatian, Lucian, and the Second Sophistic." *HTR* 98 (2005): 283–314.

Nesselrath, Heinz-Günther. "Later Greek Voices on the Predicament of Exile." Pp. 87–108 in *Writing Exile: The Discourse of Displacement in Greco-Roman Antiquity and Beyond*, ed. Jan Felix Gaertner. Leiden: Brill, 2007.

Newsom, Carol A. "Bakhtin." Pp. 20–27 in *Handbook of Postmodern Biblical Interpretation*, ed. A. K. M. Adam. St. Louis: Chalice Press, 2000.

The Nicene and Post-Nicene Fathers. 14 vols. Series 1. Ed. Philip Schaff, 1886–89. Repr. Peabody, Mass.: Hendrickson, 1994.

Nichols, Francis W., ed. *Christianity and the Stranger: Historical Essays*. Atlanta: Scholars Press, 1995.

Nielsen, Thomas Heine, ed. *Once Again: Studies in the Ancient Greek Polis*. Stuttgart: Franz Steiner, 2004.

Norelli, Enrico. *A Diogneto: Introduzione, traduzione, e note*. Letture cristiane del primo millennio 11. Milan: Figlie di S. Paolo, 1991.

Noy, David. *Foreigners at Rome: Citizens and Strangers*. London: Duckworth, 2000.

Olyan, Saul. *Rites and Rank: Hierarchy in Biblical Representations of Cult*. Princeton, N.J.: Princeton University Press, 2000.

Osiek, Carolyn. "The Genre and Function of *The Shepherd of Hermas*." *Semeia* 36 (1986): 113–21.

———. "The Oral World of Early Christianity in Rome: The Case of Hermas." Pp. 151–72 in *Judaism and Christianity in First-Century Rome*, ed. Karl P. Donfried and Peter Richardson. Grand Rapids, Mich.: Eerdmans, 1998.

———. "The Ransom of Captives: Evolution of a Tradition." *HTR* 74 (1981): 365–86.

———. *Rich and Poor in the Shepherd of Hermas: An Exegetical-Social Investigation*. CBQMS 15. Washington, D.C.: Catholic Biblical Association of America, 1983.

———. "The Second Century Through the Eyes of Hermas: Continuity and Change." *Biblical Theology Bulletin* 20 (1990): 116–22.

———. *Shepherd of Hermas*. Hermeneia: A Critical and Historical Commentary on the Bible. Minneapolis: Fortress Press, 1999.

Ovid. *Ovid*. Translated by Grant Showerman, Frank Justus Miller, J. H. Mozley, Arthur Leslie Wheeler and James George Frazer, ed. G. P. Goold. 2nd ed. LCL. Cambridge, Mass.: Harvard University Press, 1977–89.

———. *The Poems of Exile: Tristia and the Black Sea Letters*. Trans. Peter Green. Berkeley: University of California Press, 2005.

Pagels, Elaine. *The Gnostic Gospels*. New York: Random House, 1979.

Painter, John. *Just James: The Brother of Jesus in History and Tradition*. 2nd ed. Columbia: University of South Carolina Press, 2004.

Parker, David. *The Living Text of the Gospels*. Cambridge: Cambridge University Press, 1997.

Parrott, Douglas M. "Gnostic and Orthodox Disciples in the Second and Third Centuries." Pp. 193–219 in *Nag Hammadi, Gnosticism & Early Christianity*, ed. Charles W. Hedrick and Robert Hodgson, Jr. Peabody, Mass.: Hendrickson, 1986.

Pauly, A. F. *Paulys Realencyclopädie der classischen Altertumswissenschaft*. 49 vols. Munich: Druckenmüller, 1980. (New edition G. Wissowa.)

Perdue, Leo. "The Social Character of Paraenesis and Paraenetic Literature." *Semeia* 50 (1990): 5–39.

Perkins, Judith. *The Suffering Self: Pain and Narrative Representation in the Early Christian Era*. London: Routledge, 1995.

Perkins, Pheme. *The Gnostic Dialogue: The Early Church and the Crisis of Gnosticism*. New York: Paulist, 1980.

———. "Johannine Traditions in *Ap. Jas*. (NHC I,2)." *JBL* 101 (1982): 403–14.

Pernveden, Lage. *The Concept of the Church in the Shepherd of Hermas*. Studia Theologica Lundensia 27. Lund: Gleerup, 1966.

Philo. *Philo*. Trans. F. H. Colson and G. H. Whitaker. 12 vols. LCL. Cambridge, Mass.: Harvard University Press, 1929–53.

Pilch, John J. " 'Visiting Strangers' and 'Resident Aliens'." *TBT* 29 (1991): 357–61.

Plato. *Plato*. Trans. H. N. Fowler et al. 12 vols. LCL. Cambridge, Mass.: Harvard University Press, 1914–90.

Plümacher, Eckhard. *Identitätsverlust und Identitätsgewinn: Studien zum Verhältnis von kaiserzeitlicher Stadt und frühem Christentum*. Biblisch-Theologische Studien 11. Neukirchen-Vluyn: Neukirchener Verlag, 1987.

Plutarch. *Moralia*. Trans. F. H. Sandback. 16 vols. LCL. Cambridge, Mass.: Harvard University Press, 1927–1969.

Poirier, Paul-Hubert. "Eléments de polémique anti-juive dans l'Ad Diognetum." *Vigiliae Christianae* 40 (1986): 218–25.

Pomeroy, Sarah B. "Infanticide in Hellenistic Greece." Pp. 207–22 in *Images of Women in Antiquity*, ed. Averil Cameron and Amélie Kuhrt. Detroit: Wayne State University Press, 1983.

Pons, Jacques. "La Référence au séjour en Égypte et à la sortie d'Égypte dans les codes de loi de L'Ancien Testament." *ETR* 63 (1988): 169–82.

Puech, Henri-Charles, and Gilles Quispel. "Les Écrits gnostiques du Codex Jung." *VC* 8 (1954): 1–51.

Puig Tàrrech, Armand. "Le milieu de la Première épître de Pierre." *RCT* 5 (1980): 95–129, 331–402.

Rabello, Alfredo M. "The Legal Condition of the Jews in the Roman Empire." *ANRW* II.3 (1980): 662–762.

Reinhartz, Adele. "Philo on Infanticide." *SPhilo* 4 (1992): 42–58.

Richard, Earl. *Jesus: One and Many: The Christological Concept of New Testament Authors*. Wilmington, Del.: Michael Glazier, 1988.

Riesenberg, Peter. *Citizenship in the Western Tradition: Plato to Rousseau*. Chapel Hill: University of North Carolina Press, 1992.

Roldanus, Johannes. "Références patristiques au 'chrétien-étranger' dans les trois premiers siècles." *CBP* 1 (1987): 27–52.

Romm, James. *The Edges of the Earth in Ancient Thought: Geography, Exploration, and Fiction*. Princeton, N.J.: Princeton University Press, 1992.

Rorty, Richard. *Contingency, Irony, and Solidarity*. Cambridge: Cambridge University Press, 1989.

———. "The Pragmatist's Progress." Pp. 89–108 in *Interpretation and Over-*

interpretation, ed. Stefano Collini. Cambridge: Cambridge University Press, 1992.

Rotenstreich, Nathan. *Alienation: The Concept and Its Reception.* Leiden: Brill, 19898.

Rouleau, Donald. *L'Épître Apocryphe de Jacques.* Bibliothèque Copte de Nag Hammadi, ed. Jacques Ménard, Paul-Hubert Poirier, and Michel Roberge. Québec: Presses de l'Université Laval, 1987.

Röwekamp, G. "James (the younger), Literature About." Pp. 316–8 in *Dictionary of Early Christian Literature*, ed. Siegmar Döpp and Wilhelm Geerlings. Trans. Matthew O'Connell. New York: Crossroad, 2000.

Rudolph, Kurt. "Der gnostische Dialog als literarische Genus." Pp. 85–107 in *Probleme der koptischen Literatur*, ed. Peter Nagel. Halle-Wittenberg: Wissenschaftliche Beiträge der Martin-Luther-Universität, 1968.

Saddington, D.B. "Race Relations in the Early Roman Empire." *ANRW* II.3 (1975): 112–37.

Schneemelcher, Wilhelm. *New Testament Apocrypha.* Trans. R. McL. McWilson. 2 vols. rev. ed. Cambridge: James Clarke, 1991. German original: *Neutestamentliche Apokryphen.* Tübingen: Mohr Siebeck, 1990.

Schüssler Fiorenza, Elisabeth. *Rhetoric and Ethic: The Politics of Biblical Studies.* Minneapolis: Fortress Press, 1999.

Scott, James C. *Domination and the Arts of Resistance: Hidden Transcripts.* New Haven, Conn.: Yale University Press, 1990.

Scott, James M., ed. *Exile: Old Testament, Jewish and Christian Conceptions.* Supplements to the *Journal for the Study of Judaism* 56. Leiden: Brill, 1997.

Scullard, H. H. *Festivals and Ceremonies of the Roman Republic.* Ithaca, N.Y.: Cornell University Press, 1981.

Seeberg, Alfred. *Der Brief an die Hebräer.* Leipzig: Quelle & Meyer, 1912.

Seitz, Oscar J. F. "Antecedents and Signification of the Term *Dipsuchos.*" *JBL* 66 (1947): 211–19.

———. "Relationship of the Shepherd of Hermas to the Epistle of James." *JBL* 63 (1944): 131–40.

Selwyn, Edward G. *The First Epistle of St. Peter.* London: Macmillan, 1946.

Seneca. *Seneca.* Trans. John W. Basore, Richard M. Gummere, Thomas H. Corcoran, and Franks Justus Miller. 10 vols. LCL. Cambridge, Mass.: Harvard University Press, 1917–1972.

Senior, Donald. "The Conduct of Christians in the World (1 Pet 2:11–3:12)." *RevExp* 79 (1982): 427–38.

Sherwin-White, Adrian N. *The Roman Citizenship.* 2nd ed. Oxford: Clarendon Press, 1973.

———. "The Roman Citizenship: A Survey of Its Development into a World Franchise." *ANRW* I.2 (1972): 23–58.

Siker, Jeffrey S. *Disinheriting the Jews: Abraham in Early Christian Controversy.* Louisville, Ky.: Westminster/John Knox, 1991.

Sisti, A. "Il cristiano nel mondo (1 Pt. 2:11–19)." *BeO* 8 (1966): 70–79.

Smith, Jonathan Z. "Differential Equations: On Constructing the 'Other'." Paper presented at the Thirteenth Annual University Lecture in Religion, Arizona State University, Department of Religious Studies, 5 March 1992.

———. "Fences and Neighbors: Some Contours of Early Judaism." Pp. 1–18 in Smith, *Imagining Religion: From Babylon to Jonestown.* Chicago: University of Chicago Press, 1982.

———. *Relating Religion: Essays in the Study of Religion.* Chicago: University of Chicago Press, 2004.

————. "The Social Description of Early Christianity." *RelSRev* 1 (1975): 19–25.

————. "What a Difference a Difference Makes." Pp. 3–48 in *"To See Ourselves as Others See Us": Christians, Jews, "Others" in Late Antiquity*, ed. Jacob Neusner and Ernest S. Frerichs. Chico, Calif.: Scholars Press, 1985.

Snyder, Graydon F. *The Shepherd of Hermas*. Ed. Robert M. Grant. Apostolic Fathers 6. London: Nelson, 1968.

Spicq, Ceslas. *L'Épître aux Hébreux*. 2 vols. EBib. Paris: Gabalda, 1952.

————. *Les Épîtres de Saint Pierre*. Sources Bibliques. Paris: Librairie Lecoffre, 1966.

Spiegel, Gabrielle M. *The Past as Text: The Theory and Practice of Medieval Historiography*. Baltimore: Johns Hopkins University Press, 1997.

Spina, F. A. "Israelites as *gerim*, 'Sojourners' in Social and Historical Context." Pp. 321–35 in *The Word of the Lord Shall Go Forth: Essays in Honor of David Noel Freedman*, ed. Carol L. Meyers and M. O'Connor. Minona Lake, Ind.: Eisenbrauns, 1983.

Spivak, Gayatri Chakravorty. "Theory in the Margin: Coetzee's *Foe* Reading Defoe's *Crusoe/Roxana*." Pp. 154–80 in *Consequences of Theory*, ed. Jonathan Arac and Barbara Johnson. Baltimore: Johns Hopkins University Press, 1991.

Stählin, Otto, ed. *Clemens Alexandrinus*. Vol. 1. Die griechischen christlichen Schriftsteller der ersten Jahrhunderte. Berlin: Akademie-Verlag, 1972.

Stanford, W. B. *The Sound of Greek: Studies in the Greek Theory and Practice of Euphony*. Sather Classical Lectures 38. Berkeley: University of California Press, 1967.

Stoler, Ann Laura. *Race and the Education of Desire: Foucault's History of Sexuality and the Colonial Order of Things*. Durham, N.C.: Duke University Press, 1995.

Stowers, Stanley K. *The Diatribe and Paul's Letter to the Romans*. Chico, Calif.: Scholars Press, 1981.

Suetonius. *Suetonius*. Trans. J. C. Rolfe. 2 vols. LCL. Cambridge, Mass.: Harvard University Press, 1997–1998.

Tacitus. *Tacitus*. Trans. M. Hutton et al. LCL. Cambridge, Mass.: Harvard University Press, 1970–1981.

Tanner, R. G. "The Epistle to Diognetus and Contemporary Greek Thought." Pp. 495–508 in *Studia Patristica*, vol. 15. Berlin: Akademie-Verlag, 1984.

ter Haar, Gerrie, ed. *Strangers and Sojourners: Religious Communities in the Diaspora*. Leuven: Peeters, 1998.

Theissen, Gerd. *Soziologie der Jesusbewegung: Ein Beitrag zur Entstehungsgeschichte des Urchristentums*. Munich: Kaiser, 1977.

————. *Untersuchungen zum Hebräerbrief*. Studien zum Neuen Testament 2. Gütersloh: Mohn, 1969.

Theissen, Gerd, and Annette Merz. *The Historical Jesus: A Comprehensive Guide*. Trans. John Bowden. Minneapolis: Fortress Press, 1998. German original: *Der historische Jesus: Ein Lehrbuch*. Göttingen: Vandenhoeck & Ruprecht, 1996.

Thierry, J. J. *The Epistle to Diognetus*. Textus minores 33. Leiden: Brill, 1964.

Thucydides. *History of the Peloponnesian War*. Trans. Rex Warner. London: Penguin, 1954.

Tibiletti, Carlo. "Azione cosmica dei cristiani in 'A Diogneto' 6, 7." *Orpheus* 4 (1983): 32–41.

Turcan, Robert. *The Cults of the Roman Empire*. Trans. Antonia Nevill. Oxford: Blackwell, 1996.

Turner, Victor. *The Ritual Process: Structure and Anti-Structure*. Chicago: Aldine, 1969.

Unnik, W. C. van. *Newly Discovered Gnostic Writings: A Preliminary Survey of the Nag-Hammadi Find*. Naperville, Ill.: Alec R. Allenson, 1960. Dutch original: *Open-*

baringen uit Egyptisch Zand. Den Haag: Uitgeverij van Keulen N.V., 1958.
———. "The Origin of the Recently Discovered 'Apocryphon Jacobi'." *VC* 10 (1956): 149–56.
———. "The Teaching of Good Works in 1 Peter." *NTS* 1 (1954–55): 92–110.
van Aarde, Andries G. "The *Evangelium Infantium,* the Abandonment of Children, and the Infancy Narrative in Matthew 1 and 2 from a Social Scientific Perspective." Pp. 435–53 in *Society of Biblical Literature 1992 Seminar Papers,* ed. Eugene H. Lovering. Atlanta: Scholars Press, 1992.
van der Horst, P.W., ed. *The Sentences of Pseudo-Phocylides.* Leiden: Brill, 1978.
van der Vliet, J. "Spirit and Prophecy in the Epistula Iacobi Apocrypha (NHC I,2)." *VC* 44 (1990): 25–53.
van Rensburg, Fika J. "Christians as 'Resident and Visiting Aliens': Implications of the Exhortations to the *paroikoi* and *parepidēmoi* in 1 Peter for the Church in South Africa." *Neotestamentica* 32 (1998): 573–83.
Vanhoye, Albert. *La structure littéraire de l'Épître aux Hébreux.* 2nd ed. Paris: Desclée de Brouwer, 1976.
Vermaseren, Maarten J. *Cybele and Attis: The Myth and the Cult.* Trans. A. M. H. Lemmers. London: Thames and Hudson, 1977.
Vermes, Geza, ed. *The Dead Sea Scrolls in English.* 4th ed. Sheffield: Sheffield Academic Press, 1995.
Versnel, H.S. *Inconsistencies in Greek and Roman Religion* Vol. 1: *Ter Unus; Isis, Dionysos, Hermes; Three Studies in Henotheism.* Leiden: Brill, 1990.
Vesser, H. Aram, ed. *The New Historicism.* New York: Routledge, 1989.
Volf, Miroslav. "Soft Difference: Theological Reflections on the Relation Between Church and Culture in 1 Peter." *ExAud* 10 (1994): 15–30.
Voloshinov, V. N. *Marxism and the Philosophy of Language.* Trans. Ladislav Matejka and I. R. Titunick. Cambridge, Mass.: Harvard University Press, 1986.
Weidmann, Frederick W. " 'To Sojourn' or 'To Dwell'? Scripture and Identity in *The Martyrdom of Polycarp*." Pp. 29–40 in *Reading in Christian Communities: Essays on Interpretation in the Early Church,* ed. Charles A. Bobertz and David Brakke. Notre Dame, Ind.: University of Notre Dame Press, 2002.
Wells, Colin. *The Roman Empire.* 2nd ed. Cambridge, Mass.: Harvard University Press, 1992.
Wengst, Klaus. *Didache (Apostellehre), Barnabasbrief, Zweiter Klemensbrief, Schrift an Diognet.* Schriften des Urchristentums 2. Darmstadt: Wissenschaftliche Buchgesellschaft, 1984.
———. " 'Paulinismus' und 'Gnosis' in der Schrift an Diognet." *Zeitschrift für Kirchengeschichte* 90 (1979): 41–61.
Wettstein, Howard, ed. *Diasporas and Exiles: Varieties of Jewish Identity.* Berkeley: University of California Press, 2002.
White, Hayden. *The Content of the Form: Narrative Discourse and Historical Representation.* Baltimore: Johns Hopkins University Press, 1987.
———. *Metahistory.* Baltimore: Johns Hopkins University Press, 1973.
———. *Tropics of Discourse: Essays in Cultural Criticism.* Baltimore: Johns Hopkins University Press, 1978.
Whitmarsh, Tim. " 'Greece Is the World': Exile and Identity in the Second Sophistic." Pp. 269–305 in *Being Greek Under Rome: Cultural Identity, the Second Sophistic and the Development of Empire,* ed. Simon Goldhill. Cambridge: Cambridge University Press, 2001.
———. *Greek Literature and the Roman Empire: The Politics of Imitation.* Oxford: Oxford University Press, 2001.

Whittaker, Molly, ed. *Der Hirt des Hermas*. Die Apostolischen Väter 1. Berlin: Akademie-Verlag, 1956.

Wilken, Robert L. *The Christians as the Romans Saw Them*. New Haven, Conn.: Yale University Press, 1984.

Williams, Derek. *Romans and Barbarians: Four Views from the Empire's Edge, 1st Century AD*. London: Constable, 1998.

Williams, Francis E. "The Apocryphon of James." Pp. 1.13–53, 2.7–37 in *Nag Hammadi Codex I (The Jung Codex): Introductions, Texts, Translations, Notes*, ed. Harold W. Attridge. 2 vols. NHS 22–23. Leiden: Brill, 1985.

Williams, Michael. *The Immovable Race: A Gnostic Designation and the Theme of Stability in Late Antiquity*. NHS 29. Leiden: Brill, 1985.

————. *Rethinking "Gnosticism": An Argument for Dismantling a Dubious Category*. Princeton, N.J.: Princeton University Press, 1996.

Wills, Lawrence. "The Form of the Sermon in Hellenistic Judaism and Early Christianity." *HTR* 77 (1984): 277–99.

Wilson, J. Christian. *Five Problems in the Interpretation of the Shepherd of Hermas*. Mellen Biblical Press Series 34. Lewiston, N.Y.: Mellen Biblical Press, 1995.

Wimbush, Vincent. "'. . . Not of This World . . .': Early Christianities as Rhetorical and Social Formation." Pp. 23–36 in *Reimagining Christian Origins: A Colloquium Honoring Burton Mack*, ed. Elizabeth Castelli and Hal Taussig. Valley Forge, Pa.: Trinity Press International, 1996.

Windisch, Hans. *Der Hebräerbrief*. HNT 14. Tübingen: Mohr (Siebeck), 1931.

Wisse, Frederik. "Indirect Textual Evidence for the History of Early Christianity and Gnosticism." Pp. 215–25 in *For the Children, Perfect Instruction: Studies in Honor of Hans-Martin Schenke*, ed. Hans-Gebhard Bethge, Stephen Emmel, Karen L. King, and Imke Schletterer. Leiden: Brill, 2002.

Wolfe, Alan. *The Transformation of American Religion: How We Actually Live Our Faith*. New York: Free Press, 2003.

Woolf, Gregory. "Polis-Religion and Its Alternatives in the Roman Provinces." Pp. 71–84 in *Römische Reichsreligion und Provinzialreligion*, ed. Hubert Cancik and Jörg Rüpke. Tübingen: Mohr Siebeck, 1997.

Zangenberg, Jürgen, and Michael Labahn, eds. *Christians as a Religious Minority in a Multicultural City*. London: T&T Clark, 2004.

Index

Abel (biblical), 2, 49, 111
Abraham (biblical), 3, 52, 111, 141 n.21; alien status of, 43–44, 46–49, 63; collective memory of, 22; discourse of common identity and, 50–51
Aelian, 69
Aeneas (mythological), 37
Aeneid (Virgil), 37
agency, 15, 17, 40, 83–85
Alexander the Great, 85
alienation, 5, 63, 91, 98–101, 105
aliens/alien status: biblical heroes and, 51; citizens/citizenship and, 26, 44, 103; communal identity and, 22; confession to, 52–53; contextualization of, 116; critique of, 114–15; exile and, 41; in Greco-Roman views, 6; historical narrative and, 104–8; identity formation and, 92; misrecognition and, 19, 62; modern Christianity and, 111; relational nature of, 81; rhetoricity and, 15; suffering of, 4. *See also* resident alien topos
Allen, Graham, 20
allophylos/allophyloi (aliens/foreigners), 73
allotrios, 25, 80, 98
alterity, 3, 23, 81–82, 111–13, 116; exile and, 41; identity formation and, 5; Jesus outside the camp, 55, 61–62; in 1 Peter, 9–12; resident alien topos and, 1; self as other, 6; theological responsibility and, 115; travelers' narratives of, 31
Anabaptist movement, 3, 109
Anacharsis, 31–32
apocalyptic literature, 78
Apocryphon of James, 7, 8, 23, 91–92, 108; alienation in, 98–101; alien-stranger topos in, 101–2; constructed nature of Christian alien identity and, 116–17;

dialogue and authority in, 92–94; as post-resurrection dialogue, 92, 155–56 n.5; salvation viewed in, 94–98. *See also* Nag Hammadi texts
apologetic literature, 64–65, 72, 144 n.2
Aristotle, 33, 38, 149 n.50
asceticism, 89, 146–47 n.20
Athens, classical, 27
Attridge, Harold, 47, 51, 56, 143 n.61
Augustine, 2, 3, 103, 109, 124 n.19, 138 n.3
Aune, David, 65, 145–46 n.6, 146 n.7
Austin, J. L., 17, 41

Bainton, Roland, 1–3
Bakhtin, Mikhail, 19–20, 91, 102, 129 n.83
Balch, David, 11–12
barbarians, 65, 135 n.55; Germanic tribes, 34; binary with Greeks, 34–35, 67, 73, 146 n.14; Jews seen as, 146 n.14; Roman citizenship and, 27
Barthes, Roland, 20–21, 26, 57, 130 n.6
Beard, Mary, 58–59
Bhabha, Homi, 35–36
Bible, Hebrew: Deuteronomy, 42, 137 n.96; exile imagery in, 38; Genesis, 43, 48; Leviticus, 56, 115; on resident aliens, 42–43; translation into Greek, 3, 22, 43
biblical studies, 9, 13, 104
Bonhoeffer, Dietrich, 3, 109
Book of Mormon, 4
Boswell, John, 69, 70, 147 n.28
boundaries, 6, 12, 27, 32, 36, 142 n.45
Bourdieu, Pierre, 15–19, 22, 47, 62, 89, 144 n.67; on choice of words, 90; on group self-representation, 83–84; on "space of possibles," 26, 130–31 n.7; on symbolic power, 77
Boyarin, Daniel, 26, 107–8, 114, 130 n.6

Essenes, 105
essentialism, 29
Ethiopic language, 83, 154 n.34
ethnicity, 18, 25, 29–31. *See also* race
Eusebius of Caesarea, 103, 108
exegesis, 9, 13, 43, 110
exhortation. *See* paraenesis
exile, 18, 27, 99; Babylonian exile of Jews,
    38, 42, 43; discursive possibilities of,
    37–40; Greek writers on, 136 n.83;
    terms of alterity and, 41–42

Favorinus of Arelate, 38
Feldmeier, Reinhard, 10–11, 14; on Abra-
    ham's foreignness, 48; on Christians'
    foreign status, 143 n.61; on internal/ex-
    ternal polarity, 68; on Israelites' experi-
    ence of exile, 137 n.98; on *Shepherd of
    Hermas*, 88
field, 15–17
Fish, Stanley, 20
foreigners/foreignness, 1, 23, 111; cultic
    discourse and, 57–58; cultural ambiguity
    and, 32; cultural politics and, 103; eco-
    nomic practices and, 87–88; in Greco-
    Roman views of, 6; identity formation
    and, 112; Roman citizenship and, 27
Foucault, Michel, 14–15, 62, 116, 140 n.10
Fox, Robin Lane, 57
Francis, James, 89

Gaertner, Jan Felix, 37, 39
ger (foreigner/alien/sojourner), 42–43
Germania (Tacitus), 34
Gnosticism, 8, 92–93, 139 n.7
grace, 2, 53, 55, 98
Grant, Robert, 65
Greek language, 24, 30, 35, 98; *Epistle to
    Diognetus* written in, 64; Hebrew Bible
    translated into, 3, 22, 43
Greeks, ancient: binary with barbarians,
    34–35, 67, 73, 146 n.14; Christian po-
    lemics against, 65; Christians persecuted
    by, 66, 73; Roman identity and, 34–36
Greenblatt, Stephen, 14
Greer, Rowan, 103
group formation, 13, 18–19
Gruen, Eric, 39
Guthrie, George, 110–12

habitus, 15–17
Hall, Jonathan, 29

Hall, Stuart, 113
Hartog, François, 31–32, 34–35, 134 n.36
Hauerwas, Stanley, 2–3, 109, 112–13, 116
Hebrew language, 24, 42, 156 n.5
Hebrews, Epistle to the, 7, 46–47, 64, 80,
    102, 112; Abraham as alien, 47–49; alien
    status in, 52–54, 144 n.1; authorship
    of, 47, 138–39 n.3; as canonical text,
    110; cultic discourse and, 54–57, 58–60;
    dating of, 47, 139 n.4; *Epistle to Diognetus*
    compared with, 65–66, 76–77; heroes
    in, 49–50; on Jesus outside the camp,
    80; paraenesis in, 22, 60–61, 65, 68, 70,
    72, 100; resident alien topos in, 9; on
    stranger/alien status, 2
Hellenistic philosophy, 7, 10, 22, 138 n.101
Hengel, Martin, 105–7, 154 n.33
Heracles (mythological), 37
hermeneutics, 5, 20, 50, 54–57
Herodotus, 31–32, 36, 134 n.34
heroes, biblical, 49–50
history, 15
Hittites, 43, 48
Hollyday, Joyce, 110
*A Home for the Homeless: A Sociological
    Exegesis of 1 Peter, Its Situation and Strategy*
    (Elliott), 9–10
homiletic literature, 47, 116
Honig, Bonnie, 103
hospitality, 70, 154 n.35

identity, 6, 104; alien status and, 92;
    catalogs of heroes and, 50; civic and
    ethnoracial, 26; cultural, 113; insider
    status and, 40; Israelite/Jewish, 39, 42;
    language and, 18–19; martyrdom as
    discourse of, 114; of multigenerational
    group, 49; outsider status and, 2; rheto-
    ric of alienation and, 5; Roman, 34–35,
    58–59; sociology of, 15; sojourner status
    and, 44; theological, 113–14, 116. *See
    also* "usable social identity"
identity, Christian, 3, 70, 102, 108; alien
    status and, 61, 77; American, 2; con-
    structed and plural nature of, 116–17;
    cultic discourse and, 59; dichotomy of
    two cities and, 81, 84; difference and,
    46–47, 110; financial practice and,
    86–87; formation of, 15, 21, 57, 63;
    Greek/barbarian dichotomy and, 67,
    73; insider status and, 90, 101; non-iden-
    tity as, 10; in Roman social order,

Acknowledgments

This book would not have been possible without the support and encouragement of numerous people and institutions. First and foremost, I wish to thank Karen L. King. Karen has been a rigorous but always encouraging mentor, and I cannot imagine this book without her. Her insights have influenced and improved the project from beginning to end. I also want to thank François Bovon of Harvard University and Ellen Aitken of McGill University, both of whom read versions of the manuscript at a much earlier stage and offered invaluable feedback that propelled the project forward. In later phases of my research, I benefited from the kindness of numerous colleagues who were willing to read and comment on the entire manuscript in something closer to its current form. These include Daniel Boyarin, Denise Buell, Virginia Burrus, Bob Davis, Stephen Dunning, Amy Hollywood, and Jennifer Knust. I am grateful for their critiques and suggestions and have done my best to incorporate as many of their recommendations as possible. I especially want to thank Virginia Burrus for serving as a stimulating and challenging conversation partner and Amy Hollywood for helping me navigate a crucial theoretical shift in the project.

Various seminars and public forums have offered me the opportunity to present different portions of this research. These include talks and presentations at Drew University, Fordham University, Harvard Divinity School, Muhlenberg College, and various sections of the Society of Biblical Literature at the New England, national, and international meetings. I am grateful for all the feedback, helpful critique, and encouragement that I received in these various venues.

Portions of this book were previously published in different form. Material from the introduction and Chapter One appeared in "Strangers and Aliens No Longer: Negotiating Identity and Different in Ephesians 2," *HTR* 99 (2006): 1–16. Chapter Two was published in a somewhat modified form as "The Intersection of Alien Status and Cultic Discourse in the Epistle to the Hebrews" in Gabriella Gelardini, ed. *Hebrews: Contemporary Methods – New Insights* (Leiden: Brill, 2005), 177–198. Thanks to *Harvard Theological Review* and Koninklijke Brill N.V. for their permission to reprint this material here.

Jerry Singerman, Alison Anderson, the editorial board of Divinations, and the staff at the University of Pennsylvania Press have been a pleasure to work with throughout. I am indebted to them for their interest in the project and the numerous ways in which they have helped me navigate the ins and outs of the publishing process.

In addition, there are numerous friends and colleagues from various institutional contexts that have supported me in this work. While I cannot hope to be exhaustive, Carly Daniel-Hughes, Susanna Drake, Brent Landau, Taylor Petrey, and Charles Stang all deserve special mention for the ways that they have helped with different aspects of this project. During the year I spent teaching at Harvard College, I was supported by a fantastic group of colleagues in the Study of Religion including Carole Bundy, Tamsin Jones, Tal Lewis (now of Brown University), and Robert Orsi (now of Northwestern University),

Since relocating to New York City, my colleagues in Fordham University's Theology Department have provided a wonderful institutional home and intellectual community. Throughout the year I spent at the Rose Hill campus, Mary Callaway, Christophe Chalamet, George Demacopoulos, Jeannine Hill Fletcher, Brad Hinze, Christine Firer Hinze, and Mark Massa all went out of their way to reach out to me and smooth my transition to a new academic environment. I am also grateful to my chair, Terry Tilley, for his tireless work on behalf of junior faculty. In my new home at Fordham's Lincoln Center campus, I have joined an outstanding group of colleagues who love to bring intellectual engagement together with the fun of living in New York. I am especially grateful for the emotional support and friendship of Karina Hogan, Terry Klein, Maureen O'Connell, and Telly Papanikolaou. Thanks also to Fordham University Graduate School of Arts and Sciences for an Ames Fund Grant for Junior Faculty that helped subsidize some of this book's production costs.

On a personal note, I want to thank my parents, Roxy and Stephen Dunning, and my siblings, Sarah and David, for their support and love throughout the many transitions that took place for me during the writing of this project. Thanks also to Ashley Dunning who has been one of my best friends as I wrote this book and continues to be so. She more than anyone understands what is at stake for me in the topic that the book explores. And Bob Davis has read every word of this project too many times to count—and talked about it for more hours than he probably cares to remember. He has helped me sharpen my thinking in numerous ways and pushed me to make the final form of this project far better than it would have been otherwise. I dedicate this book to him.